KANTIANISM, POSTMODERNISM AND CRITICAL LEGAL THOUGHT

Law and Philosophy Library

VOLUME 31

The titles published in this series are listed at the end of this volume.

IAN WARD
Department of Law,
University of Dundee,
United Kingdom

KANTIANISM, POSTMODERNISM AND CRITICAL LEGAL THOUGHT

KLUWER ACADEMIC PUBLISHERS
DORDRECHT / BOSTON / LONDON

A C.I.P. Catalogue record for this book is available from the Library of Congress.

ISBN 0-7923-4745-5

Published by Kluwer Academic Publishers,
P.O. Box 17, 3300 AA Dordrecht, The Netherlands.

Sold and distributed in the U.S.A. and Canada
by Kluwer Academic Publishers,
101 Philip Drive, Norwell, MA 02061, U.S.A.

In all other countries, sold and distributed
by Kluwer Academic Publishers,
P.O. Box 322, 3300 AH Dordrecht, The Netherlands.

Printed on acid-free paper

Printed in the Netherlands

TABLE OF CONTENTS

INTRODUCTION 1

CHAPTER 1
Immanuel Kant and the Foundations of Critique 4

CHAPTER 2
Freedom, Responsibility and Judgment 36

CHAPTER 3
The Crisis of Judgment 57

CHAPTER 4
Postmodern Bourgeois Liberalism 78

CHAPTER 5
Critical Legal Studies and Beyond 113

CHAPTER 6
Relativism and the Return of the Moral Self 133

BIBLIOGRAPHY 158

INDEX 169

INTRODUCTION

It has been recently suggested that Kantian legal thought resembles a 'heresy driven underground' (Weinrib 1988, p.950). In one sense this is true. There are few confessed Kantian legal theorists, and relatively little overt Kantian legal writing. It is, however, the purpose of this book to suggest that there is a considerable amount of covert Kantianism abroad in contemporary legal thought. Indeed, it will be suggested that, aside from the already established schools of Kantian relativism and formalism, much of the current writings of critical and postmodern legal thought are firmly established upon Kantian foundations. This book will proceed as a genealogy, tracing the descent of a particular family of legal thought. To an extent, it will be an exercise in the history of legal theory, though without any of the grander claims to universality which such histories tend to pronounce, and without making any claim that the genealogy requires a consistent historical context. Ultimately, it will be suggested that the genealogy reveals a far greater degree of common ground in contemporary legal thought than is often surmised. Rather than perceiving Kantianism and critical legal thought to be polar opposites, it will be suggested that they merely represent varieties of thought which enjoy a number of common genealogical characteristics. Kantians are not, then, heretics. An alternative metaphor sees Kantians, postmodern and critical legal scholars as siblings, prone to squabbling, questioning relative legitimacy, and threatening ostracism, but, ultimately, all members of the same family, sharing certain family characteristics ensured by a common ancestry.

The book is comprised of six chapters. The first chapter re-examines Kant. It seeks to place Kant's legal writings, most obviously found in *The Metaphysics of Morals* and a number of other political essays, in the wider context of his critical project. Most obviously, such a context includes each of the three major *Critiques*. One of the central themes of this chapter is the suggestion that the most important of these is the third *Critique*, of *Judgement*. It is in this *Critique* that Kant addresses most immediately the faculty most suited to political judgment, and his presentation of the *sensus communis* and related provisions for communicative rationality should be seen as the most pertinent philosophical context with which the *Metaphysics* and other political essays should be read. It will be suggested that the entire genus for the postmodern project, and the more reconstructive elements of critical legal thought, lies in Kant's third *Critique*.

The following five chapters chart the development of Kantianism across various twentieth century approaches to legal and political thought. The second chapter suggests that one particular engagement with Kant is of pivotal importance to the emergence of both critical political and postmodern legal thought. This engagement is commonly termed the Heidegger-Kant 'dialogue'. Heidegger, as we shall see, repeatedly acknowledged that his reading of Kant provided the essential impulse for his philosophical endeavours. His *Rektorat*, a text which has caused so much recent controversy, can only be understood in the context of this 'dialogue'. The same is certainly true of Heidegger's much vaunted 'turn' to language and aesthetics, which has provided the foundation for the postmodernism of Derrida, Lyotard, Rorty and host of others we shall consider in subsequent chapters. The second part of this chapter will consider the work of Hannah Arendt, perhaps Heidegger's most famous pupil. It has been suggested that it is Arendt who writes the political thought from which Heidegger shied away. Arendt provided the political analogue to the Heidegger-Kant 'dialogue', and she did so by rewriting political theory in the express terms of Kant's third *Critique* and the conception of judgment.

Chapters three and four reconsider the two dominant contemporary strands of postmodern political thought. The first charts the development of postmodernism in French philosophy, from Sartre to Foucault, and from Derrida to Lyotard; a development which has become commonly known as the 'crisis of judgment'. It will be suggested that each of Sartre, Foucault, Derrida and Lyotard write as an engagement not just with Kant, but more precisely with the Heidegger-Kant 'dialogue'. Sartre tried to recover a Heideggerian humanism by returning to Kant, before finally abandoning the project to follow Heidegger into language. Foucault's later political writings are all confessed engagements with Kant's later essays, most particularly *What is Enlightenment?*. Lyotard and Derrida, so often pronounced as the leading figures of postmodernism, both acknowledge that their writings are underpinned by a determination to extrapolate the ramifications of Kant's admission of the concept of judgment to political thought. Justice, Derrida concludes, is judgment.

Chapter four considers an alternative postmodern engagement; that which Richard Rorty has termed 'postmodern bourgeois liberalism'. According to Rorty, not only he, but also a number of other contemporary North American philosophers are writing in response to Heidegger's engagement with Kant. It is this which makes them 'postmodern' liberals. Two of these perceived Heideggerians are John Rawls and Roberto Unger. It is the purpose of this chapter to examine the veracity of Rorty's claim. In the case of Rawls, so often pronounced to be the most influential of contemporary Kantians, the Heidegger-Kant 'dialogue' provides an essential context by which his controversial shift from a 'theory' of justice to a 'political' liberalism can be understood. At the same time, Unger's movement towards an analogue of 'politics' and 'passion' enjoys a similar context when compared to precisely the same movement made by Kant, towards a metaphysics of morality which is at once an analogue of right and virtue. It is certainly no coincidence that Unger's final resting place, upon a conception of responsibility in law and in ethics, is precisely that mapped out by Heidegger's engagement with Kant.

The final two chapters return to the more immediately jurisprudential, considering contemporary critical and Kantian legal thought. Chapter five charts the development of critical legal theory, from its earlier political manifestations to its later turn towards textualism and postmodernism. This turn, it is suggested, is precisely that determined by the Heidegger-Kant 'dialogue' and it evolution in the alternative postmodernisms examined in chapters three and four. Specific consideration of the writings of 'critical' legal scholars, such as Peter Gabel, Allan Hutchinson and Drucilla Cornell, provide evidence of precisely such an evolution. Rather than presenting a radical alternative to Kantianism, it can be seen that such critical legal scholarship is in fact written as part of the Kantian genealogy. This suggestion is reinforced by the affinities which such a writing enjoys with the orthodox and received Kantianism considered in the final chapter. The first part of this chapter examines the relativist and formalist alternatives presented by Ernst Cassirer, Gustav Radbruch and Ernest Weinrib. Their emphasis on legal form does not preclude the critical emphasis on political substance. It merely defines it. The codeterminative compatibility of form and substance, as the essential feature of an entire Kantian legal philosophy, is appreciated by the most influential exponent of Kantianism in contemporary legal thought, Ronald Dworkin. Dworkin's presentation of law's 'empire' and life's 'dominion' describes both the form and the substance of a Kantian legal theory, of right and of respect. It is, as we shall see, precisely the same analogue as that presented, not just by Kant, but by such as Arendt, Unger and Rorty.

It is, of course, necessary in concluding this introduction to emphasise that the purpose of this book is not to erase distinction. It would be absurd to suggest a precise congruence between any of the theories and theorists to be shortly considered. Even those who would recognise a common affinity, such as Kant and Weinrib, or Heidegger and Arendt, are distinct in many important ways. Rather, the essential ambition of this study is to emphasise certain common characteristics which can serve to bind together a number of theories which are too often presumed to be absolutely distinct. The Kantian engagement, or genealogy, provides a common foundation. It may not be the only one. But it is one.

CHAPTER 1

IMMANUEL KANT AND THE FOUNDATIONS OF CRITIQUE

1 Critical Moral Philosophy

The Origins of Kant's Critique

Like any philosopher, Immanuel Kant spent his intellectual life picking and choosing certain things with which he had sympathy and certain things with which he had not. He was brought up and educated in an uncompromisingly Pietist protestant environment. As an extreme Lutheran theology, Pietism stressed the practice of religion, and a practical religion. It was a populist Protestantism, which emphasised the individuality and the 'dignity' of the ordinary person. Equally importantly, Pietism also stressed the destiny of the individual to strive for a highest good of moral perfection. It was an active 'lived' theology, and Kant's subsequent religious writings were to reveal a deep distrust of dogmatic theology. The impulse towards moral virtue came from within, and this was to become the central assertion of Kant's theory of duty and obligation, around which he built his critique of practical reason.

In the wider world, Kant was caught in the midst of the Enlightenment. The power of reason, it was suggested, would enable mankind to push back the barriers of every science and every art. The drive for determination geared German culture and learning. It was this over-confidence which Kant, crucially, came to doubt (Velkley 1993, p.81). The greatest influence was undoubtedly that of Rousseau. Kant read *Emile* with a peculiar intensity, because it, more than any other book, convinced him of the need to respect the individual, and its capacity as a self-governing moral agent. In notes which he made on first reading *Emile* and *The Social Contract*, Kant commented: 'Rousseau set me straight... I learn to honour men, and I would find myself more useless than a common labourer if I did not believe this observation could give everyone a value which restores the rights of humanity.' (Schneewind 1992, pp.312-4) Above all he remained a committed believer in the idea of human progress, that which in *What is Enlightenment?* he referred to as 'man's emergence from his self-imposed immaturity.' (Reiss 1991, pp.58-9) And he certainly retained a fervent belief in the need to progress beyond established philosophical dogmas, if humankind was itself to progess towards Enlightenment. Emancipation would be self-emancipation. It was the idea that the logic of pure reason alone would somehow suffice in the presentation of an active practical philosophy which troubled Kant. Like the Pietist influence, it was the Enlightenment attitude, as represented by Rousseau, which convinced Kant that nothing was sacred, and above all, that it was the individual, as the source of criticism, who really mattered.

At the same time as doubting the certainty of pure reason, Kant was equally troubled by the march of Humean scepticism and its utilitarian undercurrents. According to Hume we could only know our sensations, and nothing more, and according to the utilitarians, we should then aim purely to please the greatest number in any way our instinct should care to drive us. But for Kant there had to be more. There had to be an order, and there had to be a determining ground. He rejected pure subjectivity with the same conviction that he doubted pure objectivity. Critical philosophy was directed towards establishing the parameters of both, and placing them within a discrete philosophical system. It was not a matter of choosing between alternatives, and taking a relative stance. It was a matter of rendering the alternatives irrelevant to philosophical thought (Arendt 1982, p.32).

Critical theory was not of course a new idea, and Kant never pretended that it was. Certainly for Kant the original and overriding influence was Socratic, and Kant himself acknowledged that the critical exercise would itself proceed 'in Socratic fashion' (Kant 1781, pp.xxxi). He was impressed by Socrates's refusal to ally himself with established sects and dogmas, and by his determination to render philosophical thought practical. Like Socrates, Kant wanted to perfect the rigour of critical method. As Hannah Arendt has suggested, Kant did indeed want to become the 'all-destroyer' of established metaphysics, but at the same time, he wanted to reconstruct (Arendt 1982, pp.36-9). Moreover, as Socrates had done, Kant wanted to open up the possibilities of reconstruction to the ordinary man. Critical theory would be both a populist and a practical theory, just as Pietism and the Enlightenment demanded. Following the publication of the *Critique of Pure Reason* in 1781, he expressed the hope that he could revise it to make it more digestible for the ordinary reader, and two years later commented, 'every philosophical work must be susceptible of popularity; if not, it probably conceals nonsense beneath a fog of seeming sophistication.' (Arendt 1982, p.39) Only the active practical use of moral reason could avoid the stagnation of a dogmatic analysis. The need to describe and determine a practical reason became the driving force behind Kant's later critical work, and the desire to present a workable metaphysics of morals remained an ambition from his earliest days, only to be realised finally in 1797.

Prior to his critical 'turn' Kant's research had concentrated on the philosophy of science. Yet, even by 1760 he was convinced of the need for a critical philosophy and the following decade was spent exploring the possibilities of critique, and by 1765 Kant was totally unsure about the role that metaphysics had to play in philosophy, particularly a practical philosophy. By now Kant's ambition was to design a practical metaphysic of morals. In the process of trying to pin down a practical metaphysics, and exploring these ideas for his *Dissertation*, published in 1770, 'a great light', or so he subsequently described it, dawned upon him (Beiser 1992, p.51). This 'great light' was the possibility of a dichotomy between reason and sensibility, which could prevent sensibility from infecting moral laws. What Kant now suspected, and directed his energies towards during what has become known as the 'silent decade' of the 1770s, was the possibilities of thus preserving the principle of internal freedom.

The Critique of Pure Reason

Eleven years after the *Dissertation* the *The Critique of Pure Reason* announced the arrival of Kant's re-modelled critical philosophy, based on this distinction between reason and understanding, and sensibility, and the locus of freedom. In doing so, as has been suggested, he set the agenda for philosophical debate for the following two centuries. It was to be followed seven years later by the *Critique of Practical Reason*. The third of the three major Critiques, *of Judgement* was published in 1790. The three *Critiques*, together with the *Groundwork of the Metaphysic of Morals*, published in 1785, define the critical philosophical project. It is important to realise that Kant never envisioned any grand sequence of Critiques directed towards some unified goal (Henrich 1992, p.6). Each *Critique* was designed to be discrete. The simple truth is that each time Kant felt the need to revise his critical philosophy. But from its very first expression in 1781 this critical philosophy represented a fundamental assault on the traditional metaphysical position. The classical Greek metaphysics had sought meaning outside the individual. For Kant it was certainly not a question of abandoning metaphysics; 'it would survive even if all other sciences were swallowed in the abyss of an all-destroying barbarism.' (Kant 1787, pp.xiv) But dogmatism had led rational metaphysics into dispute and created what Kant called a 'need of reason', an 'irresistible necessity' to critically reconstruct metaphysics. Kant welcomed the opportunity that the age presented to the critically aware philosopher, and in the Preface to the first edition to the *Critique of Pure Reason*, he established the critical programme. The sceptical reaction against metaphysics was, he suggested:

> not produced by lightness of mind, but by judgement of the age, which has matured and no longer tolerates being put off with illusory modes of knowledge... Our age is the genuine Age of Criticism, to which everything must submit... This calls upon reason to undertake anew the most difficult of tasks - that of knowing itself - and to institute a tribunal that will assure to reason its legitimate claims while dismissing its groundless pretensions; not by enforced decrees, but in accordance with its eternal and unalterable laws. This tribunal is the critique of reason itself. (Kant 1787, p.xi)

It is clear that the concern with the political, and thus the jurisprudential, was pervasive even at the very outset of the critical project. Onora O'Neill has stressed the presence and power of juridical metaphor, and in particular its ability to convey the centrality of a communicated and communicative political ethics, geared to the accommodation of plurality. Kant thought in terms of 'tribunals', of 'debate' and of 'community'. The limits of reason are those described by the 'tribunal'; in other words, by those who engage in its constructive capacity (O'Neill 1986, 1992).

In rejecting Hume's scepticism Kant acknowledged that it aroused him from a 'dogmatic slumber'. In refuting Hume, Kant was forced to concentrate on the mind, and its powers of apperception. We subjectively perceive objects, and we do so critically. The process was necessarily inter-relational. By the first 1781 edition of the *Critique of Pure Reason* Kant was committed to the distinction between objects themselves and our critical perception and understanding of them. At the same time Kant wanted to provide foundations for the laws of science as a metaphysics of experience. This would leave space for, and be complemented by, a free-will bound only by moral laws, and not by the laws of nature. As rational agents men could not be constrained by scientific knowledge or experience, in the guise of laws of nature. The *Critique*, as its Preface suggested, was geared to maintaining this distinction between objective reason and sensibility (Kant 1987, pp.xxiv-v).

For Kant, then, meaning lay not outside but, rather, within the morally driven individual. It was a matter of reason, not logic. Because we alone have a pure practical moral reason, we alone can self-govern, self-create and self-determine. Understanding now required a creative contribution by the cognising subject, and this contribution required the accommodation of experience as a parallel to reason:

Understanding may be regarded as a faculty which secures the unity of appearances by means of rules, and reason as being the faculty which secures the unity of rules of understanding under principles. Accordingly, reason never applies itself directly to experience or to any object, but to understanding, in order to give to the manifold knowledge of the latter an *a priori* unity by means of concepts, a unity which may be called a unity of reason, and which is quite different in kind from any unity that can be accomplished by the understanding. (Kant 1781, p.302)

It was only an accommodation. The idea of metaphysics was still the right one, but a critique was necessary in order 'to lay down the complete architectonic plan... to guarantee...the completeness and certainty of the structure in all its parts.' (Kant 1787, p.27) Kant remained convinced of the need to reinvest and reconstruct a rational metaphysics that was at the same time critical. If critical philosophy concentrated upon reason rather than objects, as Kant advocated that it must, then it would need to investigate the *a priori* conditions of causal knowledge. Causal knowledge is always experiential knowledge: 'When we experience something, we always pre-suppose that something else has gone before which it follows according to some rule.' (Kant 1787, p.240) Critical philosophy was thus directed towards addressing the nature of this causal synthetic theory of understanding, the given *a priori* objects and the creative empirically generated subject. The burning question for Kant was how the synthetic *a priori* concepts were possible.

The three distinct sections of the *Critique* set out to re-establish the position for a metaphysics that was not determined solely by nature. In doing so, it has been suggested, Kant opened the door for the critical relativism of the following three centuries (Parsons 1992, p.90). There is certainly no doubt that the entire transcendental theory which Kant constructed destroyed the rigidity of the Cartesian divide between self-knowledge and the knowledge of objects. In the 'Transcendental Aesthetic', Kant isolated a theory of sensibility which established that experience comes to us in a spatio-temporal form, which can be thus known *a priori*. In other words, the infinitude of the spatial and temporal dictates that objects are prior to our experience of them, otherwise, as Kant suggests, 'we should be landed in the absurd conclusion that there can be appearance without anything that appears.' (Kant 1781, p.25) Sensibility is immediate. Kant began the 'Aesthetic' by suggesting: 'In whatever matter and by whatever means a mode of knowledge may relate to objects, intuition is that through which it is in immediate relation to them.' (Kant 1781, p.19) So our most immediate experience of objects is sensitive and not cognitive. Concepts, in other words general reflective representations, or as Kant calls them 'principles', are then abstracted or synthesised as *a priori* synthetic knowledge, from *a priori* intuitions.

In the 'Transcendental Analytic' he established a 'metaphysics of experience', which provided universal concepts fundamental to all knowledge, which could be called 'categories' (Kant 1781, pp.79-81). The 'Analytic' was a theory of given understanding, which added distinct *a priori* concepts of synthetic understanding and judgment to the *a priori* sensibilities. Being only 'particular determinations', the universality which experience 'provides' is 'never... strict or true, but only assumed or comparative universality' (Kant 1787, pp.3-4). The 'Analytic' renders sensible representations as empirical, in other words spatially and temporally determined, contingent concepts. The natural or empirical world is causally governed and so making sense of experience is only possible in the context of causal reality. But because experience can never 'provide' strict universality, any judgment of causation must be grounded, additionally, in an *a priori* source of knowledge. Kant's 'Analytic' furnishes form and order, so that knowledge can be constructive and synthetic, rather than just receptive, analytical and purely empirical.

Kant now develops this possibility of grounding empirical causation in the 'Transcendental Dialetic', wherein he revealed the antinomies and contradictions which follow from a purely transcendental logic of reason. Kant suggested instead a critical metaphysics of understanding, as a transcendental account of interaction. He thus provided *a priori* explanation for the need for law governed relations in the natural world, what he termed the 'universal laws of nature', and what had been identified in the 'Analytic'. In other words, there is interaction in the non-empirical sphere and a reflected interaction in the empirical or natural sphere which we experience. Kant concludes the 'Dialectic' by stressing the parallel nature of this complementary accommodation:

> We require the principle of the causality of appearances among themselves in order to seek and to be able to provide natural conditions for natural occurences ie. causes of appearance. If this is conceded and is not weakened through any exception, then the understanding, which in its empirical employment sees in all events nothing but nature and is justified in so doing, has everything that it can require, and physical explanation can proceed unhindered on their way. Now it does not do the least violence to this if one assumes, even if it is otherwise only imagined, that among natural causes there are also some that have a faculty that is intelligible only in that their determination to action never rests on empirical conditions, but on mere grounds of reason, though in such a way that the action in the appearance from this cause is in accordance with all the laws of empirical causality. (Kant 1781, p.545)

The 'mere grounds of reason', are what Kant calls 'Ideas of reason', and it is the confusion of these Ideas with experiential concepts which has characterised the 'errors of metaphysics'. Kant designs the Ideas, as part of his transcendental system, to provide principles as a 'unity of reason' (Kant 1781, pp.310-32). They will, in a sense, frame the experiential substance of understanding, but the two will remain, conceptually, rigorously apart. Although they will provide a kind of guide to virtuous moral behaviour, there will be no practical use for the Ideas of Reason. They are, he stresses, 'merely ideas' (Kant 1781, p.328). A syllogistic logic, 'will contain the origin of special *a priori* concepts which we may call pure concepts of reason, or transcendental ideas, and which will determine according to principles how understanding is to be employed in dealing with experience in its totality.' (Kant 1781, p.321)

The Ideas were determined as Kant's series of categories. It is important to stress that all the 'Ideas' were 'regulated' by the one unifying 'principle of reason'. In other words, all the 'Ideas' were 'forms' of the same 'principle'. As such the Ideas have an immanent rationality, whilst at the same time making a parallel provision for maxims of practical reason. It is only a regulatory provision, and as Kant was to re-assert as the thesis of his *Groundwork*, Ideas cannot prescribe any substantive content (Kant 1785, p.55). It is the laws of nature which, in prescribing various empirically generated contents, have the potential to externally constrain our freedom, and it is the practical nature of this constraint which Kant investigates in his *Metaphysics of Morals*. The role for a reconstituted metaphysics is to accommodate this by preserving a transcendental idea of infinite freedom, distinct from an empirically conditioned concept of freedom.

The Groundwork and the Critique of Practical Reason

It was the realisation that the idea of freedom held the key to the development of a practical critical philosophy that prompted Kant to write the *Groundwork* (Henrich 1992, pp.22-3).The purpose of the *Groundwork* was to suggest that freedom was not just theoretical, but actual, and thus could provide the construction of fundamental universal laws of morality. In the *Groundwork* Kant constructed maxims as duties, to determine the relationship between internal and external freedom. Such maxims were principles of pure practical reason - the categorical imperative being the 'supreme principle of practical reason' - because they were generated by internal laws of morality, as distinct from external empirical sensibilities or instincts. They were thus principles derived solely from the 'freedom of the will' (Kant 1785, pp.129-30).

Actual examples of behaviour could never establish principles of the moral law. According to Kant it was 'absolutely impossible for experience to establish with complete certainty a single case in which the maxim of an action in other respects right has rested solely on moral grounds and the thought of one's duty.' (Kant 1785, p.74) The moral agent then, is one who understands and exercises his free-will, because this gives him the power to act in accordance with his Idea of moral laws, or maxims:

Only a rational being has the power to act in accordance with his idea of laws - that is, in accordance with principles - and only so has he a will. Since reason is required in order to derive actions from laws, the will is nothing but practical reason. If reason infallibly determines the will, then in a being of this kind the actions which are recognised to be objectively necessary are also subjectively necessary - that is to say, the will is then a power to

> choose only that which reason independently of inclinations recognizes to be practically necessary, that is, to be good. (Kant 1785, p.80)

This is 'the formal principle of duty', which is a matter not only of freedom, but also, crucially, of responsibility.

Such a law, one which ought to be obeyed for its own sake, is a categorical imperative, which in its most basic generic form was stated by Kant to be: 'I ought never to act except in such a way that I can also will that my maxim should become a universal law.' (Kant 1785, p.70) Moreover as an internally prescribed moral law, the principle of free-will or autonomy demands: 'as the supreme condition of the will's conformity with universal practical reason - namely, the Idea of the will of every rational being as a will which makes universal law.' (Kant 1785, p.98) As a principle of pure practical reason, the categorical imperative was a principle of non-contradiction. Thus the imperative demands that each individual human being should, above all, act in such a way as not to contradict himself. Of course, in the practical empirical world of nature, this will not always be the case. In the Preface to the first *Critique* Kant had observed that human reason, whilst it may strive for unity, tends, at least initially, towards disharmony, and 'precipitates itself into darkness and contradiction.' (Kant 1781, pp.vii-viii) Thus, in the *Groundwork*, he suggests, 'the actions which are recognized to be objectively necessary are subjectively contingent, and the determining of such a will in accordance with objective laws is necessitation.' (Kant 1785, p.80) Thus, just as there is internal and external freedom, so there are internal and external constraints on freedom. There are the internal moral laws, and the external maxims or duties. They run together, but only the former, as 'Ideas', are principles of true freedom and universality.

The principle of free-will and the corresponding categorical imperative, being unconditioned, are thus synthetic *a priori* propositions, and thus require the 'synthetic use of pure practical reason.' (Kant 1785, pp.112-3) In the final section of the *Groundwork*, Kant anticipated his next project, the 'Passage from a Metaphysic of Morals to a Critique of Pure Practical Reason'. Here the parallelism of the first *Critique* is expressed most clearly with the Idea of free-will and practical reason:

> Hence, in spite of regarding myself from one point of view as a being that belongs to the sensible world, I shall have to recognize that, *qua* intelligence, I am subject to the law of the intelligible world - that is, to the reason which contains this law in the Idea of freedom, and so to the autonomy of the will - and therefore I must look on the laws of the intelligible world as imperatives for me and on the actions which conform to this principle as duties. (Kant 1785, p.121)

Three years after the publication of the *Groundwork*, which was never intended to be anything more than a 'foundation' for a practical metaphysics, Kant did indeed produce his second *Critique*, of *Practical Reason*, which revised his 'Idea' of internally generated constraints on freedom, and presented a philosophy of ethics. In essence much of the second *Critique* repeats and develops what was laid out in both the first *Critique* and in the *Groundwork*. Freedom cannot be explained by reason, as Kant had noted in the final pages of the *Groundwork*, and so all we can do is defend it against those who assert its impossibility, because they too cannot prove their claim (Kant 1785, p.127). Rather than struggling with the inability to prove the validity of pure practical reason, Kant simply suggests that we must possess a free-will because of our undeniable recognition that we are bound by the moral law. It is a presupposition of our awareness of ourselves. It is, quite simply, a 'fact of reason'. The moral law 'is given as an apodictically certain fact... of pure reason, a fact of which we are *a priori* conscious' (Kant 1788, p.47).

In concluding the *Critique*, Kant iterated perhaps the most famous lines in his entire moral philosophy: 'Two things fill the mind with ever new and increasing admiration and awe, the oftener and more steadily they are reflected on: the starry heavens above me and the moral law within me.' (Kant 1788, p.161) Practical reason, the reason within us, has replaced God: 'The same subject, who is also conscious of himself as thing in himself, considers his own existence, so far as it does not stand under conditions of time, as determinable only through laws that he gives himself through reason' (Kant 1788, pp.97-8). It is also the acknowledgement of responsibility. Human agents are so defined because they have the ability to exercise causal ie. empirical power, and the exercise will be with 'reference to an end.' It has been suggested that the idea of the purposiveness of all rational activity is the most important in Kantian philosophy (Sullivan 1989, pp.25-6). It certainly becomes the centrepiece of Kant's later writings, most obviously, the *Metaphysics of Morals*. So, as causal agents and as moral beings, we have the responsiblity of placing ourselves under our own moral laws as laws of practical reason, which preserve us from the 'empiricism of practical reason, which places the practical concepts of good and bad merely in experiential succession.' (Kant 1788, p.124) Purposive action is determined purely by the exercise of the free-will bounded only by responsibility (Riley 1986, p.555). We will act then in accord with our free-will; the exercise of absolute causal self-determination. This provides for a moral good which, separated from purely empirical good, is intrinsically good and grounds the possibility of virtue and of a practical and active virtuous existence. This presentation of morally obligatory ends as duties represented the primacy of Kant's theory of ethics. Here Kant is most clearly building upon the formula of autonomy as developed in the *Groundwork*.

In the second *Critique* Kant was thus able to reinvest happiness, not in its rampant empirical sense, but as a practical complement to virtue and which tended towards a distinct empirical collective good. Kant was always aware that there 'must be a feeling side to human morality' (Sullivan 1989, p.132). But this remains irreducibly distinct as a subjective 'side'. Here Kant is making the conceptual accommodation that constructed a complementary natural imperative as a progression to a perfect end. He does so because, as ends in ourselves, we are subject to the imperative formula of the 'Kingdom of Ends': 'For rational beings all stand under the law that each of them should treat himself and all others, never merely as a means, but always at the same time as an end in himself. But by so doing there arises a systematic union of rational beings under common objective laws - that is, a kingdom.' (Kant 1785, p.101)

The final 'end' of the moral self is 'community'. We have a duty as autonomously acting individuals to create community (Sullivan 1994, pp.85-7, 152). At the same time, we have an empirically governed 'need' for an end to each activity, and so Kant provides three imperative formulae as a theory of ethics. The three formulae of the *Groundwork*, of autonomy, of respect for other persons, and of a kingdom of ends, as principles derived from the primacy of moral law, represent Kant's theory of ethics, of what it is 'virtuous' to observe and execute. These natural imperatives, as determined by the three formulae, could 'bring an Idea of reason... nearer to feeling', but it could only be an asymptotal progression (Kant 1785, pp.103-4). 'Empirically conditioned reasoning' gave rise to its own 'prudential' or 'pragmatic' rules, but not, of course, principles or moral imperatives (Kant 1788, p.16). All such rules 'appear' as imperatives, but only universal moral imperatives obligate us absolutely and unconditionally. The categorical imperative is thus an objective and at the same time, a subjective norm. The primacy of the moral law, or course, remains unassailable: 'the concept of good and evil is not defined prior to the moral law, to which, it would seem, the former would have to serve as foundation; rather the concept of good and evil must be defined after and by means of the law.' (Kant 1788, pp.62-3)

So just as there was an intrinsic freedom separate and prior to the external freedom, so there was also an intrinsic goodness prior to empirical goodness. As Kant was to re-emphasise in his *Metaphysics of Morals*, to strive for the intrinsic good is to to be 'virtuous', and that is what the empirically good person 'ought' to do. It can only be a striving. The human moral condition prevents us from achieving 'holiness'. Moreover, as a purely formal imperative of non-contradiction, the moral law makes no statement with regard to substance. That is a question for ethics alone, and for the imperatives of the natural law.

The Critique of Judgement

Almost immediately that the *Critique of Practical Reason* was completed Kant felt the need to revise it, and the following two years between it and the third *Critique of Judgement*, were again devoted to the problem of freedom. The crucial antinomy was still there, and the concern with the subjectivity of human understanding and the accommodation with reason dominated Kant's later writings. Eight years after the completion of the third *Critique*, in 1798, Kant wrote to a friend expressing his concern that the 'scandal of reason', the fact that 'reason contradicts itself', still remained (Arendt 1982, pp.9-10). In *The Metaphysics of Morals*, he stressed that our understanding of reason is restricted to an understanding of human reason ie. practical reason, and in the third *Critique* he stressed the practical effective reduction of a theory of causation and ends to contingent ends. As Gilles Deleuze stressed, the *Critique* is a treatise about 'ends'. It thus becomes an irreducibly political treatise. Only individuals could provide a contingent 'final end' (Deleuze 1995, pp.62-3). The third *Critique* represents the culmination of Kant's critique of reason because it concentrates on the individual. Kant is unequivocal: 'without man...the whole of creation would be a mere wilderness, a thing in vain, and have no final end.' (Kant 1790, vol.1 p.108) In this sense it is a Copernican treatise of philosophy or, as has been suggested, the first truly existential treatise (Jaspers 1962, pp.78-88). In the words of Hannah Arendt, having worked through reason, 'Kant had found an entirely new human faculty, namely, judgment; but at the same time, he withdrew moral propositions from the competence of this new faculty.' (Arendt 1982, p.10) In part, then, it was the inevitable response to the determined limits, even the 'failure', of reason. Hans-Georg Gadamer suggests that the third *Critique* becomes 'the Critique of Critiques' (Gadamer 1975, p.40). In doing so it becomes the most political of the Critiques.

The whole tenor of the third *Critique* became one of reflection rather than truth. 'Thinking the particular' is itself reflection. The gap between sensibility and reason, nature and freedom, had widened into a 'great abyss'. The central problem was still how to bridge this gap, but the construction of a purely rational systematicity, by which he had hoped to bridge the gap in the *Critique of Practical Reason* was abandoned. In its stead Kant now strove to construct a mirror constitution for his faculty of judgment, what he termed 'a unity of affinity'. Nature enjoyed its own system. The faculty of judgment enjoyed the twin aspect of objective and subjective universal validity. Only judgments 'upon the good' possessed objective validity. Judgments of taste were subjective, but still enjoyed the 'possibility' of being 'valid for every one' (Kant 1790, vol.1 pp.55-7). It was no longer a matter of furnishing objective measures of understanding. The *Critique of Judgement* was concerned solely with furnishing a method of understanding. It was now a question of placing reflective hypotheses in particular social and historical contexts.

At the same time, Kant was clearly reluctant to abandon everything that had gone before. It was still essential that the individual's experience remained firmly grounded in reason. Otherwise the only alternative was an experience based on instinct, and this could provide only conditional goods (Kant 1790, vol.1 pp.435, 443). So in the third *Critique* Kant affirmed that 'it is, then, only as a moral being that we acknowledge man to be the end of creation.' (Kant 1790, vol.1 p.444) The solution which Kant presented in section 21 and primarily in section 40 of the *Critique* was the idea of communicative rationality or, as he termed it, a *sensus communis*:

> a critical faculty which in its reflective act takes account of the mode of reflection of every one else, in order, as it were, to weight its judgement with the collective reason of mankind... This is accomplished by weighing the judgement, not so much with actual, as rather with the merely possible, judgements of others, and by putting ourselves in the position of every one else, as the result of a mere abstraction from the limitations which contingently affect our own estimate. (Kant 1790, vol.1 p.151)

In section 38 he had suggested that there were 'formal conditions' for judgment. In other words communication creates its own kind of uniformity in its conditions of understanding; its own kind of rationality. The centrality of communication to the critical project cannot be overemphasised. As Deleuze suggests, it is absolutely pivotal; any universality claims are dependant upon the communicability of the *sensus communis*, as something which is itself 'implied' by the theory of knowledge. It alone can ensure the ultimate harmony of the faculties (Deleuze 1995, pp.21-3). O'Neill similarly emphasises the presence of communicability as the fulcrum of the entire critical project; its presence in the third *Critique* serves to effect the final balance. What it means, she suggests, is that there is 'no lofty position above the debate, as perhaps there might be if human reason had a transcendent source. There is only the position of one who strives to reach and understand the perspectives of others and to communicate with rather than past them.' (O'Neill 1986, p.544)

The accommodation of a purely subjective faculty, even if it was constrained by its own kind of rationality, together with the assertion of historically conditioned contingent ends, most particularly in the second part of the *Critique*, represented the most extreme position in Kant's critical philosophy. Judgment, he asserted, was 'the faculty of thinking the particular', adding moreover, acutely aware of his earlier conclusions with regard to the imperative, that 'the particular cannot be derived from the universal law alone' (Kant 1790, vol.1 p.407). Kant's increasing concentration on the subjective represented an equivalent concern with the practicalities of a moral philosophy. Kant was turning his attention, more and more, to the possibilities of a practical philosophy of ethics, and the third *Critique* provided a bridge into that.

The third *Critique* was primarily constructed as two 'Critiques', firstly of Aesthetics, and secondly, and it is here that the historicity in Kant's entire critical project is seen in its most explicit, of Teleology. Both Critiques are perceived by Kant to be the purest expressions of subjective judgment in the practical world. It is no longer a judgment on the 'perfection of anything' (Gadamer 1975, p.43). The development of the aesthetic experience was, for Kant, a return to a pre-critical interest in the subject, and was also a tacit admission that the fundamental questions raised by the nature of aesthetic judgment remained unanswered. In the 'Critique of Aesthetic Judgement', Kant stressed that aesthetics existed apart from reason. It's systematicity was purely reflective, and as such determined solely by contingent factors. It was then a symbol of freedom, and a pure subjectivity of freedom. In his treatment of our experience of the sublime, Kant suggests that our preparedness to accept this pure freedom is a testimony to the power of our internal practical reason. Sublimity is the harmony of an object of the imagination with reason. The locus of this harmony lies clearly with the individual. Experiencing the infinity of the sublime, enables us to appreciate the infinity of our position in the world as historical purposive beings. It is our infinity of creative possibilities in the pursuit of the highest possible good. A similar conclusion is reached in consideration of our experience of beauty. Again it is given by freedom, by the 'free play' of our imagination as it interacts with an object, and as such is a symbol of our freedom in morality (Kant 1790, vol.2 pp.67-74, 114-21).

Whereas sublimity was the harmony of sensibility and reason, our appreciation of beauty and its freedom is a representation of harmony between sensibility and understanding. The stress on Kant's treatment of both the sublime and beauty is twofold; freedom and, from it, harmony. Certainly both the freedom and the harmony are directly subjective, constituted by singular judgment. However, as Kant stresses in the Preface to the *Critique*, that judgment is also made in relation to the general. Beauty is judged with regard to the 'form of purposiveness' visible in an object, but aesthetic judgment, even of beauty, is not purely experiential (Kant 1790, vol.1 pp.3-7). If it was simply experiential, of course, it could not be free. The analogy with the idea of practical reason is very clear. Judgments of the sublime and of beauty, though immediately subjective, are still synthetic *a priori* judgments. The truly free, truly creative, individual is the one who is capable of purely original work and ideas. Kant refers to this potential as 'genius'. A 'genius' is one who exists by his subjectivity alone, doing so by pure self-determination. The 'genius' is also the one capable of 'virtue' and the pursuit of the highest good, and as such represents a model for both art and for politics (Kant 1790, vol.1 pp.168-9).

It is in the second part of the *Critique*, the 'Critique of Teleological Judgement', that Kant emphasised the contingent nature of individual finite ends, and presented a critical moral philosophy which itself provided a bridge into his critical political philosophy. The 'Critique' builds on Kant's enduring concerns with causation and with the purpose of existence. The question that Kant asks: 'Why is it necessary that men should exist at all?' is the question which has come to dominate critical theory. By 1790 Kant was convinced that the relation of objects can only be understood if it is assumed that each object is relationally determined by an antecedent conception of the whole. It follows from this that the designer of any object must have acted with 'purpose'. It is here that Kant synthesises the alternative 'cunning of nature' with the modern Copernican belief in self as the centre of motion, which had come to dominate his later critical philosophy. Although we cannot know the universal purposes of nature, we can and do know the reflective contingent purposes of human activity, which can only be freedom: 'there remains as that which in respect to nature can be the final purpose that lies beyond it and in which its ultimate purpose can be seen only [our] formal, subjective condition, namely capacity to set our own ends in general.' (Kant 1790, vol.2 p.98)

Freedom is thus both an external force to, and an intrinsic purpose of, nature. It remains a 'regulative' imperative. Freedom maintains its pivotal role in the synthesis of the moral and the empirical highest good: 'the union of the greatest welfare of the rational beings in the world with the supreme condition of their good, or, in other words, the union of universal happiness with the strictest morality.' (Kant 1790, vol.2 p.122) But at the same time, like all 'ideas of reason' it is now an historical idea of reason. By including a synthetic ethical-historical conception of the highest good in his *Critique of Judgement*, Kant is able refine this highest good to be 'the existence of rational beings under moral laws', which in turn necessitates a virtuous conduct, both towards the self and towards the highest good in the world (Kant 1790, vol.2 p.111). Man has an existential dimension within history. He reflects upon history and directs himself towards the highest good accordingly. This is what makes the third *Critique*, as Gadamer suggests, such a devastating Critique of the first two. It is also the kernel for Hegel's subsequent development of a dynamic and progressively moral philosophy of history. The highest good is now a fully integrated historical idea of reason, wherein critical moral philosophy becomes, at the same time, a critical ethical and political philosophy (Gadamer 1975, p.40).

The remaining years of Kant's writings were devoted to investigating further this synthesis, the subjectivity of the individual and its application to a political philosophy, and the realisation of his long-cherished ambition of a unified metaphysics of morals, and it will be these writings which will be examined in the second part of this chapter. The critical moral philosophy which Kant bequeathed was, then, one based finally upon reflective judgment. No longer was there any object out there, a 'thing in itself', separate from our perception of it. There was simply our perception. There was still a system, certainly, but it was a system that existed, indeed was constructed, precisely to undercut the Cartesian metaphysics. The role of critical philosophy was simply to continue the process of reflection, as generated by each contingent event, with a purpose of attaining an empirically reflected virtue as a historically determined contingent *telos*. In other words, any truth was only cognisable when brought into reflective judgment by intuition or sensibility ie. as a 'particular'.

As Gadamer suggests, the critical project had resulted in a critical systematic relativism. Through his attempts to invest it with universal idea of community judgment, Kant hoped to avoid the idea of a 'judgment' operating from contingency to contingency. He hoped to depoliticize judgment. But as Gadamer further points out, the aesthetic element in every judgment had fundamentally undermined the possibility of either pure theoretical or practical reason. The *Critique of Judgement* 'constituted a turning point' because, with it, Kant attempted to systematise taste and sensibility. But he attempted to systematise it by setting it totally apart from reason, and by denying in it any cognitive significance of objects. In doing so Kant set up 'a critique of critique', that questioned the entire critical project. By encouraging the pure subjectivity of individuality, and the total unrestricted 'free play of imagination and understanding', he placed the supremacy of freedom above all else, and granted it its own powers of structure. The pure *a priori* principle existed in its most acutely and purely subjective form and, as Gadamer emphasised, Kant thus opened the door to ever more acute relativism in subsequent critical philosophy (Gadamer 1975, pp.29-51). It is an opinion shared by Hannah Arendt, who suggests that in completing his critical philosophical project with the third *Critique*, 'Kant himself did not see the clearly destructive side of his enterprise. He did not understand that he had actually dismantled the whole machinery that had lasted, though often under attack, for many centuries, deep into the modern age.' (Arendt 1982, p.34)

In a sense, however, Kant was acutely aware of the potentialities of critical theory, and he certainly appreciated the responsibilities which accrued to it. Reason must subject itself to criticism precisely because it is based on freedom. Only this reasoned criticism can prevent dogmatism. But it must be done correctly, that is by exercising the proper critical method. To dabble with critical theory, but to do so carelessly, was, for Kant, the worst possible sin. When one of his former students,

Gottfried Herder, in his *Ideas on the Philosophy of the History of Ideas*, appeared to commit such a sin, the retribution was swift and damning. Herder attacked the notion of universally valid principles of philosophy and, in doing so, levelled the pure subjectivity of the aesthetic against the very possibility of the Enlightenment project. For Herder, the only thing that could reveal and be revealed was the instance. Here Kant detected a movement towards the position of both Hume and the utilitarians, and he was quick to emphasise the incoherence of a philosophy based on instincts such as happiness (Reiss 1991, pp.219-20). By entirely abandoning the possibility of universal values, and with it the conceptual rigour of critique, Herder had abandoned philosophy. In reply, Kant stressed that he was convinced that these materials [for a history of philosophy] 'are not to be found in metaphysics nor in a museum of natural history... On the contrary, these materials are to be found only in human actions, in which the human character is revealed.' (Reiss 1991, p.212) In 1784, the year of the review, three years before the second edition of the *Critique of Pure Reason*, and six before the *Critique of Judgement*, Kant was clearly already conscious of the need to ground the inevitable historicity of philosophy, and to do so by empirical investigation of human activity and judgment.

The attempt to ground aesthetics through history, the possibility of which Herder had denied, and which Kant had thus perceived to be his most serious failing, came to dominate Kant's later writings, and at the same time earned him the lasting enmity of the German romantic movement (Jaspers 1962, pp.150-4). At the same time, it showed the increasing importance that the role of the subjective and its accommodation was taking in Kant's own later critical work. Both Kant and his critics realised that the success or failure of the entire project rested on his ability to make the accommodation. It was with the *Critique of Judgement* that Kant directly addressed the problem, and it was with this *Critique* that Kant re-addressed the possibilities of critical political philosophy (Deleuze 1995, pp.68-9).

For the immediate purposes of any study of Kant's legal and political thought, it is the third *Critique* which emerges as pivotal. The validity of this assertion has recently gained greater and greater acceptance amongst Kantian scholars. Gilles Deleuze reawakened an interest in Kant's critical theory during the 1960s based essentially on this premise (Deleuze 1995). Howard Caygill emphasises that it remains the most overtly political of Kant's texts (Caygill 1989). Paul Guyer attests to its emergence as the 'archetypal work for a distinctive postmodern political vision'; a vision founded on aesthetics rather than solely on ethics (Guyer 1993). Paul Crowther has developed this thesis still further. According to Crowther, Kant's treatment of the 'sublime', as the purest form of freedom and thus of morality, represents the apogee of the Kantian critical project. What Kant appreciated was that the 'aesthetic experience - and the sublime in particular - has the capacity to humanize'. It overcomes the alienation of the moral self by demanding a communicable interaction in the exercise of judgment. In this appreciation, Kant first established the 'beginnnings of the sublime in the postmodern era' (Crowther 1989, pp.165, 172-4). It is the realisation of this which, Crowther suggests, has fired critical philosophy since Heidegger, through to the contemporary ideas of such as Derrida and Lyotard. Rather than representing the ultimately indeterminate and inarticulatable, the sublime effects 'existential insights of moral import'. The sublime is thus synthetically 'reconstructive'. By 'grounding his aesthetic on synthesis', Kant 'ties aesthetic experience to constants in the human condition' (Crowther 1993, pp.40-55, 151-2).

Aside, then, from the intrinsic merits of the *Critique* as an essentially political treatise, its pivotal status is enshrined in its impact upon contemporary critical and postmodern political philosophy. Aside from Crowther's assertions, Ronald Beiner has stressed the 'stunning implications' of the third *Critique* and Kant's analysis of subjective judgment, and its impact on the (anti)humanisms of such as Heidegger, Arendt, Derrida and so on (Beiner 1993, pp.276-84). Most recently, Kimberly Hutchings has emphasised the role of reflective judgment in laying the foundations of a 'critique of politics'; which has itself been built upon by twentieth century critical philosophers, from Arendt to Foucault to Lyotard. The infinite variety of Kantianisms itself attests to the veracity of the third *Critique*. Reflective judgment enshrines variety. It is the essential text of modern political and legal thought; the only one with which any subsequent political or jurisprudential treatise must be read (Hutchings 1996).

2 Critical Political Philosophy

Philosophy, History and Purpose

Kant had an acute political awareness. His political philosophy was consciously geared to the perceived need to provide a practical workable model of political government. For this reason he remained supremely impressed by the workability of Plato's model in the *Republic*. There was no point in providing a political theory which would not work, one that was 'impossible according to practical rules' (Kant 1788, pp.109-14). At the same time, Kant remained acutely conscious of the limitations of his position, as a loyal, and wary, subject of monarchial despots. In 1784, he was able to praise Frederick of Prussia for permitting free public debate. Frederick's instruction, to 'argue as much as you like and about whatever you like, but obey', won Kant's wholehearted approval. Such was the spirit of Enlightenment. Once again, in practice as in theory, the key was communication. The duty of the philosopher was to communicate and thus to encourage communication within a community (Reiss 1991, pp.58-9, Laursen 1986, pp.593-600).

Two recent events which had shaken the complacency of the *ancien* regimes of western Europe impressed Kant immensely - the American and French revolutions. Kant's interest in purely political and constitutional issues appears to intensify following the experience of these two revolutions, both of which clearly made him increasingly confident of the strength of a rationally constrained evolving community. In both revolutions Kant perceived the vindication of his philosophy of autonomy and self-assertion, and the model for his political ideal of freedom, equality, and tolerance, governed by a system of rights. He was particularly impressed by the way in which the two revolutions had revealed an ability of peoples to change their constitution in accord with an evolving idea of community. In Kant's perception these were revolutions of the Enlightenment for enlightenment. Unlike the revolutions of the seventeenth century, they were populist and secular, and represented the realisation of the fundamental strands of Enlightenment ideology. Most importantly they suggested the attainable resolution of current political deficiencies and the corresponding evolution of an emerging political maturity.

In *The Contest of Faculties*, Kant referred to the French revolution as: 'An occurrence in our own times which proves this moral tendency fo the human race.' It was a 'drama of great political changes'. The means of their attainment, of course, and the desirability or otherwise of revolution, remained a subject of great difficulty for Kant. Nevertheless, despite this ambiguity, the historical events of 1789 in particular, to Kant, represented the fulfilment of Rousseau's prophesy, and also, in doing so, presented themselves as signs of profound hope: 'But I maintain that this revolution has aroused in the hearts and desires of all spectators who are not themselves caught up in it a sympathy which borders almost on enthusiasm, although the very utterance of this sympathy was fraught with danger. It cannot therefore have been caused by anything other than a moral disposition within the human race.' (Reiss 1991, p.182) The importance of the French revolution lay not in the events themselves, but in their reception by the 'spectators', and in the reactions that they might generate.

It has been suggested that Kant's entire critical project is founded upon a historical idea of reason (Yovel 1980). We have already seen the extent to which teleology and 'contingent ends' gave the third *Critique* a distinctively historicist underpining. The role which Kant gives to history set the tone for the historicity advocated by subsequent Kantian philosophers of history. According to Arendt the 'infinity' of history is the final 'contradiction' which Kant could never overcome, or indeed want to. In this sense Kant was the first of the 'end of philosophy' philosophers (Arendt 1982, p.77). At the end of the first *Critique* he hoped that 'before the end of the century' philosophy would achieve 'what many centuries have not been able to accomplish, namely, to secure for human reason complete satisfaction in regard to that which it has all along so eagerly occupied itself.' (Kant 1781, p.856) In 1781, Kant wanted to overcome history with a restructured critical metaphysics. Well before the end of the century, by 1790, he realised that in fact it would be history which would overcome metaphysics itself.

For Kant, history has the dual role of shaping and re-shaping both the world and itself (Knippenberg 1993, p.165). Kant sees the shaping of the world designed alternatively by what he termed 'the cunning of nature', which crucially was devolved into a matter of 'reflection' in the third *Critique*, and also as a history of religious belief, and breaking down of various religious dogmas, to be replaced by a rational knowledge that is both rationally creative and critical. This is the vital importance, for Kant, of a Critique of reason; it will instill in us a historically aware critical method. Crucially, just as the world works itself purer, so does our practical understanding of reason. It is this dynamic conception of reason, a self-determining reason, which destroys the Platonic-Cartesian theories of reason, and which makes Kant's philosophy of reason truly critical. It represents a 'Copernican revolution in rationality' which sets itself as the impulse for the Hegelian-Heideggerian project to follow (Yovel 1980, pp.12-13). Reason is not out there, ready-made for us; reason is constituted as an immanent process with its own architectonic or, most strongly in the third *Critique*, its own communicative and teleological structures. Because it is causally constituted and teleologically directed, human reason is also interest-directed and thus finite in conception.

The idea of the highest good, and the purposiveness of practical philosophy is thus not only explicit in practical reason, but implicit in pure practical reason. A teleological historicity is immanent to Kant's critical philosophy of reason (Jaspers 1962, pp.103-7). The critical project is directed towards its accommodation within the architectonic. As the third *Critique* reveals, the irreducibility of this historicity finally overcomes the critical project almost despite itself. As we have already seen, it is in this *Critique* that Kant most expressly concentrates on the idea of the highest good as a part of the empirical-natural world, rather than just the transcendent, whilst at the same time ascribing to the progressive power of history both the 'cunning of nature' and also the immanent development of a practical reason itself. The highest good is a synthesis of the moral and the empirical, of freedom and nature. History is no longer simply a matter of nature alone.

Three years after the third *Critique*, in his essay *Religion Within the Limits of Reason Alone*, Kant re-emphasised the practical historical need of reason: 'to conceive of some sort of final end for all our actions and abstentions, taken as a whole'. This will provide 'a special point of focus for the unification of all ends.' (Yovel 1980, p.5) This process leads the pure form of free-will to a synthesis with the contingent historical *telos* of man's practical finite existence. History thus becomes an idea of history. As Kant repeats in *Religion*, 'it cannot be a matter of unconcern to morality as to whether or not it forms for itself the concept of a final end.' (Yovel 1980, p.5) So, by 1790 and 1793, Kant is attempting to use reason not only to determine the form of moral action, but also its substance. The 'need' for a philosophy of ethics was appreciated as early as the first *Critique*, but had to wait for the construction of a complete critical moral philosophy (Kant 1781, pp.808-9). The resolution of the critical project established the possibility of a historical rational practical philosophy. Once Kant was in possession of the categorical imperative with its idea of universal duty, then a philosophy of ethics became possible as an historical idea (Yovel 1980, pp.61-8). In 1797, in the *Metaphysics of Morals*, this project reaches its most mature conclusion, with both a philosophy of politics and right, and of ethics. All three represented the role of history in philosophy, and the ability of the historically determined rational individual to determine both its own and the world's final end.

Philosophical-Political Writings

For Kant politics and philosophy existed for one another, and constituted together the foundations for a critical philosophy of ethics. The immediate practical justification for philosophical-political studies is a theme common to all of them. Kant opened *What is Orientation in Thinking?*: 'However exalted we may wish our concepts to be, and however abstract we may make them in relation to the realm of the senses, they will continue to be associated with figurative notions. The proper function of these is to make such concepts, which are not in other respects derived from experience, suitable for use in the experiential world.' (Reiss 1991, p.237) The essay was written to purge reason of the 'speculative' capacity and to replace it with a practical 'orientation' through pure practical reason. In doing so understanding is placed beyond the realms of pure experientialism. This is the 'theoretical use' of 'the need of reason', to be followed next by the 'practical use'. The 'practical use' of reason consisted in 'the formulation of moral laws' which could then 'lead' towards 'the idea of the highest good possible in the world, in so far as it is attainable by means of freedom alone.' Written in 1786, in the midst of his Critiques of reason, much of *Orientation* has a very familiar ring about it. The 'ultimate touchstone of the reliability' of a practical judgment, Kant stressed, 'is to be found in reason alone' (Reiss 1991, pp.237-43). Philosophy revealed the possibility of freedom in politics, and it was for politics to realise that freedom. In a final footnote to the essay, Kant echoed the existential imperative conclusions which he had just outlined in the *Groundwork*:

> To think for oneself means to look within oneself (ie. in one's own reason) for the supreme touchstone of truth; and the maxim of thinking for oneself at all times is enlightenment... To employ one's own reason means simply to ask oneself, whenever one is urged to accept something, whether one finds it possible to transform the reason for accepting it, or the rule which follows from what is accepted, into a universal principle governing the use of one's reason. (Reiss 1991, p.249)

Both *Orientation* and *What is Enlightenment?* were concerned with the purposive nature of philosophy. *What Is Enlightenment?* opened with the confident assertion: 'Enlightenment is man's emergence from his self-incurred immaturity.' This immaturity, moreover, was 'the inability to use one's own understanding without the guidance of another.' (Reiss 1991, p.54) In other words, Enlightenment philosophy would overcome the failure to exercise autonomy and to self-determine. Writing before the composition of the third *Critique*, Kant was already committed to the contingency of the free-acting individual. In the *Idea for a Universal History*, Kant prescribed the role of the philosopher, to 'attempt to find a purpose in nature behind this senseless course of human events'. And, even though it might seem 'admittedly a strange and at first sight absurd proposition', this was an inevitably historical task (Reiss 1991, pp.42, 51-2). In both the *Idea for a Universal History* and *Conjectures on the Beginning of Human History*, Kant testified to the influence of Rousseau and his commitment to the idea of a unified historical purposefulness (Reiss 1991, p.227).

The immediate practical effect of Kant's teleological theory of the philosophy of history was the inevitability of change. The *Idea for a Universal History* is a series of Propositions which describe the evolution of a society towards a highest good. Thus, not only did the philosophy of history reveal change to be inevitable, but the purposiveness of the highest good, rendered it a duty also. The third Proposition asserts: 'Nature has willed that man should produce entirely by his own initiative everything which goes beyond the mechanical ordering of his animal existence, and that he should not partake of any other happiness or perfection than that which he has procured for himself without instinct and by his own reason.' (Reiss 1991, p.43)

Just as Kant's critical moral philosophy had led him to the conclusion that man has a duty to change himself in accord with his progress towards the highest good, which, as he suggested in the third *Critique*, was for man to bring himself 'and every other rational creature, under moral laws', so there was a moral duty, incumbent upon all men, to change the institutions of government within the ethical community. In *Conjectures*, Kant makes quite clear the futility of inactive yearning for a 'golden age'. It is man's ultimate responsibility to assert himself, using his own practical reason: 'Consequently, he must continue to ascribe his present condition and all its hardships to himself and his own choice... each individual is for his own part called upon by nature itself to contribute towards this progress to the best of his ability.' (Reiss 1991, pp.233-4) For Kant the Enlightenment was more than a form of consciousness. It was a real political force. The strength of that force, however, lay not with the individual, but with the community. In *What is Enlightenment?*, Kant observed that the greatest chance lay with 'an entire public enlightening itself.' (Reiss 1991, p.55)

In Kant's opinion the most dogmatic philosophies are theological, and as such are amongst the most strongest denials of implicit historicity. Much of *Religion Within the Limits of Reason Alone* is a critique of 'historical religions' and their inflexibility. Christianity has proved to be one of the more flexible, because it has concentrated the power of God within us. But Kant is still critical of the concentration of some faiths on especial supernatural powers embodied in statutory laws and rituals. Ultimately Kant reaches the same conclusion that he had reached in the second and third *Critiques* with regard to the attainment of the highest good. Morality 'leads ineluctably to religion', for only God can supply what we cannot. But because relations with God are transcendent and unknowable, no one can claim any especial knowledge of them. God can only be 'postulated'. And so true religious enlightenment is, then, the appreciation that all we can do is preserve our own freedom as an idea of reason. In other words the 'idea' of God that we have, will be our idea, and as such moral goodness is our responsibility.

The concept of God sits particularly comfortably with the 'reflective' nature of 'judgment' which Kant had presented only three years before. The relationship, for Kant, is one of mutual dependence. The force that is within us is clearly God's spirit and, as such, the ethics and the ethical community that we design are Christian in origin. Kant's ethical philosophy was built on this idea of the inevitability of the ethical community which he had first considered in some depth in the *Groundwork*, and then developed as a highest good in the third *Critique*. As early as 1784, in the *Idea for a Universal History* Kant had stressed that nature purposed man toward the 'establishing... [of] a perfect civil constitution', which was 'both the most difficult' problem, and 'the last to be solved by the human race.' It is the 'most difficult' problem because, 'nothing straight can be constructed from such warped wood as that which man is made of', so 'nature only requires of us that we should approximate to this idea.' (Reiss 1991, pp.46-7) It is the last because it will represent the end of conflict, the resolution of the 'antagonism' which history has revealed to be the characteristic of the human condition.

As Hannah Arendt perceptively stresses, for Kant, because communicative ethics is at root a philosophical construct, it is at once both the end and the origin of human progression. It is this which determines the inevitability of the ethical community. The idea of the ethical community was the only possible solution to resolving the perceived tension between the individual and the need to live in a social situation. It was not, Kant determined, a 'need'. Rather, it was an inevitability of existence. We live as part of our community, and our 'judgments' are reflections on the *sensus communis* of our community. As we have already noted, section 40 of the third *Critique* establishes the conditions for a wholly non-foundational community, presenting three maxims of the *sensus communis* which enjoin each individual within the community to think for themselves, to think from the perspective of others, and to think consistently. In *Religion*, Kant equates such a community with 'the kingdom of God on earth', which had come to represent a fleshing out of the 'kingdom of ends' suggested in the *Groundwork*. In *Religion*, he asserted: 'The highest good cannot be achieved merely by the exertions of the single individual toward his own moral perfection, but instead requires a union of such individuals into a whole working towards the same end - a system of well - disposed human beings, in which and through whose unity alone the highest moral good can come to pass.' All of Kant's political writings were directed towards the ultimate establishment of such a community (Ward 1972, p.142).

The mechanism for self-determination and for change, in an ethical community, is communication. This is the inter-subjective rational and essentially reflective communication which had emerged as the core thesis in sections 21, 39 and 40 of the third *Critique*. In fact, as early as the first edition of the first *Critique*, Kant had shown an awareness of the importance of communication as a constraint upon reason: 'For reason has no dictatorial authority; its verdict is always simply the agreement of free citizens, of whom each one must be permitted to express, without let or hindrance, his objection or veto.' (Kant 1781, pp.738-9) We have already noted that, as the years had progressed, Kant had clearly become increasingly aware that communication was a purely subjective method of understanding, and as such, an irreducible constraint upon it. In *What Is Enlightenment?* Kant characterised the Enlightenment not as a form of understanding, but as a purposive method of communicative understanding: 'The public use of man's reason must always be free, and it alone can bring enlightenment among men' (Reiss 1991, p.55). In *What Is*

Orientation in Thinking?, Kant again stressed that a critique of reason was simply a critique of the method of understanding (Reiss 1991, p.247).

Kant's political writings after 1790 confirm his concern with validating a practical philosophical approach to political and legal theory. At the same time they also reveal an intensification in his desire to portray a purposive natural evolution towards a state of universal peace. *On the Common Saying*, written three years after the publication of the *Critique of Judgement*, betrays Kant's determination to reaffirm the usefulness of a refined critical philosophy in political debate. The faculty of judgment, he asserts, exists to guide the individual from the universal to the particular:

> It is obvious that no matter how complete the theory may be, a middle term is required between theory and practice, providing a link and a transition from one to the other. For a concept of the understanding, which contains the general rule, must be supplemented by an act of judgement whereby the practitioner distinguishes instances where the rule applies from those where it does not. And since rules cannot in turn be provided on every occasion to direct the judgement in subsuming each instance under the previous rule (for this would involve an infinite regress) theoreticians will be found who can never in all their lives become practical, since they lack judgement... It is therefore not the fault of the theory if it is of little practical use in such cases. The fault is that there is not enough theory; the person concerned ought to have learnt from experience. (Reiss 1991, p.61)

Criticisms against theory, Kant suggests, are invariably criticisms against vague idealistic philosophies, but 'in a theory founded on the concept of duty, any worries about the empty ideality of the concept completely disappear.' Kant is particularly keen to assert that matters of law and justice must be based on duty, for 'all is lost if the empirical (hence contingent) conditions governing the execution of the law are made into conditions of the law itself.' (Reiss 1991, pp.62-3)

Kant develops his argument by suggesting that the fact that the social contract is 'derived entirely from the concept of freedom in the mutual relationships of human beings, and has nothing to do with the end which all men have by nature', means that 'a civil constitution is a relationship among free men who are subject to coercive laws, while they retain their freedom within the general union with their fellows.' Moreover, such 'is the requirement of pure reason, which legislates *a priori*, regardless of all empirical ends' (Reiss 1991, p.73). This civil state is based on three such *a priori* principles; the freedom, equality and independence of each member of the community. They 'alone' can establish a state 'in accordance with pure rational principles of external human right.' (Reiss 1991, p.74) If the legislator operates within the constraints of pure reason, he cannot err with regard to the form or rightfulness of law, only its content. It is because of this legislative infallibility that Kant can so vigorously deny any right to active disobedience. To rebel against the commonwealth would be incoherent and irrational, because it would represent self-destruction, the destruction of the idea of freedom itself. Those who advocate active disobedience do so because they mistake the social contract for reality, rather than merely an idea. However, active criticism of a constitutional ruler and the substantive rules of the constitution, in other words the communicative 'freedom of the pen', is permitted. Indeed, such an attitude represents the essential 'spirit of freedom', necessary in all such enlightened rational societies (Reiss 1991, pp.80-5).

The ultimate ambition for Kant's theory of communities and communicative reason was the idea of an international order, and it is this which he addresses in the final section of *On the Common Saying*. In the *Idea for a Universal History*, he had established 'the problem of a law-governed external relationship with other states' as the ultimate problem to be addressed. In the same essay, Kant also stressed the 'antagonistic' nature of the evolution of international order in its initial, more 'imperfect' forms. The repeated willingness of nations to engage each other in warfare reveals that 'we are still a long way from the point where we could consider ourselves morally mature.' (Reiss 1991, p.49) Kant still shares this basic premise of immaturity in 1793, but at the same time, presents a much more assertive description of the inevitability of man's progressive 'moral improvement'. An international order, he suggests, will inevitably emerge, and will do so as an idea of 'practical moral reason' (Reiss 1991, pp.87-92).

In 1785 Kant presented *Perpetual Peace*, in which constitutions derived from the idea of an original contract, were based on the three *a priori* principles, freedom, equality and independence (Reiss 1991, pp.99-101). It is the detailed presentation of the 'Preliminary' and 'Definitive Articles of a Perpetual Peace' which represents a development in Kant's treatment of international order, and which, at the same time represents a still clearer determination to present a philosophy which had a practical immediacy. 'Perpetual Peace' would be constructed upon three constituent rights; civil, international and cosmopolitan. The cosmopolitan state was the ultimate idea of 'universal hospitality' shown towards all members of all constituent states. The notion that there is a 'purposive' progression towards such universal harmony is 'guaranteed by... nature' (Reiss 1991, pp.93-111).

In his last major political treatise, *The Contest of Faculties*, Kant repeated his now familiar vindication of philosophical study, together with another assertion of the historicity of human progress. The essay is subtitled 'A Renewed Attempt to Answer the Question: Is the Human Race Continually Improving?', and is dedicated to attaining 'a history of future times', which cannot be discovered by experience, but only by reason. Although the problem of progress cannot be solved by experience alone, the 'prophetic history' Kant asserts 'must nevertheless start from some sort of experience'. In making this assertion, Kant repeats his theory of causation and change. The central section of the essay concentrates on the French revolution which could not have been 'caused by anything other than a moral disposition within the human race.' The event had clearly inspired great confidence in Kant, for whom the revolution represented, not a rebellion, but an 'evolution of a constitution governed by natural right.' So much so that he could comment:

Even without the mind of a seer, I now maintain that I can predict from the aspects and signs of our times that the human race will achieve this end, and that it will henceforth progressively improve without any more total reversals. For a phenomenon of this kind which has taken place in human history can never be forgotten, since it has revealed in human nature an aptitude and power for improvement of a kind which no politician could have thought up by examining the course of events in the past. Only nature and freedom, combined with principles of right, have enabled us to forecast it; but the precise time at which it will occur must remain indefinite and dependent upon chance. (Reiss 1991, pp.184-5)

It is perhaps fitting that Kant's political writings concluded with a testament to chance.

The Metaphysics of Morals

The Metaphysics of Morals represented the culmination of Kant's long held ambition to present a practical guide to how man might achieve his contingent highest good. It was also his final major work, and thus contains his most mature and comprehensive theories of ethics, politics and law. As such the *Metaphysics* represented the culmination of Kant's critical philosophy as history. In the 'Preface' Kant made it quite clear that the presentation of a 'system' of 'the metaphysics of morals' represented a culmination of the 'critique of practical reason'. It was a 'metaphysics' because it was a 'system derived from reason'. The philosophy of history emphasises that the ultimate purpose of philosophy is praxis. In other words the 'Idea' that man progresses towards a highest attainable good. As early as the first edition of the *Critique of Pure Reason*, Kant had prescribed a proto-type imperative: 'Do that through which thou becomest worthy to be happy' (Kant 1781, pp.808-9). But it took another sixteen years before Kant, equipped with a critical moral philosophy, could finally provide a philosophy of ethics. It cannot be overemphasised that the theoretical underpinnings of the *Metaphysics* are established by many of the key concepts which Kant had refined in the major critical works - the three *Critiques* and the *Groundwork* - freedom, duties, imperatives, ends in themselves, causality, and, most importantly, community, communication, subjective judgment and the particular in relation to the universal.

The fulcrum role of these ideas and concepts is stressed in the 'Introduction to the Metaphysics of Morals'. Section Four of the 'Introduction' makes it quite clear that the *Metaphysics* is to be based upon the concept of freedom, and the 'imperatives' or constraints upon it, obligations and duties (Kant 1797, pp.48-51). Earlier in the first Section, Kant describes the nature of moral laws, as worked out in critical moral philosophy. Practical reason is concerned with accommodating the 'capacity for desire'. So, Kant asserts: 'The capacity for desire whose inner determining ground, hence even what pleases it, lies within the subject's reason is called the will.' The will, of course, 'is practical reason itself'. So, if 'reason can determine the capacity for desire', it can determine it as 'free choice'. This is freedom from determination by natural inclinations: 'In contrast to laws of nature, these laws of freedom are called moral laws.' It is also the 'capacity of pure reason to be of itself practical.' Re-emphasising what he had determined in the *Groundwork*, Kant states that, in terms of the imperative, this is the capacity of every maxim of action to qualify as a universal law. As such it is a 'capacity' of form, and not of substance (Kant 1797, pp.41-2). In the second section, Kant repeats that morality 'command[s] for everyone, without taking account of his inclinations, merely because and insofar as he is free and has practical reason.' If, therefore, there is a 'system of *a priori* knowledge from concepts alone', in other words a 'metaphysics', then 'it is itself a duty to have such a metaphysics, and every man also has it within himself' (Kant 1797, p.44). Making explicit reference to the third *Critique*, Kant emphasises that the metaphysics of morals lies within each individual, and as such it is at once a metaphysics of freedom, and a practical philosophy (Kant 1797, p.45).

The main part of the *Metaphysics* is divided into a 'Doctrine of Right', and a 'Doctrine of Virtue'. The two are quite separate realms, but are united in the sense that they represent the two 'practical' applications of a critical moral philosophy. In the *Groundwork*, Kant had restricted himself primarily to establishing the form of duties, and once again this is the primary force of the 'Doctrine of Virtue', but with the complementary 'Doctrine of Right' in particular, Kant presents a substance for the ethical community which he wishes to promote. Any attempt to understand what is Kant's most elaborate and mature philosophy of law, politics and society, necessitates an integral appreciation of the two sections. What both sections of the *Metaphysics of Morals* investigate is the nature of freedom and its constraints, both political and ethical, external and internal. In the 'Introduction' Kant suggests that the distinction between the two 'Doctrines' is defined by 'incentive' and constraint: 'That lawgiving which makes an action a duty and also makes this duty the incentive is ethical. But that lawgiving which does not include the incentive of duty in the law and so admits an incentive other than the Idea of duty itself is juridical.' (Kant 1797, p.46) There is thus the one concept of duty, but the practical effects of this duty can be either ethical alone, or both ethical and juridical: 'Ethical lawgiving (even if the duties might be external) is that which cannot be external; juridical lawgiving is that which can also be external.' (Kant 1797, p.47)

In the *Groundwork*, Kant had concentrated on the subject who imposed the obligation. In the *Metaphysics*, however, he addresses the subject upon whom the constraints or obligations are imposed. The former is the pure practical reason; the latter is a subject enjoying the 'capacity for free choice'. It is from the latter that practical maxims of action are derived. Kant refers to 'practical reason putting itself under obligation.' (Kant 1797, p.235) In the *Groundwork*, Kant had impressed the contingent nature of man as an end in himself. Again in the *Metaphysics*, Kant repeats that it is its capacity to set any end whatsoever which 'characterizes humanity (as distinguished from animality)' (Kant 1797, pp.195-6). An end, moreover, is 'an object of free choice, the representation of which determines it to an action (by which the object is brought about)' (Kant 1797, p.189). The idea of determined action is derived from the theory of causality which became increasingly important in the second and third *Critiques* in particular. The moral action is the one derived from the freewill, and the maxims which govern action are those which the individual chooses to adopt in the pursuit of the ends which it wills.

The bridge between the critical moral and critical political philosophy is then established by the concept of 'duty' as constraint which, following the first two *Critiques*, was firmly established as an Idea of Reason. It was quite clear from the

Groundwork, of 1785, that Kant saw 'duty' as the synthetic *a priori* principle upon which he could construct both a political and an ethical theory. These duties were, of course, derived from the individual and the individual's moral law, in other words from his freewill. The freewill is free because it is pure practical reason. It is neither guided by the moral law, nor any empirical laws. As such, the only constraint on duties as freedom, is the freewill itself. The pure practical reason provides the categorical imperative, from which the obligated subject then creates its maxims or imperatives (Kant 1797, p.51). The categorical imperative is thus the keystone of the entire structure. As a concept, or Idea of reason, the duty which it prescribes provides a universal consistency of form. It transcends any subjective contingency inherent in the human condition. Any maxim which does not conform to the universality of the categorical imperative 'is contrary to morals' (Kant 1797, p.51). It is, however, the presence of this subjective contingency in practical 'free choice', the co-existence of a transcendent imperative with the subjective multitude of possible maxims, which necessitates Kant's consideration of the substance as well as the form of the community, and it is this which makes the *Metaphysics* the essential culmination of Kant's entire critical project.

The Doctrine of Right

For Kant the problem of ordering society had always been intimately connected with the problems of freedom and justice. The first 'Doctrine', of 'Right', is devoted to the just ordering of society; in other words the constraints demanded by the existence of individuals in the ethical community. By concentrating on the specific problem of constraint, Kant was enjoining a debate which had long troubled natural right theorists for whom the presence of external constraint had never been easy to justify. Kant determines natural right as innate right, which is the right to freedom of action. This is the one and only natural right, and thus the only non-acquired right. Moreover, Kant adds, this principle of innate freedom inheres the quality of 'innate equality, that is, independence from being bound by others to more that one can in turn bind them.' (Kant 1797, p.63)

Kant enshrines this innate freedom as a 'concept of Right' which, being a concept, is thus a matter of form, not of substance. The 'Doctrine of Right', then, like the subsequent 'Doctrine of Virtue' is grounded in critical moral philosophy. The 'concept of Right' is an 'Idea' of reason: 'All that is in question is the form in the relation of choice on the part of both, insofar as choice is regarded merely as free, and whether the action of one can be united with the freedom of the other in accordance with a universal law.' It is following this statement that Kant can then posit the 'Universal Principle of Right': 'Any action is right if it can coexist with everyone's freedom in accordance with a universal law, or if on its maxim the freedom of choice of each can coexist with everyone's freedom in accordance with a universal law.' (Kant 1797, p.56) This is the one maxim which cannot itself be the subject of external constraint. As an *a priori* concept of practical reason, that 'I make it my maxim to act rightly is a demand that ethics makes on me.' (Kant 1797, p.56) If anyone exercises their freedom in such a way that it will infringe upon the freedom of another, then, and only then, can the actions of the first person be constrained, because to use freedom in such a way, to use it to restrict the freedom of another, is fundamentally incoherent: 'Hence there is connected with Right by the principle of contradiction an authorization to coerce someone who infringes upon it [ie. freedom].' (Kant 1797, pp.56-7) External constraint is only used to preserve internal freedom, and the 'contradiction', as such, is a synthetic one.

The 'one innate right' is contrasted with 'acquired right', which are rights which have to be established by 'an act'. In the civil situation this 'act' will be the 'positive' law of a legislator. Having distinguished the principles and the concept of right in the three introductory sections, Kant then devotes the first 'Doctrine' to justifying the obligation placed by the legislator upon the subject. He defines this positive law precisely by its constraining power, and by its contingent nature. The distinction between the form and the substance of Right remains at the heart of the 'Doctrine'. The substantive external law is no longer one's own moral law of the freewill, but a collective ethical law of a collective freewill. External law thus constrains the actions of the individual, not the act of free choice itself. This is, of course, the essence of the categorical imperative. By placing morality apart from substantive external legislation, and by underlining the contingent nature of all such legislation, Kant is presenting a theory of external law which is at once both positivist and critical.

The first part of the 'Doctrine of Right' considers the nature of private right. Here Kant is concerned with rationally justifying the possession of something external. There is no purely rational justification for private possession. The only justification is that of pure practical reason. The subjectivity of choice is thus determined as 'a synthetic *a priori* proposition'; 'Right is a pure practical rational concept of choice under laws of freedom.' (Kant 1797, p.71) Because there can be 'no theoretical deduction...for the possibility of freedom', possession of an external object, as a right, 'can only be inferred from the practical law of reason (the categorical imperative), as a fact of reason.' (Kant 1797, p.74) The substantive matter takes on the formal characteristics of right, and possession thus becomes an 'idea of reason' just as law is. The synthetic *a priori* nature of choice and possession is the keystone to Kant's entire theory of right, and as such employs all the building materials of the critical metaphysical project.

The laws of causality demand that the use of any object requires its possession by the user. This use, of course, is relational and must be one which is compatible with the freedom of others. The choice is then a communal choice, made in relation to other members of society. It is this relation with these other external members which removes possession of an external object from the empirical sphere to the *a priori*. It is Kant's assertion that nothing is by nature free in a society. Everything is possessed by someone or some group of individuals (Kant 1797, pp.69, 72). As such, use and possession determine their own practical rationality and, in turn, it is the practical concept of use and possession which determines the nature of a society. Only a society governed by a civil constitution can regulate use and possession in accordance with the principles of practical reason.

The natural right becomes a civil right and thus a rational right. In the following three sections of chapter two of the 'Doctrine of Right', Kant discusses property, contract and family as relational concepts of possession grounded as rights; in other words, as synthetic *a priori* concepts determined by, and determinative of, a community situation. Thus when discussing the original right to property, Kant suggests that the idea of community is defined by possession, and that a 'conclusive' acquisition (ie. not a 'provisional' or original right) is determined by the presence of a civil constitution, 'which alone determines what is right, what is rightful, and what is laid down as right.' The relation of possession, Kant stresses, is purely formal as an idea of community (Kant 1797, pp.84-9). So just as a right over property is a right held against others and thus a constraint on their freedom, only justifiable as a community right of pure practical reason, a contract in turn is the acquisition of someone else's promise, and thus a constraint on their choice, and justifiable only by the rationality of the relationship (Kant 1797, pp.93-5).

A right to possess something is by implication a right against everyone else, and as such a constraint upon them, and it is only a 'universal' rule which can regulate such a right. It is thus the postulate of 'Public Right' which demands that we enter the civil society, and submit ourselves to the civil constitution, so that our rights to possession are themselves subject to practical universal maxims. Possession is, then, no longer a matter of choice, but of duty. In the final chapter of the first section of the 'Doctrine of Right', Kant emphasises that the civil community is characterised by the power of a 'Public Court of Justice' to administer the 'distribution' of justice. This court makes 'judgments', which for the Kant of 1797 were teleological historical judgments of practical reason. The court judges issues of right and rightful possession in the community. In other words, it judges the coherence of relationships between individuals in a bid to decide whether or not they are practically rational (Kant 1797, pp.118, 122).

In the second part of the 'Doctrine of Right' Kant considers 'Public Right'. It is here that he describes his idea of the 'just state'. The establishment of a 'constitution' unites individuals in a 'civil condition' ie. an *ad hoc* community. There are then three Rights, of the State, of Nations and of all Nations, and all three are 'Ideas' of Right; in other words, a series of communities, each defined in relation to one another. Kant first discusses the nature of the 'state'. The 'state', as 'a union of a multitude of men under laws of Right', is itself an 'Idea' of Right. In describing the 'authorities' in the state, Kant invokes a classical separation of powers thesis - sovereign, executive and judicial authorities. In the 'just' state, the state as a synthetic *a priori* idea of Right, the individual retains three qualities, lawful freedom, civil equality and civil independence. In preserving these qualities a state will remain rightful (Kant 1797, pp.123-6).

The civil constitution is described as a contract, although it is clear that, as an instrument of private right, Kant uses the contract in public law strictly as an analogy.

The use of the contract analogy stresses the inter-relational nature of community rationality. The original contract is established as an Idea of Reason, and thus as a synthetic *a priori* principle. Possession can only be preserved and protected once the possessor has acknowledged the constraints immanent to the original contract. The contract is, thus, not a document of state, but a document of practical reason. The state, and the creation of the rational community exists purely as and, in practical terms, for the sake of, external freedom and the freedom to possess. Each 'citizen' is then 'in possession of himself and is not dependant upon the absolute will of another alongside him or above him.' (Kant 1797, p.128, Hoeffe 1992, pp.120-42, Kersting 1992, pp.149-52) As a synthetic *a priori* concept, the state of the original contract is representative of both internal and external freedom. The contingency of the external freedom is theoretically quite distinct from the coherence of the internal freedom. The state, and the original contract, are ultimate expressions of Kant's critical philosophy.

As to the nature of the authority of the state, monarchy, aristocracy or democracy, Kant is equivocal. The matter is purely one of effectiveness. It is futile to inquire further, because the immediate premise of the inquiry is wholly contingent. A constitution is an 'idea' of reason; the best constitution is a matter of practical politics. The constitution itelf is determined by its rightfulness, that is its internal coherence as a structure of freedom and equality. But that is as far as a critical philosophy extends - further questions are outside its remit. Kant's emphasis on the historical evolutionary nature of the establishment of such a government is significant (Kant 1797, pp.147-9). A state governed by a rule of law is an end in itself - a contingent end which, being contingent, can be achieved. Indeed, it must and will be achieved. Appreciation of the true critical nature of pure practical freedom will make this end inevitable. There will be constant evolution and change until this end is realised, and once realised, history will have overcome itself.

Kant's two sections on the Right of Nations and of all Nations then develop the basic constructively rational model and its limits. The Right of Nations is the right of states in relation to one another. Just as a state is determined by its own relational *a priori* rationality, so states can determine a rationality between one another. However, according to Kant, such a rationality is not as developed as the rationality of the state, essentially because it lacks the coherence of a sovereign authority. There is thus no united will which can express itself in authority. As such there is no concept of internal freedom and no corresponding 'right' of possession between states in international law. Such states remain in 'the state of nature', and their 'rights' to possession remain only provisional. Devoid of this essential 'rightfulness', the rationality between states lacks the internal constraints of pure practical reason. There is constant conflict between states, both physical and non-physical. In order to secure external freedom and the right to possess, the Right of Nations must evolve as an internally rational and coherent concept of law; as, Kant suggests, a 'league of nations'. Once again, this evolution is inevitable and, once achieved, will lead inexorably to a historically determined, and historically determinable, end in itself, of peace: 'Only in a universal association of states (analogous to that by which a people becomes a state) can rights come to hold conclusively and a true condition of peace come about.' (Kant 1797, p.156) The end, however, is a contingent one, and falls short of a universal Nation and a universal peace. The impossibility of an ultimate Nation leads Kant to discuss the practical alternative of a 'Cosmopolitan Right'. The idea of mutual association between individual communities, though contingent, is still an idea of pure practical reason, an idea of critical political philosophy. Such an association is demanded by peaceful interaction between communities, and as such creates its own practical rationality (Kant 1797, pp.158-9).

In conclusion, then, Kant's theory of 'Public Right' is essentially a theory of sovereignty, and that sovereignty belongs to the united will of the people. This fundamental position is reasserted in Kant's published reply to a critique of the *Metaphysics* which appeared in the Goettingen Journal (Kant 1797, pp.176-7). It is a self-determined and self-asserted sovereignty. As such the people give the law to themselves as the principles of pure practical reason and duty would demand. These laws, as enacted by a legislative and executed by an executive, will be necessarily contingent. This contingency, however, in no way detracts from the internal coherence that each community as a state can enjoy. As an 'idea' of reason, each community will be constituted by its own synthetic *a priori* rationality.

The Doctrine of Virtue

If the 'Doctrine of Right' expresses a positivistic and critical analysis of external constraints, the 'Doctrine of Virtue' presents an analysis of internal constraints based on the 'ought' concerns more familiar to natural rights theorists. This is the essential distinction between the two 'Doctrines': 'Ethical duties involve a constraint for which only internal lawgiving is possible whereas duties of Right involve a constraint for which external lawgiving is also possible. Both, therefore, involve constraint, whether it be self-constraint or constraint by another.' (Kant 1797, p.198) The second 'Doctrine' is, of course, still a metaphysics, and it is the fact that the 'Supreme Principle'of ethics is synthetic, as a form of internal constraint, that further distinguishes it from the analytic 'Doctrine of Right'. Kant reemphasises that both 'Doctrines' present 'metaphysical first principles'in the Preface to the second 'Doctrine', commenting that any 'moral principle' upon which action is based is 'really an obscurely thought metaphysics that is inherent in every man because of his rational disposition' (Kant 1797, pp.181-2). The second 'Doctrine' is, thus, most sharply a critical metaphysics.

The duties upon which the second 'Doctrine' is based are then once again principles of pure practical reason, and more explicitly duties of 'inner freedom': 'the part of the general doctrine of duties that brings inner, rather than outer, freedom under laws is a doctrine of virtue.' (Kant 1797, 186) Kant is concerned with the ethical development and qualities of the individual, and the self-constraint which determines these qualities. It is no longer a question of actions and possession, but of development and lasting dispositions. In other words, these are duties which are self-determined, and exist quite apart from the external duties discussed in the 'Doctrine of Right': 'Ethics considered in terms of its formal principle is the science of how one is under obligation even without regard for possible external lawgiving.' (Kant 1797, p.211) An ethical maxim is determined if, as an inclination, it could qualify as a universal law, and so the inter-relationship between the two 'Doctrines' is established by the ethical obligation to make the universal law of right a maxim of action. In other words, the maxims of virtue exist as guides to virtuous behaviour: 'Maxims are here regarded as subjective principles which merely qualify for a giving of universal law'. Maxims do not prescribe ends of behaviour or action; they establish themselves as ethical duties (Kant 1797, p.193). It is for the 'Doctrine of Right' to provide the substantive content of Kant's philosophy of ethics, just as the 'Doctrine of Virtue' will itself provide the substance for the philosophy of right.

It is the nature of the 'end' which distinguished the second 'Doctrine' from the first. In the 'Doctrine of Virtue' the end and the duty are one. As a synthetic concept this 'end' is 'an end of pure reason that is presented as an end which is also objectively necessary, that is, an end which, as far as men are concerned, it is a duty to have.' (Kant 1797, p.186) Whereas the external constraints were provided by an external legislator - albeit as an expression of 'general will' - and as such could not be determined by specific incentive, the internal constraints of virtue, as self-imposed constraints, are necessarily ends orientated. The incentive is determined by one's own will, and it is an ethical disposition which leads the individual to adopt ends which are determined as duties themselves. The ends are derived from the duty; they are not pre-determinative of it. At the same time, this 'end' is, as an active 'object of choice' - every end is causally generated - based on the same premises of purposiveness, contingency and practical rationality which had provided the gears to the 'Doctrine of Right' and to the entire critical moral philosophy. The second 'Doctrine' is a synthetic theory of contingent individual ends, and it is the synthetic character of these ends as duties which presents a critical philosophy of ethics: 'among these ends there must be some that are also (ie. by their concept) duties. For were there no such ends, then all ends would hold for practical reason only as means to other ends; and since there can be no action without an end, a categorical imperative would be impossible. This would do away with any doctrine of morals.' (Kant 1797, p.190)

The two ends that are also duties, are 'one's own perfection' and 'the happiness of others'. Both are 'concept[s] belonging to teleology' and, as such, duties of pure practical reason. Man has a 'duty' to cultivate his own faculties, and in doing so increase the sum of human happiness (Kant 1797, pp.191-2). This he does by acknowledging the responsibility of ethical duties as maxims of ends-orientated actions. The variability of these ends, of the substance of the ethics, creates what Kant terms 'wide obligations'. These are obligations determined by broad maxims of behaviour, not by the narrower constraints of political right (Kant 1797, pp.194-7).The assumption of internal constraints is virtue, and the supreme virtue remains the constraint of self-government through the exercise of reason: 'Since virtue is based on inner freedom, it contains a positive command to man, namely to bring all his capacities and inclinations under his (reason's) control and so to rule over himself...for unless reason holds the reins of government in its own hands, man's feelings and inclinations play the master over him.' (Kant 1797, p.208) This is the ethical concept of responsiblity which complements the concept of political responsibility advanced as the centrepiece of the first Doctrine.

Following the 'Introduction', the remainder of the 'Doctrine of Virtue' is divided into the larger first part, the 'Elements of Ethics', in which are derived the specific ethical duties, and a smaller second part, the 'Method of Ethics', which discusses the practice of virtue. As outlined in the 'Introduction', there are two types of ethical 'duty', to oneself and to others. The idea of constraining oneself is, of course, a contradiction, and Kant acknowledges this potential antinomy at the very start of his deeper examination of duties to the self. The antinomy is an inevitability of the synthetic nature of the duty, and so is the solution. The resolution, as propounded by each and every subsequent Kantian theorist, lies within the nature of internal freedom as free-will. The following list of duties to oneself which Kant then presents are determined as duties which prevent one's own freedom and lead to a denial of self-constraint, from the most extreme example of 'murdering oneself' to excessive drinking and servility. All such vices are fundamentally irrational and incoherent, and lead to the ultimate self-negation and denial of responsibility for and to oneself. Each of these vices also leads to the dissolution of the community of which one is a member (Kant 1797, pp.214-32).

In possession of conscience, man has the innate ability to judge his own conduct. Indeed man will be the ultimate judge of his own virtuous behaviour, guided by the constraint of a rational conception of God. These are not then universal standards of virtue but standards of practical reason, judging the form or coherence of activity, not its substantive quality: 'the Idea is not given to him objectively, by theoretical reason, but only subjectively, by practical reason, putting itself under obligation to act in keeping with this Idea (Kant 1797, p.235). Man can thus strive towards his own moral perfection. Of course, given the manifold nature of the duties of virtue, he can never attain it. He is destined instead to an existence of 'continual progress' towards to an unattainable end (Kant 1797, pp.241-2). Such was the conclusion that Kant had derived from the third *Critique*.

The coherence of the community is the primary ethical duty incumbent upon all members within it. The feelings which accompany the duties owed to other members of the community are those of love and, most importantly, of respect; the feelings necessary to maintain the coherence and stability of inter-relationships which create the community. Hatred and disrespect will lead to the dissolution of the community. Mutual respect will create its own series of obligations upon which a community can be constructed. So the importance of the community is once again central in Kant's philosophy of ethics. In the practical world of politics and ethics, a rationally constructed community is not only an inevitability, it is a rational duty (Kant 1797, pp.256, 265).

The *Metaphysics of Morals* represents the first discrete piece of modern critical legal and social thought. The intensity of self-assertion, responsibility and the exercise of free-will as the constituents of rational action, and the construction of the communicatively determined community are emphasised again and again, and nowhere more forcefully than in the final 'Doctrine of Virtue'; another Kantian text all too readily ignored by those in search of a Kantian jurisprudence. As Karl Jaspers emphasised, it is the 'Doctrine of Virtue' which best encapsulates the existential nature of Kant's critical political philosophy. It is the openness of the Doctrine which demands the continuing development of the Kantian critique; it recognises that critique can never be foreclosed (Jaspers 1962). According to Paul Guyer, the 'Doctrine of Virtue' is Kant's ultimate political-ethical statement, revealing in its concentration on duties to the self, more than any other political text, the pervasive influence of the third *Critique*. Critical political philosophies founded on 'duties of love', such as those of Unger and Lyotard, take their inspiration from this doctrine (Guyer 1992, pp.31-2, 304-84). As Roger Sullivan has recently emphasised, no one before Kant had placed reciprocal duties to the self and to others at the very heart of a political and ethical philosophy. In this way Kantian political philosophy goes beyond politics in order to accommodate the dignity of the self (Sullivan 1994, pp.15, 32, 127-8).

A Kantian political and legal theory cannot, of course, be located in the 'Doctrine of Virtue' alone. Neither can it be located in the *Metaphysics of Morals*. Neither can it be found in the *Critique of Judgement*, or any of the other *Critiques*. Kant's critical political and legal philosophy can only be located in the entirety of his texts. Any assertion that another Kantian politics can be ascertained simply from the third *Critique* is as mistaken as the contrary assertion that it can be found in a simple reading of the *Metaphysics* in the context of the *Groundwork* and the second *Critique*. The purpose of this chapter has been to show that the 'politics of critique' demands a holistic approach to Kant. Yet, as Hutchings has recently emphasised, such an approach does not furnish a consistent or easily accessible Kant. Indeed, it reveals a 'volatile and paradoxical' political philosophy. Yet this only serves to emphasise its veracity. The writing of a critical political philosophy was a constant 'struggle' for Kant, and one which ultimately eluded him; as any such critique must (Hutchings 1995, pp.12, 39, 55-7). Rather than leaving us with a completed philosophy, Kant actually leaves a wholly incomplete philosophy; that is his greatest achievement. Kant confirmed that the politics of critique cannot be foreclosed. The varieties of Kantianism which have followed, and which are considered in the following chapters, bear testimony to this achievement.

CHAPTER 2

FREEDOM, RESPONSIBILITY AND JUDGMENT

1 The Heidegger-Kant Dialogue

The Question of Ethics

The interest in a Heideggerian ethics was first suggested by Charles Sherover in 1972, but has only really received an impetus first from Daniel Dahlstrom and then most recently and most substantively from Frank Schalow in his important and influential study, *The Renewal of the Heidegger-Kant Dialogue* (Sherover 1972, Dahlstrom 1991, Schalow 1992). For all three the starting point, if only as an immediate symbol, is Heidegger's oft-cited comments made in the spring of 1928: 'Some years ago, as I studied the *Kritik der reinen Vernunft* anew and read it against the backdrop of Husserl's phenomenology, it as, as it were, as though the scales fell from my eyes and Kant became for me an essential confirmation of the rightness of the path on which I searched.' (Dahlstrom 1991, p.329). It is generally recognised that the Kantian turn prefigured Heidegger's ensuing Nietzschean turn, which was an attempt to jump the 'abyss' from which he had perceived Kant to have recoiled.

Recent commentators on Heidegger's engagement with Kant have unsurprisingly supported the received view that his monumental *Being and Time*, published in 1927, was generated as a critique of Kant's architectonic of reason. Two years later Heidegger published a a philosophical codicil as *Kant and the Problem of Metaphysics*. For some this represents the culmination of the engagement, but for others it is merely a stage in a continuing dialogue which occupied Heidegger right up until his death. According to Dahlstrom, Heidegger's statement appears in the middle of 'roughly a decade' during which he was thoroughly 'preoccupied with Kant's critical philosophy' (Dahlstrom 1991, p.329). Schalow suggests that Kant is the only consistency in Heidegger's work, ever present in the ontology, the ethics, the politics and the later concerns with technology and language. Heidegger's work, he says succinctly, is a continuing 'appropriation of Kant'. Moreover, the development in Heidegger's own thinking very conspicuously reflects his successive encounters with Kant's various *Critiques*. In 1927 Heidegger used Kant to retrieve an ontology. Two decades later he was still using Kant as a means to accessing an effective praxis (Schalow 1992, pp.xi-xviii).

Although Heidegger will go on to make serious dispute with much of what he terms 'Kant's ontology' in the first *Critique* in particular, from the very opening pages of *Being and Time*, his admiration for Kant is clear (Heidegger 1962, pp.30-1). Kant had established the direction for critical philosophy, the 'path' along which it must travel. Kant had made three particular moves which had broken from the established metaphysical tradition. He had identified time as the source of ontology, he had distinguished time from the determination of particular beings, and he had suggested time as the basis of experience. Self-consciousness, Heidegger went on to suggest, could then be determined with regard to time (Dahlstrom 1991, p.351). It was this which distinguished his own brand of sentient philosophy from the more explicitly neo-Kantian epistemology of such as Ernst Cassirer. Both parties shared the conviction that the key to unlocking a critical Kantian philosophy lay with the concept of judgment, but whereas Cassirer pursued the established line of 'logical judgment', Heidegger developed the alternative of a judgment determined by intuition. According to Cassirer, of course, this was the critical distinction, and anyone following Heidegger was abandoning Kant and any possibility of reason (Cassirer 1967). Yet, Heidegger himself suggested that Kant was his closest ally in the campaign to reestablish human finitude, and it is directly from the Kantian hermeneutic that Heidegger develops his own theory of hermeneutics and historicity.

The later, post-*Rektorat* Heidegger, increasingly immersed in the related problems of language, technology and history, turned to the third *Critique*. But the earlier ontological Heidegger remained with the first *Critique*, because it was in this work, and in this work alone in two thousand years of philosophical inquiry, that Heidegger thought that he could see a way of 'extracting' the individual, by reexamining the relationship or 'space' between the 'knower' and the 'object' (Heidegger 1990, p.31). This was the circle described by the Kantian hermeneutic. Heidegger's determination to follow this 'path' is revealed in his earliest lectures. Already Heidegger had identified the central issue in critical philosophy, indeterminacy, and had directed himself to effecting its accommodation. By the 1925-26 lectures, he had decided that its resolution could only be effected in time, by man's essential finitude. Even in these pre-*Being and Time* years, Heidegger was firmly immersed in the nature of the hermeneutic, and the historical 'evolutionary character of meaning'. Thinking, he repeatedly observed, was always an engagement with previous thinkers. It was in the following lecture series that Heidegger made his famous already noted comment about the need to follow the 'path' determined by Kant. This alignment with Kant, as Heidegger knew only too well, necessitated either the abandonment or the accommodation of both interpretation and ethics. The essential question of this period in Heidegger's thinking was 'What is the role of ethics?' The solution which was to emerge from *Being and Time* was an ethics which originated in 'the factical dimension of lived experience' (Schalow 1992, p.39).

The 'rift' between truth and judgment was the essential element which Heidegger drew from Kant. He had noted this before *Being and Time*. By the time of its completion he knew, just as Kant had a century and a half before, that any continuing ontological inquiry would need to address, increasingly, the concept of judgment (Schalow 1992, pp.21-2, 45-79). The famous 'Truth Problematic' had emerged as the heart of *Being and Time*, and the critique of Kant's first *Critique* had increasingly become a critique of the problem of *a priori* judgment. By the time Heidegger emerged from *Being and Time*, truth was firmly remodelled as a 'being' thing rather than an 'object' thing. This was 'truth in its relational sense'. Heidegger's conscious dissociation with neo-Kantianism has erroneously led a number of commentators to underestimate the nature of Heideggerian relativism. Relativism is the concept which determines the nature of any neo-Kantian philosophy. For Heidegger relativity was central because it geared the mutually creative relationship between persons and objects (Heidegger 1990, pp.81, 135-8).

This recognition becomes a hallmark of subsequent attempts to determine a Heideggerian ethics. Thus, as Arendt comments, judgment is always an interpretive strategy (Arendt 1982, p.4). It is however most clearly in the *Kant* book that Heidegger presents 'imagination' as the derivative of judgment and as the centrepiece for a future philosophy of ethics. It is here that Heidegger wrestles most vigorously with the synthetic model as he bids to internalise knowledge with an experiential fore-understanding (Heidegger 1990, pp.357-68). Thus, as Schalow observes, although Heidegger champions 'imagination' as the conceptual centrepiece, the real key to the *Kant* book is 'experience'. By the time of its completion the 'path' was again redirected, from the first to the third *Critique*. By the end of 1928 Heidegger's ultimate ambition had crystallised still further. His ambition and that of any critical philosophy, had to be one of achieving the mediation of the theoretical and the practical; in other words, a praxis (Schalow 1992, pp.77-9). It was the same ambition, of course, as Kant's.

From 1929 onwards the later Heidegger, post-*Being and Time*, abandoned his ontological inquiry about the essence of being, which is taken for granted, and instead reformed the question so that it addresses the relations between beings and objects. At this stage, he was also better able to disinguish his project from that of the neo-Kantians. Whereas neo-Kantianism develops 'from' the relativism of being, in other words it describes, Heidegger wants to go further back, to the 'roots' or 'essence of being', and question the very foundations of man's finitude; thus his increased interest, during this period, in the pre-Socratics. The *Kant* book had reorientated critical philosophy from epistemology to ontology, and so now it undergoes a complementary reorientation, from the logical to the aesthetic. To stress this movement, at this time, Heidegger entered a vigorous debate to defend Kant's transcendental aesthetic against Scheler. Some commentators suggest that this represents Heidegger's firmest commitment to a Kantian critique, and at the same time an explicit ackowledgment that the third *Critique* represented the 'point of departure for critical philosophy' (Schalow 1992, pp.107-23, Sallis 1987, pp.67-75). In the *Kant* book Heidegger clearly declared that his ambition was to extend critical philosophy along the same path, but beyond the point that Kant was prepared to go, declaring famously: 'In the radicalism of his questions, Kant brought the 'possibility' of metaphysics to this abyss. He saw the unknown. He had to shrink back.' (Heidegger 1990, p.115) Judgment lay beyond pure reason, and it was there that Heidegger hoped to locate the essence of being.

Examination of the third *Critique* reinforced Heidegger's confidence that a synthetic idea of judgment would lead inexorably to relativism and then to a theory of existence. This process he termed the 'synthesis of perception'. It was, he also realised, echoing both Kant and the neo-Kantians, a matter of 'reflection' as opposed to 'determination'. The key to praxis lay in accessing a 'consensus' of 'judgment', because such a consensus was 'world-formative'. The 're-trieving' of this conception of judgment would be effected by historical and communicative thinking. Kant, he recognised, had an 'inhibition' with regard to the 'forefront of language'. It was language, Heidegger increasingly came to believe, which would enable him to negotiate the abyss from which Kant had recoiled. Language, more than anything else, would 'unlock the subject'. The ambition was the same as Kant, but the concentration on language was very much Heidegger's own critique of the third *Critique*, because language held the key to communication and thus to 'consensus' (Schalow 1992, pp.156-60, 188-97). An understanding of judgment could facilitate an understanding of praxis.

What Schalow terms the 'frontiers' of praxis, and the possibility of a Heideggerian ethics, were defined by the concept of freedom; the critical conception in any Kantian ethics. In *On The Essence of Truth*, Heidegger suggested that freedom lay at the heart of a Kantian view of the world, thus represented the active corollary of praxis (Heidegger 1978). According to Arendt, Heidegger's move towards a praxis was primarily a response to the increasingly purposive notion of man which emerged as the first *Critique* evolved into the third. From the purposive man emerged the conceptions of self-assertion and responsibility which become the key components of a Heideggerian ethics. It is here, according to Schalow, that Heidegger and Kant are indistinguishable in their attempt to link freedom with obligation (Schalow 1992, pp.258-60). The interface is most clearly and most famously expressed in Heidegger's *Letter on Humanism*, where he articulated his belief in the evolution of 'practical freedom' into a concept of 'self-responsibility'. Heidegger quite deliberately adapted Kant's concept of 'self-respect' as the genesis of 'self-responsibility'. This, of course, is also the genesis of the Kantian moral person, who respects the moral law because it represents respect for oneself (Heidegger 1978). As Schalow asserts, what Heidegger realised, from Kant, was that a 'de-emphasis on the universality of the law and its rational origin... marks an important concern in uncovering a viable ethics capable of meeting the challenges of the contemporary age' (Schalow 1992, pp.274-8). It was this realisation which convinced Heidegger to construct what was essentially a Kantian theory of ethics. As Heidegger himself observed in *Basic Problems of Phenomenology*: 'In subjecting myself to the law, I subject myself to myself as pure reason; but to say that in subjection to myself I raise myself to myself as the free, self-determining being. The submissive self-elevation to myself reveals, discloses as such, me to myself in my dignity.' (Heidegger 1992, p.135)

An awareness of the nature of the Kantian moral self was thus evident from Heidegger's earliest writings. In the *Kant* book he observed that: 'To the extent that the essence of the subjectivity of the subject lies in its personality, which, however, is synonymous with moral reason, the rational character of pure knowledge and of action must be solidified. All pure synthesis and synthesis in general must, as spontaneity, fall to the faculty which in a proper sense is free, the acting reason'. (Heidegger 1990, p.115) Morality is something done as opposed to something that simply is, and the 'awakening to moral obligation' is an expression of self-responsibility (Heidegger 1990, pp.108-9). Morality is thus the 'synthesis' of 'imagination', of accommodation of receptivity and creativity. Freedom is responsibility, the freedom to do something, and this is what Heidegger determines as an ethics of praxis: 'The essence of a person, personhood, consists in self-responsibility... Practical freedom as autonomy is self-responsibility, the essence of the personality of the person, the authentic essence, the humanity of man.' (Heidegger 1990, p.167) It is this vision of praxis which provides the springboard for a host of various Heideggerian ethics, as presented perhaps most coherently by Hannah Arendt and Herbert Marcuse, who both took a particular interest in developing Heidegger's movement towards a community ethics, and the social dimension of freedom.

The years following the *Letter on Humanism*, published in 1946, saw a continuation with the problems of praxis, building on the ethics which he had constructed. At the same time, the foreground of Heidegger's thought was now occupied by a deeper investigation into the historicity of technology and language. This was a clear response to increasing engagement with the aesthetics of the third *Critique*. The question of ethics was famously redefined as *The Question Concerning Technology* (Heidegger 1978). Questioning becomes central after the 1930s, and the redefinition of human finitude and judgment. It is here that some, most famously Derrida, have detected the ethics shaken by a deconstructionist turn and an increasingly radical historical contingency.

Heidegger's 'path' certainly took many turns, but it remained the one which Kant had established, and to which Heidegger had declared his early allegiance. The power remained with the creative individual despite the threat of modern society. In continuing his opposition to modern ethics, including that which he perceived as presented by the neo-Kantians, Heidegger maintained that his 'ethics' was the properly developed Kantian praxis, where the individual, and not metaphysics, determined the 'ends' of individual endeavour, and the nature of his relations with others. This was the practical ethical 'meaning of Being'; consensus based on freedom. According to Sherover, it is this ultimate resolution of the ethical problem which designates Heidegger's praxis as unavoidably liberal in spirit and in substance (Sherover 1972, p.46) It is, ultimately, imaginative freedom which empowers the individual against the potentially alienating conditions of modern society. As we shall see shortly, it was upon these foundations that Hannah Arendt was to attempt to establish a more liberal Heideggerian ethics.

Heidegger's Political Speeches, 1933

Following his controversial appointment to the rectorship of Freiburg University in spring 1933, Heidegger made a series of speeches in which he articulated a political 'ethics'. Whether, of course, this was a genuine Heideggerian ethics, has remained an issue of vigorous debate, as has the more general problem of his association with National Socialism (Ott 1994). These issues will be considered shortly. But first we must look at the speeches themselves, starting with the most notorious, the *Rektorat*. For some, the *Rektorat* was the classic exposition of a Heideggerian-Kantian ethics. For others it also represents the moment of ambivalence in Heidegger's project, after which he finally tries to abandon any hopes of an ethical praxis (Ott 1994, pp.133-66). The *Rektorat* is itself a deeply controversial and ambiguous text, stressing at once the power of the individual and the constraints on that power. During it, Heidegger made what is undoubtedly his most (in)famous quasi-jurisprudential comment: 'To give the law to oneself is the highest freedom.' (Heidegger 1985, p.476) But what did Heidegger mean by this statement ?

Before trying to answer this question it is necessary to establish a perspective. There can be little doubting the importance which Heidegger attributed to his position at Freiburg. In *Facts and Thoughts*, composed after the war, he emphasised his 'plan for founding the essence of the university in a primordial manner' (Heidegger 1983, pp.483-4). Heidegger wanted to be nothing less that the *eminence grise*, the spiritual *Fuehrer*, of National Socialism. He wanted to revolutionize the German university, and with it the German people (Ott 1994, pp.21, 147-64). When asked, in the 1976 *Der Spiegel* interview, whether he had envisaged an integral relationship between the German university and 'the political situation in Germany as a whole', Heidegger unequivocally replied in the affirmative (Heidegger 1981, p.47). Heidegger's assumption of the Rectorship offered an opportunity to play a role in the design of a National Socialist political ethics.

The *Rektorat* was entitled 'The Self-Assertion of the German University'. As the title suggests the key idea is that of self-determination. There can only be self-determination if 'we know who we ourselves are' (Heidegger 1985, p.470). The correlation between the essential determination of man and truth, as he repeated throughout both the Kant and the Nietzsche lectures, was the 'impulse' behind everything, before and after *Being and Time*. It was certainly the impulse in 1933: 'The Self-Assertion of the German University is the primordial will to its essence' (Heidegger 1985, p.471). 'Essence' was a principle Heideggerian construct, because it represented something internal and thus beyond metaphysics, and at the same time, something determinative. Throughout the *Rektorat* there is constant comparison between the truly 'essential' and the contemporary complacency of metaphysical *Wissenschaft*. The new German constitution was to be immanently determinative, and not a metaphysical structure of inessential rules and morals.

The 'Self-Assertion', the taking responsibility which it described, was the primary statement which Heidegger wanted to emphasise in May 1933. In the same way as the German students, the German people were to 'assert' themselves and to come to 'presence' as a cultural and historical people, so that they would then 'give the law to' themselves. In this sense the 'Self-Assertion', as the assumption of responsibility, represented both the first step towards a 'presencing' and also to its completion or 're-trieval'. These two concepts, 'presencing' and 're-trieval', were critical. In *The End of Philosophy and the Task of Thinking*, written in 1962, Heidegger revised the 'task of thinking' from 'Being and Time' to 'Opening and Presence'. Heidegger retrospectively suggested that the desire to 're-trieve' a space for thought, and the possibility of 'presencing', or coming-to-oneself, was the consistent thread throughout his writings

(Heidegger 1978). The idea was immanently historical, and Heidegger attributed it to the combined influences of Kierkegaard and Kant.

In his favourite metaphor, Heidegger described the process of 'presencing' and 're-trieval' in terms of retracing certain 'pathways' or *Holzwege*, which would lead to the 'opening'. The specific term for the process is *Wiederholung*: *Wieder* as the 'self-again', and *holung* as the 'fetching'. This, then, is what Heidegger meant when he urged the German students to 'give the law to themselves'. They should take the responsibility to assert their law, by 're-trieving' an authentic understanding of law. What Heidegger meant was that they should cast aside understandings of law which were irrevocably prejudiced by existing liberal notions of *Recht*. What it also meant, of course, was that the German people must always recognise their own potential to construct the integrated principles of law and morality. 'Self-Assertion' would enable them to create space and possibilities, within which they could then access and realize a more 'essential' understanding of law.

This was only the first part of the praxis which Heidegger presented in the *Rektorat*. The second part concerned the 'freedom' which the German students would then access by taking the responsibility to self-assert. 'Freedom', as has already been noted, was the ultimate foundation in Heidegger's attempt to redesign an alternative Kantian ethics. To continue the metaphor, 'freedom' was that which was found in the 'opening'. In *On the Essence of Truth*, conceived around 1933, Heidegger concentrated on this conception of 'freedom', as distinct from an unrealizable metaphysical freedom, and its humanistic import. Towards the end of the *Rektorat*, Heidegger uncompromisingly rejects the contemporary neo-Kantian alliance of freedom with humanism: 'The much celebrated academic freedom is being banished from the German university: for this freedom was not genuine, since it was only negative.'(Heidegger 1985, p.476) Heidegger's freedom is a freedom of praxis, an embracing of responsibility of the 'spiritual mission' to self-determination. As with each and every Heideggerian construct, this 'freedom' enjoyed a reciprocal internal and external aspect. Freedom is both a power and a constraint; the freedom to be always relative. This was the crux for any thinker engaged in a 'dialogue' with Kant. According to Derrida and Lacoue-Labarthe, it was this accommodation which remained unresolved and which continued to haunt Heidegger long after 1933 (Lacoue-Labarthe 1990).

During the summer of 1933 Heidegger taught a course at Freiburg entitled 'The Fundamental Questions of Philosophy'. It continued his attempt to retrieve an essential understanding of Being, and also represented an intensification of his engagement with Kant. At the same time it continued the theme, from the *Rektorat*, of the 'self-assertion' of the historical German people: 'The German people found itself and also found at its head a *Fuehrung*. Thanks to this, the people, now returned to itself, created itself.' But, he added, it was only the 'difficult dawning of a still obscure future.' The theme was complemented by his continuing desire to reformulate the 'Question', from pure ontology to praxis. During the course of these lectures, Heidegger forcefully allied the question of Law with the Question of law: 'The fundamental

Question' was 'the Question of Law and the structure of Being' (Farias 1987). In the place of metaphysics, the 'structure of principles and ideas', there would be a new Questioning of Law.

The possibility of the Question was, of course, critical. The means to accessing 'opening' or space, what Heidegger termed 'impoverished' thought, lay with 'authentic' questioning. The very first lines of *Being and Time* had asserted that the 'Question has today been forgotten'. Applying a Husserlian methodology, Heidegger could assert that, 'Questioning is a knowing search for beings in their thatness and whatness... the meaning of Being is the question to be formulated.' (Heidegger 1978, pp.316-7) In *The End of Philosophy* he reformulated the proposition, so that 'Questions are paths towards an answer. If the answer could be given it would consist in a transformation of thinking, not in a perpetual statement about a matter at stake.' His whole thinking, he acknowledged, had been driven by the desire to strip away 'prejudices' and to shape the Question more 'primordially' (Heidegger 1978, p.373, 381, 392).

Authentic thinking was Questioning. In the *Rektorat* Heidegger was unequivocal; 'questioning becomes the highest form of knowing.' *What is Metaphysics?*, the text built from the 1933 lectures, was devoted to redefining the nature of questioning, as determined by indeterminacy. The construct of *Being and Time*, *Dasein*, could never of course determine Being, only the Question of Being, for it was itself the determination of temporality. It defined itself and did so when it inquired about Being. The 'space' where the Question would be 'presenced' must be sought both externally and transcendentally; thought is an 'internal quality', and one that is reflective. In his *Discourse on Thinking*, Heidegger stresses the reflective quality of 'meditative thought', which he perceived as having been usurped by 'calculative thought', and which it was now the job of critical philosophy to re-trieve, as a condition of Questioning. As the 1930s progressed, the Question became something more than it was in 1927. In 1927 it was just the method of thinking, but by 1933 the Question was everything, method and matter. It was in Questioning that being came-to-itself; it 'presenced'. In the *Der Spiegel* interview, at the end of his life, Heidegger commented: 'The only measure for thought comes from the thing itself to be thought. But this is, above all, the Questionable.' (Heidegger 1981, p.64) Only a reformulation of the Question could overcome metaphysics, and that Question was the Question of Law, not the metaphysical question of *Recht*; the critical Question of the moral and ethical law, the immanent and principled law that had been presented by Kant in the three *Critiques*. The manifestation of our Being, our *Dasein*, such as political or ethical laws, can have no determination save that made recognisable by the Question.

If the summer 1933 lectures, and their central theme, represented a 'metaphysical' antidote to the *Rektorat*, Heidegger's most controversial political comments were reserved for his address to the 'Students of Germany'. Here, in its rawest form, was a Heideggerian praxis. With regard to the problem of law, Heidegger was unequivocal: 'Do not let principles and ideas be the rulers of your existence. The *Fuehrer* himself, and he alone, is the German reality of today, and of the future, and its law.' The statement went to the very heart of legal philosophy, dispensing with the metaphysical conceptions of liberal legalism, and instead presenting a legal politics which could realize a Heideggerian neo-Kantian praxis. It is the first sentence which warrants especial attention. Here Heidegger advocates the abandonment of external metaphysics, to be replaced by the immanent morality of the essential existential person. Again, authentic law is self-asserted law. In the *Der Spiegel* interview, Heidegger repeated his view presented most famously in *The End of Philosophy and the Task of Thinking*, that philosophy as metaphysics had come to an end. It was, he suggested, a mere 'distraction', albeit a considerable one. In its stead was 'another thinking', critical thinking (Heidegger 1981, p.59).

So philosophy was 'ended'. The word that Heidegger used is *vollendung*, which more suggestively translates as full-ness. Philosophy was 'full', and there was no room left for essential critical thinking. Legal philosophy too was *vollendung*. It would be overcome, but not by an alternative metaphysical conception of law, not by ideas. Law would become real and existential, the product of concrete experience, not somebody else's ideas. It would thus be self-asserted law. It was here, of course, that Heidegger veered most sharply from the Kant of the *Metaphysics of Morals*. Although, as a number of commentators have noted, the *Rektorat* in some ways crystallised Heidegger's confrontation with Kant, following 1933-35, Heidegger continued to operate with the same conceptions provided by critical philosophy. The destruction of the Kantian idea was the reconstruction of the Heideggerian praxis (Harries 1975, p.643).

The political reality of the praxis is presented in the second sentence. The *Fuehrer* was the 'reality of today, and of the future, and its law.' Hitler was to be the political *Fuehrer*, just as Heidegger was to be the philosophical *Fuehrer*. Both would guide Germany to its 'presencing' and its 'freedom'. The word *Fuehrer* has a particular meaning in German philosophy, to which the reality of Adolf Hitler is of only marginal relevance. Heidegger referred to the '*geistige Fuehrung*', or spiritual conduction, as the 're-trieval' of 'spirit'. The *Fuehrung* were 'pathways', and so *Fuehrung* and *Geist* were mutually supportive. The importance of the *Fuehrung* had been stressed at the very opening of the *Rektorat*, as 'that unyielding spiritual mission that forces the fate of the German people to bear the stamp of its history' (Heidegger 1985, pp.470-1). The *Fuehrung* was essential thinking, both necessary and temporalised. It was, of course, historical thinking. Concrete existential thinking is necessarily historical thinking. Thus there is no longer a philosophy of law, just a reality of law, and that reality is the *Fuehrer*, who, in the real existential situation, will lead Germany to the 're-trieval' of its 'essence'. In August 1932, Heidegger had invited the German jurist Carl Schmitt to join in the *Fuehrung*: 'I am very much counting on your collaberation in rebuilding the entire faculty of law from the inside out... It becomes ever more urgent to gather together the spiritual forces that can bring about what is to come.' (Habermas 1989, p.443) By 1932 Schmitt had already graphically advocated the merits of dictatorial governance against transcendental jurisprudence.

By May 1933 Heidegger was a card carrying member of the National Socialist party. By late 1934 his political ambitions were finished. The National Socialist constitution never came about, not at least in Heidegger's vision. The failure of National Socialism had a massive effect on Heidegger, coming as it did at the time of his initial engagement with Nietzsche. The capture of National Socialism by what he perceived to be metaphysical politics left him bitterly disillusioned (Ott 1994, pp.156-8). According to Poeggeler, it also convinced him to abandon his projected second volume of *Being and Time*, and also with it any continuing ontological ambitions (Poeggeler 1978, p.99). Yet, this in no way threatened the validity of a Heideggerian praxis. As Heidegger repeated after 1945, Germany was still awaiting a true National Socialism. The refusal to repent has proved to be a cause of considerable heartache to Heideggerians, who have sought to distance their intellectual mentor from his apparent aberration. Heidegger was prepared to disown Hitler, but not National Socialism, and certainly not the praxis he had prescribed for it. Ultimately, of course, Hitler failed Germany, and he failed Heidegger, because he had failed to take 'the responsibility of the entire west.' Hitler was not the *Fuehrer* that both needed, but both still needed a *Fuehrer* (Blanchot 1989, p.478).

The recent renewal of the Heidegger debate, sparked in the main by Victor Farias's implicit suggestion that any Heideggerian praxis would be inevitably fascist, has served to return Heidegger to the forefront of contemporary philosophical debate (Farias 1987). According to Ferry and Renaut, everything, particularly for the tradition in French post-structuralism and deconstructionism, hangs in the balance (Ferry and Renaut 1990). According to Karl Jaspers, Heidegger was a 'child' who 'got caught up by the juggernaut of hideous political events.' Yet, the story of Heidegger's engagement with Nazism had a 'touch of the tragedy of evil' about it (Ott 1994, p.244). For others however, such as Loewith and Lukacs, there is an implicit fascism in the Heideggerian praxis (Ott 1994, p.134). The same reluctant admission is made by Lacoue-Labarthe, and perhaps most strongly by Otto Poeggeler in his much revised and influential second edition of *Heidegger's Path of Thinking*.

Amongst others there was a more valiant attempt to rescue Heideggerianism from the Nazi taint. Hannah Arendt, though expressing distress that Heidegger, like Plato, when he 'entered into human affairs, turned to tyrants and *Fuehrers*', tried to divorce the politics from the philosophy. According to Hans-Georg Gadamer, the failures of 1933 catalysed the re-orientation in Heidegger's thinking, towards Kant's third *Critique* and towards Nietzsche (Gadamer 1989, p.428). As we shall see in the next chapter, the renewal of the Heidegger debate has forced Derrida to reexamine the whole basis of the *Rektorat* and led him similarly to conclude that the flirtation with Nazism only served to intensify Heidegger's desire to reformulate a praxis, directed more towards intuition and judgment and away from ontology and the spectre of metaphysics. The debate will continue. Like all great debates there is probably no certain answer to it, and that, of course, is precisely what Heidegger himself would have wished. Regardless of the degree to which his thinking is fascist or not, there is certainly no doubt with regard to its influence in contemporary critical thought. In the following section, and the three ensuing chapters, it will be suggested that the

Heideggerian influence extends right into the heart of contemporary critical legal thought, and does so as a conduit of the Kantian critique.

2 Hannah Arendt and the Politics of Judgment

The Philosophy of Judgment

With all major political thinkers, it is never easy to distinguish the political thinking from philosophical. Given her singularly reflective approach to thought and her correspondingly wide range of writings, the problem is particularly acute with Hannah Arendt. Recent studies of her work have tended to emphasise the overall political intent of her writings whilst implicitly acknowledging their philosophical substance and foundations (Parekh 1981, Canovan 1974, Hansen 1993, D'Entreves 1994). Four intellectual figures dominated Arendt's life; Karl Marx, her two teachers Karl Jaspers and Martin Heidegger, and Immanuel Kant. It has been recently suggested that Martin Heidegger, with whom Arendt had a brief but intense physical relationship, was the 'philosophical hero' of her early life, whilst Kant emerged as the 'philosophical hero of her adult life' (Watson 1992, pp.19-25, Young-Bruehl, 1982, pp.50-6). Certainly the formative years were of crucial importance in Arendt's intellectual development. The turn to Kant towards the end of her life, as she sought a solid philosophical basis for her political theses, was very much a re-turn. When she enrolled to study philosophy under Heidegger in 1924, like Heidegger and virtually everyone else at the Marburg Faculty, Arendt was immediately cast under the neo-Kantian spell.

After Marburg, Arendt moved to Heidelberg to continue postgraduate work, and to continue her interest in Kant under the supervision of Karl Jaspers, whom she came to perceive as 'the twentieth century's reincarnation of Kant' (Arendt 1965, pp.71-94). Rather perversely perhaps, it was following her arrival at Heidelberg that Arendt became less concerned with the individual and more concerned with the concept of social solidarity, more with political philosophy than with political science. It was nearly forty years later, as she approached *The Life of the Mind*, that Arendt came full circle and returned to Kant. The tradition in which Arendt continued was, as Sheldon Wolin observed in his review of *The Life of the Mind*, very firmly in the 'Kant-Heidegger' line (Wolin 1978). According to David Watson, Arendt's philosophy 'identified with the existential pole of the Kantian legacy...and in particular with the achievement of Heidegger.' (Watson 1992, p.107) Unsurprisingly, following both Heidegger and Kant, Arendt's philosophical thinking was primarily geared to a critique of metaphysics, and as such she was fundamentally critical of a system of thinking which established 'truth' as the goal to be achieved.

It is difficult to attempt to weigh the relative influences of Kant and Heidegger. Most recently Phillip Hansen has suggested that Arendt's philosophy is firmly grounded in the Kantian legacy and, moreover, that, in similar spirit to Kant, her later thoughts were determined by a desire to soften the rigours of the categorical imperative in the more immediate and practical world of political philosophy. Arendt's return to philosophy was in fact an attempt to provide thorough philosophical foundations for the 'fact' of reasonable 'pluralism' in modern politics (Hansen 1993, pp.195-200). Maurizio D'Entreves has similarly stressed Arendt's pivotal concentration on the modernist suppression of Kantian judgment (D'Entreves 1994, pp.12-3). Margaret Canovan has also emphasised the Kantian influence, using her lectures on Kant's third *Critique* to validate her assertion that Arendt's political philosophy was at root a neo-Kantian philosophy geared to the desire to subvert the concept of truth. In the place of truth Arendt wanted to place freedom, and it was this which inexorably led her back to Kant. At the same time, however, it was an overriding concern with the existential situation of the individual which fascinated Arendt's political inquiries (Canovan 1974, pp.110-26).

Bikhu Parekh has redefined Arendt's Kantian engagement by tracing it through the more immediate influence of Heidegger. Parekh stresses that Arendt consciously followed Heidegger in her Kantian critique, and in particular her critique of truth. In this way, Arendt was sucked into a critique of phenomenology which only served to intensify her belief that the key to developing a critical philosophy lay with a development of the Heidegger-Kant dialogue. It was with this critique of philosophy in place that Arendt engaged the various concepts of philosophical and political indeterminacy; contingency, pluralism, judgment and experience. Finally, it was with this critique completed that Arendt then moved on to search for a reconstructive critique in Kant's later writings. In this sense, Heidegger and Kant represented polar opposites, but opposites contained within the same spectrum of criticism, and between which Arendt oscillated. Heidegger's existentialism represented the 'radical end of subjectivism' in that it impressed the irreducible alienation of the human condition, whilst Kant presented the constructive alternative of reflective and communicative hermeneutics. Kantian philosophy, as Arendt realised, could still constrain the radical intersubjectivity which Heidegger had released (Parekh 1981, pp.61-72).

In reading Arendt, the two primary philosophical texts are *The Life of the Mind* and the lectures on Kant. The Heidegger-Kant dialogue dominates both (Hinchman and Hinchman 1984). *The Life of the Mind* is essentially two of a projected three part thesis, containing two studies, of 'Thinking' and of 'Willing'. The third projected part, 'Judging', for which Arendt had only written the title and two quotations before her death, has been posthumously constructed from her lectures on Kant's political philosophy. The first two treatises, on 'thinking' and 'willing' are essentially the primary critiques, and represent a rearticulation and evolution of both Heidegger's and Kant's critiques of the mechanics of metaphysics. The third treatise, on 'judging', is the more reconstructive and depends more exclusively upon Kant. The first treatise was a critique of 'thinking' as employed in the western metaphysical tradition, and it is in this treatise that the influence of Heidegger is most apparent. The strict constraints which the Socratic tradition has placed upon the individual power to think have supressed the idea of freedom and free-will. The thesis is of course, Heidegger's.

In the introduction to 'Thinking', Arendt emphasises that she is sharing the Heidegger-Kant inheritance in seeking to subvert metaphysics, and to reconcile the fact of philosophical indeterminacy by reorientating philosophical endeavour towards meaning rather than truth (Arendt 1971, pp.3-15). The first two sections of 'Thinking' continue by critiquing metaphysics as a philosophy of 'appearances', and again she acknowledges that the primary philosophical impulses for making the Being-Appearance distinction are Kant and Heidegger. The critical move, she acknowledges, was Kant's, because Kant realised that the power of thinking lay within the individual. But it was Heidegger who really developed the thesis to such an extent that the 'doubting' mind, or skepticism, became an inevitable of philosophical investigation (Arendt 1971, pp.40-65). Although Arendt never got to present a coherent third treatise, on 'judging', it is clear from the second section of 'Thinking' that her thoughts already lay in this direction. The search for 'meaning' must lie with an investigation of 'judgment', which is an 'activity' of thought. Kant was the first to advocate two related modes of thinking, 'judgment', and 'common-sense'. In a substantive commentary on Kant's theory of 'thinking', Arendt stresses the dual role of the Kantian thinking individual, at once an actor/thinker and a spectator/judge. From Kant, she immediately proceeds into a discussion of Heidegger, and particularly into the problem of language as a control of judgment and truth, which was of course the progression which characterised Heidegger's post-Nietzsche writings. Her ultimate position, that truth is a contingent relation of knowledge and object, is clearly in sympathy with Heidegger's later work. In the following final two sections of 'Thinking', Arendt continues by developing Heidegger's search for a pre-Socratic basis for thinking, which was itself triggered by the problem of language. The solution, however, lies less with the pre-Socratics, but rather with the later Kant, and the marriage of reason and judgment (Arendt 1971, pp.73-10, 111-20, 192-3, 212-6).

In the second treatise Arendt tries to present at least a partial defence of 'willing', against 'thinking'. The primary reason for this is the desire to reconstruct a conception of freedom from the idea of the free-will. It is here that Arendt begins to move more sharply away from Heidegger. Whereas Heidegger looked to the pre-Socratics in order to avoid the ramifications of the Kantian free-will, Arendt suggests that the search for a new political philosophy makes the free-will an unavoidable component (Arendt 1971, pp.3-6). Again, as with 'judgment', it was Kant who first realised the critical and 'liberating' power of the will, and its dominance in the 'modern age'. After Kant, philosophers, and here she suggests that Heidegger is a prime example, strove to define the relation between the will and Being, but paradoxically did so by thinking about willing. Kant, of course, shared the philosopher's 'embarassment' about the potential of freedom and the 'problem of spontaneity', but tried to constrain the free-will through the power of the morally driven individual and reason, rather than through thinking. This was Kant's 'discovery of the inner man', the origins of which can be traced back to the very beginnings of a philosophy of ethics, and Augustine's idea of the individual creative will (Arendt 1971, pp.20-9, 57-9, 104-9).

The conclusion to 'Willing' reveals, perhaps most clearly of all, the extent to which Arendt is describing the emergence of a critical philosophy through the Heidegger-Kant dialogue. Here she immediately reemphasises the pivotal position of freedom in 'thinking', which can thus introduce a philosophical basis for a political philosophy of action, or praxis. What Arendt wants ultimately, and what she perceives to be Heidegger's most fundamental neglect, is to present a revitalised philosophy of 'thinking' based on action, rather than a simple passive conception of the will (Arendt 1971, pp.149-51, 172-8, 197-9). This will be a political philosophy constructed around the fact of 'human plurality'. She writes:

Thus political freedom is distinct from philosophic freedom in being clearly a quality of the I-can and not the I-will. Since it is possessed by the citizen rather than by man in general, it can manifest itself only in communities, where the many who live together have their intercourse both in word and in deed regulated by the great number of *rapports* - laws, customs, habits, and the like. In other words, political freedom is possible only in the sphere of human plurality, and on the premise that this sphere is not simply an extension of the dual I-and-myself to the plural We. Action, in which a We is always engaged in changing our common world, stands in the sharpest possible opposition to the solitary business of thought, which operates in a dialogue between me and myself. (Arendt 1971, p.200)

The twentieth century is, at least intellectually, the century of 'difference' and of starting anew. This is a direct response to the Kantian critique of metaphysics. The treatise ends by suggesting that the next and final step in her reconstruction of the march of critical philosophy will be to reconstruct this political philosophy by reintroducing the idea of judgment (Arendt 1971, pp.201-7, 217).

The overriding political ambitions behind Arendt's philosophical investigations were those which framed the prospective concluding treatise on 'Judging'. Although death intervened, the publication of her *Lectures on Kant's Political Philosophy*, upon which the treatise on 'Judging' was to have been based, provide us with a comprehensive introduction to Arendt's thoughts on the subject. Above all, they provide us with conclusive evidence of a return to Kant, and more precisely to the third *Critique*. Kant, she repeatedly asserts, was the 'greatest representative' of the 'origin of critical thought', the great 'liberator' who sought to free us from intellectual 'prejudice'. Above all, when Kant thought critically, he thought politically and he thought practically (Arendt 1982, pp.36-43). The overriding purpose behind the Kant lectures is to reinvest Kant's political philosophy, as primarily articulated in *The Metaphysics of Morals*, with the perspective of the third *Critique*. This she attempts chiefly by trying to stress a particular continuity between the third *Critique* and the *Metaphysics*. Thus she notes that the *Metaphysics* as originally conceived in 1770 was to be the 'Critique of Moral Taste', and that the third *Critique* was similarly subtitled the 'Critique of Taste', which suggests that by the time of the third *Critique* Kant had firmly divorced morality from taste, and determined that political philosophy was to be developed from the latter (Arendt 1982, p.10).

It was only once Kant had accommodated the potentially devastating effects of the 'particular' that he could then, according to Arendt, progress to writing a politics. Indeed, the logic of the third *Critique* demanded the immediate tackling of two particular questions, of man's relationship with others, and the reasons for a political existence. Arendt makes particular note of Kant's increasing interest in matters political, and most especially in constitutional law (Arendt 1982, pp.10-6). The key to understanding Kant's political philosophy lies in appreciating the constructive nature of society's rationality, and in the particular role of communication in that construction. It is this which mediates the fact of 'plurality'. The only constraint upon men was man; the constraint of the morally driven individual upon the potential indeterminacy of the plural society. It is for this reason that Arendt suggests that Kant was the first to define the existential problem (Arendt 1982, pp.17-28). Kant's own solution to this problem was political 'relativism', as of course articulated by the neo-Kantian pluralists with whom Arendt moved at such close intellectual quarters whilst at Marburg. Relativism in politics is the only possible alternative to either extremes of dogmatism and skepticism. Her commentary here on the need for a constructive rationality to work itself pure, is strikingly reminiscent, not only of the neo-Kantian pluralists but also of more contemporary Kantians such as Dworkin or Rawls. It was the presentation of relativism as the only alternative that made Kant the 'all-destroyer of metaphysics'. In Arendt's words: 'Kant himself did not see the clearly destructive side of his enterprise. He did not understand that he had actually dismantled the whole machinery that had lasted, though often under attack, for many centuries, deep into the modern age.' (Arendt 1982, p.34)

She continued by suggesting that 'discord', as opposed to harmony, is man's 'natural' condition, and that man's subsequent attempt to progress by constructing a limited harmony was the essence of politics. Pluralism is thus 'the vehicle of progress', which is itself perpetual and indeterminate (Arendt 1982, p.52-8). The perspective, then, with which we should read Kant's political writings is that provided by the 'Critique of Aesthetic Judgment', because it outlined the means of understanding the relationship between taste and communicability. Such a relationship is one geared to facilitating a shared appreciation of meaning, as opposed to an assertion of truth. The communicator, or 'spectator-judge', always exists in a plural situation. Moreover, he is always judging 'something', and judgment, as Kant so peceptively noted, is nothing more than the application of 'common sense' (Arendt 1982, pp.61-4). Such an exercise objectivises to the extent that it creates objects relatively and reflectively, by comparison with other objects. Not surprisingly Arendt makes much of the critical sections in the third *Critique* where Kant himself outlined the nature of a commonly constructed sense, or *sensus communis*. In her final lectures on Kant's political philosophy, Arendt makes much of the *sensus communis* because it will lie at the heart of her own notion of 'participatory democracy', and that which will be subsequently suggested by like-minded critical political and legal theorists. The *sensus communis* is the articulation of judgment, as demanded by the fact of 'pluralism' and the essential 'sociability' of men (Arendt 1982, pp.72-7).

The Kant lectures have attracted considerable attention. According to Ronald Beiner, Arendt's return to Kant was prompted by her initial inability to resolve some of the perplexities which she had encountered in trying to account for twentieth century politics and the 'crisis in understanding'. Beiner emphasises Arendt's like of the intersubjective potential of a political theory based around a *sensus communis* of reflective judgment. Moreover in his concluding comments, Beiner suggests that it is this thesis which lies at the heart of contemporary critical political theory, whether it be of the liberal kind as enunciated by such as Rawls and Dworkin, or of the more radical Habermasian variety. Arendt's particular like of the more constrained notion of reflective judgment, he concludes, aligns her more comfortably with the radical liberal as opposed to Habermasian position (Beiner 1982, pp.119-42).

In contrast, Patrick Riley suggests that Arendt in fact is much closer to the more radical Habermasian position and that her political theory must be read in the context of the lectures on judgment, and most particularly with regard to her the idea of the *sensus communis* as constructive of a political rationality (Riley 1992). Bhikhu Parekh asserts that the Kant lectures were very much a homecoming for Arendt, emphasising that it was Kant who fashioned a theory of political relativity which Arendt used to constrain the radically indeterminate alternatives being presented by other critical interpreters of the Heidegger-Kant dialogue. Kant provided the faculty of 'opinion' as the medium for an investigation into reflective meaning. According to Arendt this was the 'crucial political category' (Parekh 1981, 9-11). Barekh has no doubt that the Kantian critique of judgment lay at heart of Arendt's mature political philosophy. More recently, a series of critics have affirmed the centrality of the third *Critique* to Arendt's political philosophy, and her pervasive search for a 'common understanding' as a 'citizen rationality', and ultimately as the basis of a 'participatory democracy' (Hansen 1993, pp.119-215, D'Entreves 1994, pp.101-27, Young-Breuhl 1982, pp.322-3).

The Politics of Judgment

Arendt was always aware of the need to address real political problems; an awareness which became concentrated after the experience of Nazism. Along with Stalinism, Nazism revealed the stark reality of totalitarianism and the essentially nihilistic potential of modernism. In terms of political philosophy, this experience of modernism realised the destruction of the public domain effected by the diminution of the faculty of judgment in modern political science. Totalitarianism was not a natural force. It was a human artefact. Nazism was our creation and, in appropriately Heideggerian terms, our responsibility. It was this realisation, articulated first in volume one of *The Origins of Totalitarianism*, which underpinned Arendt's increasingly intense concentration on the political problems of modernism (Young-Breuhl 1982, p.102, D'Entreves 1994, pp23-63, 122-4, Canovan 1992, pp.19-21, 87-91).

The original philosophical ambition, to overcome the dominance of a metaphysical conception of truth, was that which had been tentatively articulated in *Truth and Politics*, an essay which was itself written in response to the furore brought about by her account of the Eichmann trial (Arendt 1954). It was the Eichmann book and resulting controversy which convinced Arendt of the need to look beyond political history and political science, towards a philosophy of politics, and more precisely to an understanding of judgment as an alternative medium. The failure of justice is a failure of judgment, not of universal ethics. Her account of the Eichmann trial remains perhaps

Arendt's most influential, and certainly most controversial, work (Watson 1992, pp.74-82, Young-Breuhl 1982, pp.329-75). Certainly some of Arendt's passing jurisprudential observations were thought-provoking. The trial was, she asserted, more of a 'show' than a legal proceeding, brought by the Israeli premier, Ben-Gurion, in a desperate bid to absolve the 'Jewish consciousness'. Arendt also made a strident attack against a legal positivism by which the Jews had lived and died; believing in the Nuremberg laws as 'their' laws, and thus refusing to disobey them.

However, most interesting was Arendt's characterisation of Eichmann. Eichmann was the man incapable of exercising judgment. Unlike the Jews, Eichmann did not cling to any legal positivist defence. Indeed he invoked Kant as his jurisprudential idol. Eichmann did not execute the orders of the Final Solution because he feared the effects of his refusal to obey enacted law, but because he felt that it was his moral duty to do so. Eichmann's sudden invocation of the Kantian imperative, whilst under interrogation, caught the entire court by surprise. For Arendt it signalled not just Eichmann's failure to understand the proper nature of Kantian duty, but also the potential limitations of basing a jurisprudence upon this conception alone. In her account of Eichmann's use of Kant we can clearly see her own concern that Kant must be approached from an alternative angle, that of judgment and political opinion (Arendt 1963, pp.11-8, 91-3, 135-6). It has been recently intimated that the germ of all three treatises which were to have constructed *The Life of the Mind* can be detected in these paragraphs (Hansen 1993, pp.165-9). Eichmann's 'banality' was an inability to think, and was thus symbolic of the limitations of a modern philosophy which had served to alienate and to supress the individual mind.

The conditions for Eichmann's 'banality' had already been closely examined in Arendt's first major work *The Origins of Totalitarianism*, and then again in *The Human Condition*. The distinction which is clearly drawn in the three volumes of *Origins* lies between the alternatives of totalitarianism and pluralism. Nazism, it was immediately asserted, was the epitome of anti-pluralism and represented the 'frontal assault' of European modernism (Young-Breuhl 1982, p.200, D'Entreves 1994, p.3-5). Much of the first volume, *Anti-Semitism*, revolves around a commentary on the infamous Dreyfus case, which polarised intellectual opinion in late nineteenth century France. For Arendt, the Dreyfus case represented the collapse of the Jacobin ideals, of community and individual right, and was thus symbolic of the collapse of French politics and the social disintegration which was to characterise western democracies in the first part of the twentieth century. The account is suggestive, because in her condemnation of the supra-nationalism which stripped both the sense of individual and community justice and which was pervasive during the Dreyfus period, can be seen the cause of the bitterness in her 1963 account of the Eichmann trial. The ambitions behind the Eichmann trial, its naked supra-nationalism and its implicit denial of community, were precisely those which lay behind the injustices which Dreyfus suffered. Rather than ending the Dreyfus 'tragedy', the Eichmann trial perpetuated it (Arendt 1951a pp.91-120). The anti-nationalist polemic was continued in the second volume, *Imperialism*, which charted the rise of nationalism in the place of community.

Symbolically, nationalism represented the triumph of the philosophy of Hobbes over that of Kant, and the absence of legal rationalism displaced by a legal mysticism. The two concepts which imperialism sought to deny, above all else, were freedom and equality; the two core concepts which underpin any reconstructive Kantian political philosophy (Arendt 1951b, pp.19-37, 115-25, 166-82).

In the final volume, *Totalitarianism*, Arendt returned to Nazism and Stalinism in a bid to trace the tendencies of anti-semitism and imperialism in modern totalitarianism. The triumph of totalitarian politics was the 'mass atomization' of the 'doomed man', alienated from any sense of community. Ultimately, 'total domination' will always try 'to organise the infinite plurality and differentiation of human beings as if all of humanity were just one individual'. This alienation could only be achieved outside any rational conception of law. The first step always is 'to kill the juridical person in man' (Arendt 1951c, pp.21-8, 91-2, 145). From these early writings, Arendt was already convinced that law lay within the individual, and only the individual could then construct a rational community of law. In the final part of *Totalitarianism* Arendt returned to the jurisprudential theme to emphasise the suppression of legality as absolutely essential to the success of any ideological dogmatism. In her discussion of law the rejection of both legal positivism and natural law is undeniable. The only alternative is a jurisprudence based on immanent morality and internal individual duty. Her suggestion that the ultimate juridical ideal is for positive laws based upon immanent principle and a constructive rationality, again bears striking comparison to the recent work of Rawls and Dworkin. At the same time, her emphasis that no legal order should ever try to suppress 'contradictions', but instead should accommodate them and then construct from them, articulates the ethic of critical legal thought (Arendt 1951c pp.158-68).

Such an attack on the 'juridical person' was at once an 'attack on the moral person', and of course a threat to the existence of the individual: 'Totalitarian terror achieved its most horrible triumph when it succeeded in cutting the moral person off from the individualist escape and in making the decisions of conscience absolutely questionable and equivocal... After murder of the moral person and annhilation of the juridical person, the destruction of individuality is almost always successful.' (Arendt 1951c, pp.150-3) Moreover, it was the condition of the modern age:

> The totalitarian attempt to make men superfluous reflects the experience of modern masses of their superfluity on an overcrowded earth. The world of the dying, in which men are taught they are superfluous through a way of life in which punishment is meted out without connection with crime, in which exploitation is practiced without profit, and where work is performed without product, is a place where senselessness is daily produced anew. Yet, within the framework of the totalitarian ideology, nothing could be more sensible and logical; if the inmates are vermin, it is logical that they should be killed by poison gas; if they are degenerate, they should not be allowed to contaminate the population; if they have 'slave-like souls' (Himmler), no one should waste his time trying to re-educate them. Seen through the eyes of ideology, the trouble with the camps is almost that they make too much sense, that the execution of the doctrine is too consistent. (Arendt 1951c, p.155)

The articulation of totalitarianism lay with and through the unquestioned triumph of modern technology. The concern with technology was one which Arendt shared with

Heidegger, and Heidegger's notorious comment that the gas chambers were conceptually no different from agricultural machinery, in that both technologies led to the suppression of individual creative potential, makes an interesting comparison with Arendt's own comments, not only in *Totalitarianism*, but also subsequently in *The Human Condition*.

The Human Condition represented Arendt's most strident critique of the dehumanizing effects of technology, and her resultant appeal to poetry as a means of maintaining human dignity in the face of this oppression was again resonant of Heidegger (Arendt 1958, pp.140-72, Canovan 1992, pp.94-5). *The Human Condition*, published in 1958, was Arendt's first venture into political philosophy as opposed to political science, because it was the first attempt to accentuate the idea that freedom is something participated in, as opposed to granted. At the same time, *The Human Condition* remains very much a historical piece in its charting of the cultural and philosophical conditions which have led to man's 'alienation'. Margaret Canovan suggests that it is one of the first substantive pieces of historical phenomenology in modern critical thought (Canovan 1974, pp.58-9). The purpose of the study was to trace the historical treatment of the relationship between the individual and society as articulated by activity, and more especially to critique the Marxist economic analysis of this relationship. The particular failing is, of course, that of modernity. It has triumphed the state and diminished the individual's capacity to create community, not least by its suppression of the effective means and power of communication and by the diminution of public space (Arendt 1958, pp.249-320). The ambition which lay behind the study was to uncover a non-Marxist, but still radical and alternative, reconstructive praxis based upon this ability to create community.

The philosophical basis for her investigation was taken from the Heideggerian tradition as articulated by Sartre; the human condition of Being-in-the-World (Arendt 1958, pp.9-20). The crucial political tension is provided by the accommodation between the public and the private spheres. The history of politics and political philosophy is a history of the description of this accommodation. The 'emergence of society' has blurred the public-private distinction, as Arendt had emphasised in *Origins*. The possibility of reconstructive social theory lay in the direction mapped by a redefinition of society, which empowered the creative individual and applauded the creative potential of difference; the idea which Arendt continued to refine in models of solidarity and 'participatory democracy' (Arendt 1958, pp.29-77, 175-238, D'Entreves 1994, pp.3-11, 47-9, 72-6). The ultimate ambition of *The Human Condition* was to reinvest 'activity' as the means of empowering the creative individual, and to do so by widening the dimensions of public space (Young-Breuhl 1982, pp.319-20). This reinvestiture was only possible if political philosophy redirected itself to an investigation of individual freedom, as opposed to political sovereignty; precisely what Arendt was herself to do in later writings on Kant. Freedom, she suggested, echoing Heidegger's statements in 1933, was the freedom to self-assert.

If Arendt's earlier political studies were at root historical, later essays became ever more concerned with the reconstructive alternatives. Indeed, it is after *The Human*

Condition that Arendt concentrates almost solely, both in her political essays and of course in her later philosophical writings, on reconstructive politics. Most influential of the political essays was *On Revolution*, published in the same year as *Eichmann* in 1963. In the epilogue to *Eichmann*, and in the postscript published in the revised 1965 edition, Arendt presented a preliminary sketch for a reconstructive praxis based around the principles of 'public space' and the 'collective' responsibility of communities. The epilogue emphasised crimes committed against communities and not just individuals, so that the Holocaust was not just a Jewish 'thing' but a crime against the world community. The sense of a community possessed of a jurisprudence created around constructive ethical principles is, Arendt added, more important in the later twentieth century than ever before (Arendt 1963, pp.261-79).

On Revolution is, once again, very much a historical analysis. The central idea is that of reinvesting freedom and through it activity; the ambition which had been outlined in *The Human Condition* (Arendt 1990, pp.11-2). Freedom, which was the 'passion' of the Enlightenment, provides the impetus for revolution. Thus freedom is, as suggested in *The Human Condition*, the freedom to assert. It is also, of course, power. The contrast is again that of the Hobbesian theory of freedom as opposed to the Kantian. The demise of freedom, despite Kant's efforts, largely due to the oppression of the Marxist theory of revolution, was the 'lost treasure' (Arendt 1990, pp.124-33, 189-280). In her discussion of the lost Enlightenment ideals, Arendt makes early reference to the liberating potential of Kant's theory of judgment, as a means of reempowering the individual creative potential (Arendt 1990, p.229). According to Phillip Hansen, *On Revolution* represented the conclusion of Arendt's political thought, because consideration of revolution and its hitherto inadequate definition of freedom convinced her that political theory as it stood was in immediate need of a restructured philosophy. This would be a philosophy which could take account of political reality, the inevitability of pluralism and the need to create communities by means of a revitalised concept of judgment, which could authenticate a new theory of 'participatory democracy' and which, in turn, could be founded upon a redefined and effective idea of the 'public sphere'. There was an inextricable link between judgment and participatory democracy (Hansen 1993, pp.170-89).

The critique of the kind of communitarianism articulated in both Marxism and liberalism is a key component of *On Revolution*. The Marxist version, the 'council system', deliberately did not empower, but instead gradually centralised and formed hierarchies. Marxism failed as a philosophy of freedom because it possessed no adequate theory of institutions (Arendt 1990, pp.256-80). Arendt is similarly critical of the centralising tendencies in the liberal alternative, representative democracy. Modern democracy's obsession with representative democracy is in fact a betrayal of the principles of the French and American revolutions. Instead, Arendt advocates the empowerment of small decentralised communities, akin to the Jeffersonian model, and in line with those she perceived to have existed temporarily during the Hungarian uprising (Arendt 1990, pp.148-9, 189-212, 242-9, Young-Breuhl 1982, pp.202-10). It was this ideal which returned Arendt to Kant, and which correspondingly led her away from Heidegger, who consciously refused to present a politics as a theory of communities. It has been commonly suggested that the precise nature of the 'participatory democracy' is never fully explained, and it is indeed fair to say that it stands as much as an idea as a substantive thesis. This is not to diminish it, and it can be suggested that if the idea requires philosophical, as opposed to purely institutional, substance Arendt's later use of Kant's political philosophy provides it. Arendt returned to Kant because she wanted to retrieve a 'dignity' for political theory, by revitalising it and by presenting a political philosophy of particularism. It was to this ambition that Arendt directed her idea of participatory democracy as a liberating and at once empowering concept.

The ambition resurfaces throughout her later political essays. In *What is Freedom?* Arendt repeated the demand for a return to Kant and a return of freedom as the centrepiece of any political philosophy. *The Crisis in Culture*, similarly, is at root a political crisis and an institutional crisis, because it is the institutions of modern politics which suppress the voice of potential participants (Arendt 1954, pp.143-71, 197-226). In one of her final critiques of modern political culture, *Civil Disobedience*, Arendt again considered the various alternative jurisprudences available to a participatory democracy, and again came up with a Kantian variant based on the moral duty of the individual as the construct of a legal rationality (Arendt 1972, pp.82-9). Again, in *On Violence*, Arendt repeated that politics was ultimately about change, because politics was ultimately about difference and its creative accommodation, and thus famously went so far as to justify violence, where necessary, as a medium of political change (Arendt 1972, pp.124-30, 171-80). The idea of participatory democracy was perhaps most substantively, certainly most eloquently, argued in one of Arendt's final political forays, *Thoughts on Politics and Revolution*, and it serves as a fitting conclusion to a study of her particular reconstructive political philosophy:

> This new form of government is the council system, which, as we know, has perished every time and everywhere, destroyed either directly by the bureaucracy of the nation-states or by the party machines. Whether this system is a pure utopia - in any case it would be a people's utopia, not the utopia of theoreticians and ideologies - I cannot say. It seems to me, however, the single alternative that has ever appeared in history, and has reappeared time and again... In this direction, I think, there must be something to be found, a completely different principle of organization, which begins form below, continues upward, and finally leads to a parliament... The councils say: We want to participate, we want to debate, we want to make our voices heard in public, and we want to have a possibility to determine the political course of our country. Since the country is too big for all of us to come together and determine our fate, we need a number of public spaces within it. The booth in which we deposit our ballots is unquestionably too small, for this booth has room for only one. The parties are completely unsuitable; there we are, most of us, nothing but the manipulated electorate. But if only ten of us are sitting around a table, each expressing his opinion, each hearing the opinions, then a rational formation of opinion can take place through the exchange of opinion. (Arendt 1972, pp.231-3)

CHAPTER 3

THE CRISIS OF JUDGMENT

1 Politics, Language and Power

The Idea of Existential Humanism

It has recently been suggested that Sartre's 1946 lecture *Existentialism and Humanism* was the defining 'intellectual event' in post-war France (Miller 1993, p.42). Certainly Sartre's audacious attempt to appropriate the Heidegger-Kant dialogue defined the parameters for the development of French critical theory. In writing *Nausea*, with its portrayal of necessity, existence, responsibility and alienation, it has been suggested that Sartre 'was not merely popularizing the ideas of Heidegger, he was dramatizing them' (Hayman 1986, p.99). According to Iris Murdoch, it engages Sartre with a Heideggerian ethics, revealing the underlying metaphysics which runs throughout his works (Murdoch 1987, pp.35-51). The influence of Heidegger can be seen equally clearly in *Being and Nothingness*. George Steiner famously suggested that the text is itself nothing but a 'footnote' to *Being and Time*. Sartre spent much of his wartime captivity reading and translating Heidegger's works, and later expressed himself to be particularly impressed by Heidegger's working of the concepts of freedom and responsibility. It is commonly suggested that Sartre began to compose *Being and Nothingness* as an immediate response to Heidegger, and as a personal expression of self-assertion (McBride 1991, pp.24-7).

Iris Murdoch placed Sartre's writings squarely within the Heidegger-Kant dialogue. Sartre's writings are all ethical to some degree, and as such continuously flirt with Kant. Indeed, she suggests that Sartre's obsessive concern with the either/or problematic seems to 'daze his ethical sensibilities' (Murdoch 1987, pp.136-7). Certainly it is obvious in *Being and Nothingness* that Sartre was aware that any future ethics would be founded upon the twin Kantian-Heideggerian conceptions of freedom and responsibility. At the same time as he was encountering Heidegger, Sartre was deeply disturbed by the whole experience of war and of National Socialism, and it was during and then immediately after the war, that his determination to re-present a political ethics crystallized (Hayman 1986, pp.143-213). Thus, even if *Being and Nothingness* was indeed an ethical work, dimly harbouring grander ethical-political aspirations, its six hundred pages reveal far less about a Sartrean ethics than the controversial thirty page lecture which was to immediately follow the end the war entitled *Existentialism and Humanism*.

Existentialism and Humanism was, thus, written at a particular conjunction of events, at the end of the war, and as Sartre determined to revise the Heideggerian project. It set out to counter three 'reproaches' which Sartre perceived to be levelled against existentialism; that it is an invitation to despair, that it emphasises the ignominious in the human situation, and that it denies the seriousness and reality of this situation. In countering these reproaches, Sartre immediately aligned himself with what he calls the Heideggerian 'existential atheists'. It is this which, rather than condemning existentialism to pessimism, through the liberating concept of responsibility reveals an implicit humanism: 'Thus, the first effect of existentialism is that it puts every man in possession of himself as he is, and places the entire responsibility for the existence squarely upon his own shoulders. And when we say that man is responsible form himself, we do not mean that he is responsible only for his own individuality, but that he is responsible for man.' (Sartre 1989, p.29)

In classically Heideggerian prose, Sartre outlines that existentialism denies the possibility of ultimate values, then switches into Kantian prose, to present a defence of the Kantian idea of valuing people as ends (Sartre 1989, pp.33-7). Because existentialism is a philosophy based on the ethically driven individual it is a philosophy founded on 'an ethic of action and self-commitment'. What existentialism adds to Kant is an enhanced awareness of the determining nature of the 'other'. The existential Kantian world is a 'world of inter-subjectivity'. This notion is at the 'very heart and centre of existentialism' (Sartre 1989 pp.44-7). Anticipating the tenor of his subsequent *What Is Literature?*, Sartre suggests that an existential ethics, in its intersubjective 'heart', is akin to an aesthetics. Such an ethics enjoys a 'creative situation', one where the individual can create and assert the law for himself (Sartre 1989, pp.48-9). The dual echo is unmistakable. Although Sartre expressly attributes this assertion to the Kantian imperative, it is at the same time a striking invocation of Heidegger's 1933 lecture; a lecture which harboured similar aspirations to Sartre's and is flawed for precisely the same reasons. In Sartre's ensuing development of the concept of judgment as appropriate to an intersubjective ethics founded upon the unavoidably transcendental idea of free-will, the Kantian echoes become even more resonant (Sartre 1989, pp.51-2). The concluding passages of *Existentialism and Humanism* banish any final lingering doubts about Sartre's commitment in 1946 to the retrieval of a Kantian existentialism:

> There is no universe except the human universe, the universe of human subjectivity. This relation of transcendence as constitutive of man... with subjectivity... is this which we call existential humanism. This is humanism, because we remind man that there is no legislator but himself; that he himself thus abandoned, must decide for himself; also because we show that it is not by turning back upon himself, but always by seeking, beyond himself, an aim which is one of liberation or of some particular realisation, that man can realise himself as purely human. (Sartre 1989, pp.55-6)

Existentialism and Humanism is an undoubtedly Kantian text, and has been both praised and villified for it. Murdoch refers to its 'benign Kantian perspectives', noting that the introduction of a categorical imperative is a pure 'piece of Kantian ethics' (Murdoch 1987, pp.15, 134). Moreover, *Existentialism and Humanism* did not represent the end of Sartre's ethical and humanist ambitions. Indeed, in many ways it is the beginning, at least it is of his increasing concern with political and revolutionary praxis. McBride suggests that the central idea of 'free self-determination' remained the 'bedrock' in his subsequent political writings (McBride 1991, pp.8-9, 45-6). In another essay written at the same time, *Materialism and Revolution*, Sartre made the same claim as Hannah Arendt; that revolution was a 'philosophy of transcendence', itself grounding a radically transformative democratic polity (Sartre 1962, p.198).

As Sartre became increasingly engaged with literature, and then more directly with politics, ethics continued to reappear. The concept of 'solidarity' emerged as central to his later political essays. In *Cahiers*, Sartre invoked a transcendental principle of 'reflection' in order 'to introduce into the internal structure of the Person, the relation of solidarity, which will later be modified into solidarity with others.' The ethics of the *Cahiers* is important because it represented the 'blatant' switch from individual to social and, implicitly, universal ethics. The second volume of the *Cahiers* is more restrained, chiefly because it represents another quite sharp switch, this time into a specifically historical temper. But the historicity is again of an obviously Kantian variety. Ethics as historical is thoroughly Kantian (McBride 1991, pp.64-82). The *Critique* was composed in an effort to humanize Marxism, in a similar way as the 1946 lecture was given in an attempt to humanize existentialism. What orthodox positive Marxism lacked was the 'element of freedom', and it was this which a humanist existentialism could recover. The *Critique* was, thus, a treatise on freedom and praxis, incorporating much of Sartre's already articulated views on humanist ethics, solidarity and the nature of revolution. The 'practico-inert' which suffocated the possibility of transformative action was to be released by a new ethical praxis, 'the only ethical relationship of man to man.' Such a praxis emerges in the second book of the *Critique* as a kind of radical spontaneous political action (McBride 1991, pp.141-69). Again the similarities with Arendt are striking.

Murdoch suggests that Sartre's vast study of *Genet* represents a switch from the early Kant to the later (Murdoch 1987, pp.16-20). Sartre became ever more convinced that language was power, and as such political and ethical. *What Is Literature?* made it quite clear that the responsibility of the writer was always political and ethical. Moreover, in its deduction of political imperatives from human nature, *What Is Literature?* is Sartre's most obviously Kantian text after *Existentialism and Humanism*. Murdoch suggests that, in its description of aesthetic pleasure as the 'image-making' capacity of the being-in-the-world, it is a piece of 'traditional post-Kantian aesthetics' (Murdoch 1987, pp.65-79, 97-104). Certainly, Sartre himself saw his idea of aesthetics as a development of Kant's. The goal of art is to recover freedom, and in this ascribes to art an ethical and humanist import. As he concluded, 'We stand for an ethics and an art of the finite.'

In its ambition to develop a aesthetics of morality, *What is Literature?* can be seen as the first step towards the kind of postmodern textual ethics, which we shall shortly encounter with Derrida and Lyotard. Certainly Sartre was convinced that 'at the heart of the aesthetic imperative we discover the moral imperative.' (Sartre 1967, pp.33-6, 40, 238) The responsibility of the writer is to propose 'mechanisms' for effecting a politics of freedom. More precisely, Sartre vigorously advocated the writing of praxis, which he perceived to be the revolutionary reality of political and ethical transformation. It is this notion, of course, which Hannah Arendt chose to develop in her theory of revolutions and transformative politics. Sartre demanded a 'committed' writing which would overcome the 'complacency' of the bourgeois literature. It would be 'liberating' form of writing for the humanist ideal. The association of language with praxis, and thus with ethics, has been one of the key legacies of Sartrean philosophy.

Sartre's commitment to political communism in 1953 led to the partial eclipse of his intellectual reputation, if not his popular acclaim. Yet in 1968 it was Sartre who retook the centre stage, both intellectually and politically. Although lectures such as the notorious *Justice and State*, given in 1972, seemed somewhat bizarre, advocating 'wild justice' and a 'living morality' of law, Sartre was articulating alternatives which have emerged as central to the politics of critical legal thought. The same is true of his tentative suggestion that there should be a new theory of supplementary and transformative rights, articulated in a handful of lectures given at the time of Vietnam. Of course, in its concentration on the responsibility of the ethically driven individual as the fountainhead for a new democratic jurisprudence there is a continuing echo of 1946 and the Heidegger-Kant 'dialogue'. However, the centre of intellectual gravity in French critical thought was already shifting, and from the mid-1970s it was to Michel Foucault that radical politics turned for guidance.

A Genealogy of Foucault

Existentialism and Humanism was probably the single most important factor in Foucault's early contempt for philosophy as a discipline. Any philosophy, any humanism, legitimated 'techniques' of power (Simons 1995, pp.43-5, Sheridan 1980, pp.4-5). The other critical influence was Martin Heidegger. In the very final interview Foucault gave before his death, he testified that Heidegger 'has always been the essential philosopher' (Foucault 1990, p.250). Heidegger had appreciated the situation of the other. In his first major publication, *Madness and Civilization*, Foucault concentrated on the political morality of marginalization; the techniques, strategies and discourses which effected the marginalization of those designated mad. It was not a history, in the sense of traditional progressive continuous 'history', but an archaeology, which denied both continuity and progression, and most importantly objectivism. The heart of Foucault's thesis was the denial that madness could be objectivity defined. Madness was a judgment, not an objective fact. The technology of government was founded on the pretended objectivisation of judgment. *Madness and Civilization* represented the beginnings of decade of Foucaultian structuralism. Foucault became irreducibly embroiled in the Sartrean legacy, the pervasive concern with language and discourse. Language was everything, and could not be dissociated from any intellectual endeavour: 'Fiction does not exist because language is at a distance from things... Language is the distance.' (Miller 1993, pp.103-30, Dreyfus and Rabinow 1982, pp.4-12)

The 'archaeology' of discourse dominated Foucault's next and most structuralist work, *The Order of Things*, an expressly Kantian response to Sartre's *Critique of Dialectical Reason*. In wanting to make his response, Foucault had turned to Heidegger's engagement with Kant, sharing the conviction that Kant had shied away from potential repurcussions which he had revealed in his own critical philosophy. The desire to locate the structures of thought and discourse was irreducibly transcendental. It was the same ambition which fuelled *The Archaeology of Knowledge*, a text at once part Kant and part Sartre. Foucault repeated the same assertion that the origins of critical philosophy lay in the Kantian distinction between the transcendental and the empirical. Dreyfus and Rabinow emphasise the Heideggerian origins of this particular appreication of the Kantian critique (Dreyfus and Rabinow 1982, pp.32-41). In a review of *Archaeology*, Gilles Deleuze noted that in switching from philosophy to 'poetry' Foucault was consciously echoing Heidegger (Sheridan 1980, p.90). In the final passages of *Archaeology*, Foucault declared that his future research would now be directed towards politics. The move to political ethics, made a decade later, was inevitable. The abandonment of hermeneutics in favour of a post-structural adherence to radical contingency was necessitated by the return to the Heidegger-Kant dialogue. As Dreyfus and Rabinow suggest, the 'bracketing' of truth and meaning claims, left Foucault at the edge of the same 'precipice' of nihilism over which Heidegger had stared. Never again would Foucault attempt to speak from a 'position of phenomenological detachment' (Dreyfus and Rabinow 1982, pp.79-100).

There can be little doubt that Foucault's determination to address the practicalities, rather than the mere theory, of modern society, was in no small part a reaction to the events of 1968. For Foucault, as for Sartre and so many others, 1968 seemed to represent the reality of a post-Marxist revolution. Foucault was convinced that the question that had to be addressed was that of power. The growth of his friendship with and admiration for Gilles Deleuze was intensified by the common pursuit of Heidegger and Kant, and their determination to identify humanism, with its necessary diminution of the will to power and the notion of self-assertion, as the enemy. The methodology which Foucault adopted in place of 'archaeology' was 'genealogy'. Genealogy was a return to interpretation and, more precisely, to an interpretation which sought, not to uncover meaning, but to recognize itself as a formative lived experience. From 1970 onward, Foucault was obsessed by the desire to explore the genealogy of discourse, power and knowledge. In his 1975, he referred to 'a strange contest, a confrontation, a power relation, a battle among discourses and through discourses' which 'give us a key to the relations of power, domination and conflict within which discourse emerge and function, and hence provide material for a potential analysis of discourse (even of scientific discourses) which may be both tactical and political, and therefore strategic.' (Sheridan 1980, p.134).

Foucault's writings in the years following 1968 are noticeably more political in style, and both *Discipline and Punish* and *History of Sexuality*, composed throughout the second half of the 1970s, are studies of the interrelation of power and knowledge. As he subsequently acknowledged, the impulse for these works was ethical and, ultimately, Kantian. Indeed, *Discipline and Punish*, as a genealogy of morals, can be read as an immediate critique of the *Metaphysics of Morals*. Foucault revealed the genealogical and ethical ambition which lay behind his study of power and knowledge. It was the interaction of power and knowledge, and the tension between them, that effected political discourse. Foucault's essays and interviews given at this time further evidence the determination to develop a thesis which could radically subvert the rationalist discourse of power and knowledge. Both the ambition and the genealogical methodology were Heideggerian (Dreyfus and Rabinow 1982, pp.122-4). In an earlier 1972 interview, Foucault denied that his writings were anti-humanist. Rather he contested the humanism which laid claim to truth and, in its place, advocated a radical pluralist humanism. The person he chose to cite as the fundamental influence in his determination to access this post-philosophical humanism was Heidegger (Foucault 1988, pp.12-5).

In *Truth and Power* he emphasised the centrality of the Heideggerian truth problematic, observing that every society 'has its own regime of truth', and identifying 'a combat for the truth, or at least around the truth, as long as we understand by the truth not those true things which are waiting to be discovered but rather the ensemble of rules according to which we distinguish the true from the false, and attach special effects of power to the truth' (Foucault 1980, p.131). Modern jurisprudence, he suggested in a 1971 essay, is a study of rituals validated by truth claims, and effected through power relations. 'The relationship of domination' which characterizes modern political jurisprudence 'is fixed, throughout its history, in rituals, in meticulous procedures that impose rights and obligations' (Foucault 1977, p.150). In his his debate with Chomsky, also in 1971, Foucault suggested 'it seems to me that the idea of justice in itself is an idea which in effect has been invented and put to work in different types of societies as an instrument of a certain political and economic power or as a weapon against that power.' (Foucault 1984, p.6) A court of law always 'implies an ideology'. The alternative Foucaultian vision emphasised the same virtues of participatory democracy, pluralism and a decentralized juridical structure, which have proved so popular amongst critical legal scholars (Foucault 1980, pp.1-36).

The further Foucault moved towards issues of politics and ethics, the more he contemplated the jurisprudential. In a 1977 interview he suggested that the juridical was the chosen image of power in western thought (Foucault 1980, p.201). *Truth and Power* was a comment on the juridical implication of the discourses of power. In *Power and Strategies*, he reaffirmed that, 'Law is neither the truth of power, nor its alibi. It is an instrument of power which is at once complex and partial.' The juridical, he added, was a discourse, a 'strategic mode of thought' (Foucault 1980, pp.141-4). In two 1976 lectures, foreshadowing some of the themes in his subsequent lectures on 'governmentality', Foucault discussed the nature of sovereignty and the 'power, right, truth' triangle which determined its discourse: 'The system of right, the domain of law, are permanent agents of these relations of domination, these polymorphous techniques of subjugation. Right should be viewed, I believe, not in terms of a legitimacy to be established, but in terms of the methods of subjugation that it instigates.' Reform of the legal system, he suggested, must concentrate on reform of the discourse of law (Foucault 1980, pp.96, 104-6).

The ethical turn in Foucault's writings from the middle of the 1970s is clearer still in the *History of Sexuality*. The 'insurrection of subjugated knowledges', of which the history of sexuality was one, took on a whole new importance as the centrepiece of

Foucault's developing thesis. *Sexuality* is a classic example of genealogy at work; the search for 'specificity, local varieties, and texture' resulting in the presentation of a discourse suppressed because of its incompatibility with the capitalist ethic. The role of the law in enforcing the exclusion of the discourse, the 'juridico-discursive', is vital; a 'disciplinary technology' geared to the production of 'docile' individuals, a humanist ethics. The development of these ethical ambitions occupied Foucault for the rest of his life. The question that Foucault addressed, of self-identity and determination, was the same as that addressed by Heidegger, the question of self-assertion. The evolution in Foucault's thought, from the hermeneutic to the interpretive and finally to the ethical was a inexorable.

Foucault's turn towards the ethical was described in essays on liberalism and governmentality. In *Politics and the Study of Discourse*, Foucault stressed that politics is the exercise of power, and political research is the investigation into the pluralism of networks of power. Equally, Foucault was keen to emphasize the 'discontinuity' of politics which is effected by this pluralism, and the role of the 'transformative' discourses. Political practice 'transforms the conditions of existence and system of functioning of discourse'. In *Governmentality* he investigated the rise of administrative bureaucracy which, he suggested, characterised the later modern political state in which the 'art' of government had given way to the 'science'. A characteristic of modern government is that it sought to govern, not territory, but rather the relationships between men. In other words, it was concerned with the determination, or 'technology', of the self. This post-sovereignty thesis is also a post-juridical thesis, because just as government in the modern polity was no longer about exercising sovereignty, so too was it no longer about the 'discipline' of law. Administration had rendered the twin characteristics of the 'art' of government redundant. Administrative law thus became a strategy, rather than an imposition, and an encourager of behaviour, rather than a punisher of misbehaviour. Ultimately, it is the jurisprudence of modern humanist ethics and ethical rationality (Foucault 1991, p.93-8, 103). In the Tanner lectures, which Foucault gave at the same time, he presented his governmentality thesis specifically in the Heidegger-Kant tradition, concentrating on the responsibility of the self-determinative and assertive individual. Modern government, he emphasized, is not a natural or divine art, but a science of power, and the rationality which power/knowledge relations construct. Thus, the possibility of justice remained, for Foucault, nothing more than a dream, forever defeated by harsh reality (Foucault 1988, pp.145-62, Foucault 1990, pp.57-85).

Confronting Kant

Foucault's writings on political morality, on governmentality and liberalism, necessitated a more intense return to Kant. The presence of Kant, and in particular Foucault's commentary *What is Enlightement?*, is the most striking characteristic of his final writings (Simons 1995, pp.13-5). In asking the question 'what is Enlightenment?' Kant had, according to Foucault, recast the whole nature of philosophical inquiry by turning its attention internally. In presenting a critical philosophy which 'sought to reflect upon its own present', Kant's essay 'marks the discrete entrance into the history of thought of a question that modern philosophy has not been capable of answering, but that it has never managed to get rid of either' (Foucault 1984, p.32). Kant revealed a fundamental awareness of the temporality of inquiry. In comparison with the grander metaphysical inquiries of the Socratics:

> the way Kant poses the question of *Aufklaerung* is entirely different: it is neither a world era to which one belongs, nor an event whose signs are perceived, nor the dawning of an accomplishment. Kant defines *Aufklaerung* in an almost entirely negative way, as an *Ausgang*, an 'exit', a 'way out'... In the text on *Aufklaerung*, he deals with the question of contemporary reality alone. He is not seeking to understand the present on the basis of a totality or of a future achievement. He is looking for a difference: What difference does today introduce with respect to yesterday?... The hypothesis I should like to propose is that this little text is located in a sense at the crossroads of critical reflection and reflection on history. (Foucault 1984, p.34)

What is remarkable about Kant's essay is that it announces the arrival of existential questioning. Philosophy is, in the Heideggerian sense, a process of self-reflection and self-overcoming. The Enlightenment, more than anything, represents immanent critique, and in its presentation of the existential critique, *What is Enlightenment?* is a culmination of Kant's entire critical project (Foucault 1984, pp.37-8). The comparison which Foucault makes in his essay is with Baudelaire, a thinker who articulates many of the more aesthetic aspirations in current postmodern thinking. In his concentration on the temporality and contingency of modernity and its thinking, Foucault suggests that Baudelaire is Kant's heir, and postmodernism Kant's bequest. What Baudelaire realises is that the 'permanent critique of ourselves' gives way to a humanism shorn of the 'facile confusions' of transcendentalism which has characterized recent attempts to reinvigorate classical humanism, such as Sartre's. The suggestion that only modernist variants of humanism, such as Sartre's, must be rejected, once again counters the accusation that either Foucault or indeed any postmodern critique is anti-humanist in the wider sense. The historicity of Enlightenment is an ethos, or event. It is this which makes modernism at once post-modern. It is also an 'attitude', as Ronald Dworkin has more recently reaffirmed, and we, as post-modern moderns, have an attitude to ourselves. Foucault suggests:

> I shall thus characterize the philosophical ethos appropriate to the critical ontology of ourselves as a historico-practical test of the limits that we may go beyond, and thus as work carried out by ourselves upon ourselves as free beings... The critical ontology of ourselves has to be considered not, certainly, as a theory, a doctrine, nor even as a permanent body of knowledge that is accumulating; it has to be conceived as an attitude, an ethos, a philosophical life in which the critique of what we are is at one and the same time the historical analysis of the limits that are imposed on us and an experiment with the possibility of going beyond them. (Foucault 1984, pp.47, 50)

A second direct confrontation with Kant's essay is *The Art of Telling the Truth*. Kant's essay is remarkable, Foucault again emphasizes, for its concentration on the immanent nature of rational inquiry. Enlightenment is a motif for modernity in that it interrogates itself about the nature of the present. Kant answers his own rhetorical question in later works, such as the *Contest of the Faculties*, where the answer presented is the 'significance' of revolution. For Kant, what is remarkable about revolution is not just that it signifies progress. It is the fact of the existence of a revolution which is significant, and the inspiration which flows from it. What Foucault is keen to stress is Kant's willingness to embrace the practical import of critical philosophy:

Kant seems to me to have founded the two great critical traditions between which modern philosophy is divided. Let us say that in his great critical work Kant laid the foundations for that tradition of philosophy that poses the question of the conditions in which true knowledge is possible and, on that basis, it may be said that a whole stretch of modern philosophy from the nineteenth century has been presented, developed as the analytics of truth. But there is also in modern and contemporary philosophy another type of question, another kind of critical interrogation: it is the one we see emerging precisely in the question of the *Aufklaerung* or in the text on Revolution. That other critical tradition poses the question: What is our present? What is the present field of possible experiences? This is not an analytics of truth; it will concern what might be called an ontology of the present, an ontology of ourselves, and it seems to me that the philosophical choice confronting us today is this: one may opt for a critical philosophy of truth in general, or one may opt for a critical thought that will take the form of an ontology of ourselves, an ontology of the present. (Foucault 1993, pp.10-18)

In an interview given just before his death, Foucault admitted that 'in fact what interests me is much more morals than politics, in any case, politics as an ethics'. More precisely, he expanded, this is ethics as praxis, as 'manner of being' (Rabinow 1984, pp.375-6). The essential critique of modernism is a Kantian critique, and an abandonment of 'the work of Kant' left a thinker with nothing but the gaping void of 'irrationality'. Anyone who thought, he added, thought 'with Kant' (Foucault 1988, pp.248-9).

Disourse with Foucault

Not surprisingly these final lectures and interviews, concentrating on the nature of liberal governmentality and on Kant in particular, have proved to be of enormous interest. Andre Glucksmann suggested that Foucault announced the intellectual birth of a 'resurgent neo-liberalism' (Miller 1993, p.452). Colin Gordon has suggested that Foucault's idea of radical plural participatory government underpins a range of theories of solidarity which have gained momentum during the 1980s (Gordon 1991, pp.33-6). As we shall see in the next chapter, Richard Rorty has expressed an enthusiasm for the 'liberal' potential which he perceives in Foucault's lectures. Jacques Donzelot has also suggested that Foucault's thesis represents a 'tentative rapprochement' between neo-liberalism and neo-social democracy, centred around a principle of 'solidarity' (Donzelot 1991, pp.169-79). Mark Poster stresses the potential that a 'discourse praxis' possesses for a reinvigoration of the revolutionary praxis advocated in various forms by such as Sartre and Arendt (Poster 1986).

Graham Burchell has suggested that in their shared interest in the subjectivism and ethics of government, Foucault's lectures on governmentality in modern politics resemble the neo-Kantianism articulated in Ernst Cassirer's *The Philosophy of the Enlightenment*. Both Cassirer and Foucault, he suggests, wanted to use the Kantian critique as a springboard to a more radical participatory theory of political ethics

(Burchell 1991). Two decades earlier, Foucault had published a laudatory review of Cassirer's book, in which he had aligned himself unavoidably with neo-Kantianism; unavoidable in the sense that all philosophy was to some degree, he suggested, Kantian (Gordon 1991, pp.23-4). Nancy Fraser has emphasised the particularity of a Foucaultian 'post-humanism' in the Heidegger-Kant tradition, and suggests that, in his treatment of the ethics of power, presupposes the very liberal normativism which he attempts to decry (Fraser 1981, 1983, 1985). Charles Scott has similarly reaffirmed the place of ethics at the very heart of Foucault's work, emphasising its situation in the Heidegger-Kant tradition. The dominant conception for both Foucault and Heidegger is self-assertion, and it is Foucault who carries the Heideggerian project to its conclusion in the ethical constituted self-overcoming subject. It is Foucault who finally presents the radically pluralist theory of ethics which is demanded by Heidegger's engagement with Kant (Scott 1990, pp.53-93).

The Kantian dialogue is thus pivotal. According to Miller the return to Kant was made inevitable by his determination to challenge the ethics of freedom. Lawrence Kritzman suggests that the Foucault-Sartre debate on the nature of humanism was the defining event in post-war French philosophy. Foucault's success lay in presenting a Kantianism that seemed to enjoy a practical, as opposed to purely metaphysical, quality. What Foucault bequeathes to philosophy is a 'new transformative ethics' of aesthetic dimensions more immediately recognizable in the postmodernism of such as Lyotard or Derrida (Kritzman 1990, pp.xi-xxv). Gordon suggests that the proper inheritors of the neo-Kantian mantle are the neo-liberal Heideggerian Kantians such as Foucault and Unger, rather than the more familiar liberal Kantians, such as Rawls or Dworkin (Gordon 1991). Arnold Davidson has made a similar suggestion, that Foucault and Heidegger are the true 'heirs to the Kantian tradition, because unlike the Anglo-American Kantians, the Heideggerians appreciate that a Kantian ethics is an ethics of the self' (Davidson 1986, pp.231-3). Although he is distrustful of what he terms Foucault's innate 'irrationalism', Juergen Habermas has emphasised the degree to which Foucault's writings have been defined by his engagement with Kant. In spirit, the early Foucault follows the early Kant, and the later Foucault, the later Kant. The switch from the study of 'power formations' to the study of the self was, according to Habermas, demanded by Kant. In this sense, Habermas concludes that Foucault is Kant's 'legitimate heir' (Habermas 1986, pp.103-8, Simons 1995, p.110-4)

Comparative studies of Foucault and Derrida further emphasise the pervasive influence of Kantianism in contemporary critical theory. As we shall see, Richard Rorty has made much of the comparison, in his attempt to root both in the Heideggerian project. Commenting on the exchange between Foucault and Derrida, Roy Boyne suggests that their engagement is a debate about the nature of a 'Kantian ethics'. More especially, it becomes an argument about the relationship between ethics and judgment. It was Foucault's attempt to get beyond the discourse of rationality in order to critique that discourse which Derrida was unable to accept. As we shall see shortly, for Derrida there is simply no inhabitable space beyond reason which a writer can occupy. According to Boyne, Foucault's final writings can be read together with Derrida's later more political texts, because both witness a return to Kantian ethics. The trigger for both of them was that originally set by Heidegger's ambivalent treatment of the self (Boyne 1990, 28-33, 40-6, 158-69). It is to the deconstructive turn in the French Heideggerian tradition that we must now turn.

2 Deconstruction and Postmodernism.

Against the Metanarrative

Postmodernism, for Jean-Francois Lyotard, is Kantianism. The suggestion that Kant, and more precisely the Kant of the third *Critique*, might be the recourse for a post-modern philosophy originally occurs in Lyotard's *Instructions Painnes*, first published in 1977. As Geoffrey Bennington has suggested, in the ambition to redirect critical philosophy as 'ultra-critique' rather than 'anti-critique', Lyotard gave early notice of the inevitability of his later 'massive return' to a 'fundamentally Kantian' critical idea of philosophy (Bennington 1988, pp.34-5, 114). So, too, in *The Postmodern Condition*, Lyotard presents a much more obviously Heideggerian critique of contemporary society, its economics, its technology and its culture. However, at the same time, there is already a recognition that the Kantian 'aesthetic of the sublime', and the complementary nature of 'reflective judgment', may offer itself as a postmodern alternative to the modern ethical determination of 'justice'. What *The Postmodern Condition* reveals is Lyotard's strong affinity with the Kantian aesthetic. Lyotard openly advocates the virtues of aesthetics over technology, and against the implicit scientism which he sees in Habermasian communicability. The 'operativity criterion' of technology is directed essentially against 'justice', and so the ambition of postmodernism is to effect an alternative conception of justice. Postmodernism is justice. As the final passages of *The Postmodern Condition* emphasize in particular, this ambition is, unavoidably, an 'ethical-political' one. As Frederic Jameson observes, the text itself testifies to the 'protopolitical thrust' which lies behind Lyotard's recourse to aesthetics (Lyotard 1984, pp.xvii, 71-82).

It was in *The Differend* that Lyotard's return to Kant become critical. In previous works, Lyotard had concentrated on revealing philosophy as a series of narrative events, and on the necessity of constant critique of dominant meta-narratives. The key assertion in *The Differend* is that it is itself performative; it is an event (Carroll 1984). A 'differend' is determined as an incommensurable difference; something which, as Kant acknowledged, cannot be bridged. As Bennington observes, the genus of 'differend' is to be found in the Kantian idea-concept distinction (Bennington 1988, p.145). It was this acknowledgement, Lyotard affirms, which led Kant to approach the third *Critique* in an attempt to try move beyond the moral imperatives which framed the first two *Critiques*. The third *Critique* thus recognised the 'pragmatic' differentials between philosophy and politics (Lyotard 1988a, pp.118-23, 130-41). The third *Critique*, according to Lyotard, together with the fourth 'Critique' collected in Kant's subsequent essays, describe a concluding political Critique (Carroll 1984, p.79).

Following his suggestion in *The Postmodern Condition*, Lyotard directs the postmodern return to Kant to the same 'ethical-political' ambition; to present an alternative idea of 'justice' or reality of the 'multiplicity of justices'. The reality of the 'differend' demands a plurality of justices. As David Carroll has observed, 'it implies that judgments must continually be made and remade and that neutrality is impossible'. The 'differend' is, thus, an innately jurisprudential and political conception, as well as a textual one. It describes a postmodern textual ethics (Carroll 1984, p.76).

After Auschwitz, Lyotard asserts, there is a fundamental need to redetermine 'justice'. Moreover, any ultimate 'ethical-political' redefinition can only be effected as a textual redefinition. Auschwitz destroyed the 'we' of modern humanist ethics. It established that the ultimate injustice is the exluding and the silencing of the Other. In its silencing of the others, it too has been 'silenced', and so, after Auschwitz, there can only be 'sentences' (Lyotard 1988a, pp.3-8). Heidegger's silence with regard to the gas-chambers is precisely this silence. Postmodern justice is a complementary 'respect' for the textual 'differend' and the political 'dissensus'. It is also an aesthetic jurisprudence. Again returning to a Kantian text, the *Universal History*, Lyotard emphasises that such an aesthetic jurisprudence will be effected as a 'spectator' jurisprudence. An aesthetic humanism will 'look', as Kant did, for 'signs' of human development, rather than asserting them as imperatives (Lyotard 1988a, pp.133-8, 155-79). Such an aesthetics is an aesthetics of the 'sublime' rather than the beautiful, because, in Kant's words, it is a 'presentation of the infinite' rather than the determinable good, whilst at the same time being a politics in its pragmatic 'anticipation' of a community consensus, which is not effected by 'litigation'. Such a consensus, he terms, again after Kant, a '*sensus communis*', being a 'universality' in 'abeyance' or 'suspense', for which 'judgement' then becomes and ideal, but indeterminate, norm in a community (Lyotard 1988a, pp.132-3, 155-8). Accordingly:

The *sensus communis* is thus in aesthetics what the whole of practical, reasonable beings is in ethics. It is an appeal to community carried out *a priori* and judged without a rule of direct presentation. However, in the case of moral obligation, the community is required by the mediation of a concept of reason, the Idea of freedom, while in the phrase of the beautiful, the community of addressors and addressees is called forth immediately, without the mediation of any 'concept', by feeling alone, inasmuch as this feeling can be shared *a priori*. The community is already there in taste, but it is not yet there as rational consensus. (Lyotard 1988a, p.169)

In a subsequent essay entitled *Sensus communis*, Lyotard returned to the same themes. The '*sensus communis*' was, following Kant, something 'beyond' the cognitive, not a matter of mediated principled morality, but signifying an idea of community rationality geared to 'practical ethical use'. The essay thus concentrated on the analytic of the beautiful, as opposed to the sublime. The 'beautiful', he suggested, is able to represent a 'region of resistance to institutions and establishment.' It, too, can be used as a complement to the sublime in the establishment of a postmodern politics (Lyotard 1992). What Lyotard ultimately suggests in *The Differend* is that such a politics will be effected not by litigation, which can only work if the contestants are in dispute over something determinable, but by love. It is, of course, precisely the same ultimate recourse as that made by Kant, in the second 'Doctrine' of the *Metaphysics* (Lyotard 1988a, pp.160-1).

Lyotard published *Heidegger and 'the jews'*, as his contribution to the Heidegger 'debate'. As with Auschwitz, the 'jews' are representative of the 'other', or the 'forgotten' (Lyotard 1990, pp.3-48). Lyotard repeated that Heidegger's silence recognised that the fate of the Jews symbolized the end of humanism. Yet, despite this recognition, Heidegger's mistake was to cling to a residual humanism and refuse to appreciate the ever-presence of the other in the textual-political situation. Only the invocation of the sublime can evade humanism. According to Lyotard, Heidegger recognised his mistake in associating himself with Nazism, but still failed to distance himself from its metaphysical impulses. His politics and his philosophy must be approached discretely. Approving Lacoue-Labarthe's thesis, Lyotard suggests that Heidegger's genius was to realise that a post-Auschwitz postmodern political ethics must be an aesthetics. It is this which explains his refusal to make a non-aesthetic statement on the subject. Auschwitz was 'beyond' humanist discourse (Lyotard 1990, pp.51-89). What Heidegger failed to do was acknowledge that such a postmodern ethics would have to return to consider 'justice' and 'obligation'. Aesthetics could not merely concentrate on the idea of freedom alone. In other words, he refused to go far enough along the road which Kant dictated (Lyotard 1993, pp.135-47).

Ultimately, Lyotard suggests in the final passages of the book, Heidegger must be read in conjunction with Hannah Arendt, the 'great non-German German' and 'non-Jewish Jew'. Arendt, he suggests, is the intellectual 'complement' to Heidegger because she takes Heidegger's thesis back to Kant, beyond the first *Critique*, and on to a Kantian politics of the third and fourth *Critiques*, where Heidegger himself was not prepared to go. Arendt drags Heidegger back to the pragmatic inevitabilities of a postmodern politics derived from the third *Critique* (Lyotard 1990, pp.92-3). The affinity between Lyotard's present ambitions and Arendt's has been approved by Philippe Lacoue-Labarthe, noting that Lyotard seeks recourse to section 28 of the third *Critique*, and the sublime, whereas Arendt remained committed to a development, along more obviously Heideggerian lines, of section 40. Both recognised the necessity of returning to Kant in order to access a postmodern ethics (Lacoue-Labarthe 1984).

The philosophy of the 'differend' has led to an intensification of Lyotard's engagement with the later Kant. His most recent work has underlined an increasing interest in the complementary conceptions of 'reflective judgement' and the 'sublime'. In *The Faculty of Judgment*, Lyotard described himself as returning to Kant after a Marxist 'interlude', and with the ambition of producing a textual critique of the faculty of judgment. The role of judgment in postmodernism is to 'recognize and bring to light the abyss' that exists between language 'genres', and between communicators. Where modern philosophy has gone wrong is in its attempts to fill in the abyss which Kant described, rather than seeking out 'fragile passages... above' it (Lyotard 1989, pp.324-9). In *Peregrinations*, he expressed his sympathy with, and desire to refine, a philosophy of 'singular cases', and reaffirmed his suggestion that Kantian 'reflection' was the means by which to develop such a philosophy. Both ethics and aesthetics, in the

Kantian project, share common origins in 'reflective judgment': 'to respond to a case without criteria, which is reflective judgment, is itself a case in its turn, an event to which an answer, a mode of linking, will eventually have to be found. This condition may be negative, but it is the principle for all probity in politics as in art.' (Lyotard 1988b, p.27) *Peregrinations* represents Lyotard's ultimate commitment to the third *Critique*. To fail to make this commitment, and to realise that any philosophy, political, ethical or aesthetic, must now be derived from this source was Heidegger's critical mistake. Heidegger sensed where he must go, but refused to follow. In similar vein, Lyotard expresses himself to be 'amazed' that latter day critical philosophers, most particularly pragmatic conversationalists who aspire to postmodernism, have failed to appreciate that the third *Critique* is the inevitable locus for their concentration (Lyotard 1988b, pp.29-38).

The recent *Lessons on the Analytic of the Sublime*, which reprises Lyotard's writings over the previous half decade, emphasises a commitment to Kant's third and 'fourth' *Critiques* in an effort to access a textual political-ethics. The third *Critique*, in its determination to restore universality to judgment through the analytic of taste, is the only effective 'bridge' over the Kantian 'abyss'. Following Kant, Lyotard affirms that the 'reflective' faculty of judgment is the only true 'mode of critical thought': 'The reading that I advocate... consequently admits that if the third *Critique* fulfills its mission of unifying the field of philosophy, it does so, not primarily by introducing the theme of the regulative Idea of an objective finality of nature, but by making manifest, in the name of the aesthetic, the reflexive manner of thinking that is at work in the critical text as a whole.' (Lyotard 1991, p.8) What Lyotard emphasises is the constituent of 'feeling' in reflective judgment, most particularly, 'sublime feeling', which he terms the 'irruption' of thought in the 'desire for limitlessness'. It is this 'limitlessness' which distinguishes the 'sublime' from the 'beautiful'. It is also this quality which leads Lyotard to assert that the 'differend' lies at the 'heart' of the 'sublime feeling' (Lyotard 1991, pp.6-13, 50-9).

As an 'idea', the 'idea of freedom' leads directly, not to moral action, but to the 'aesthetic feeling'. A Kantian ethics is thus derived from the aesthetics. The distinction between the 'beautiful' and the 'sublime' is once again central. There is an 'analogical' relationship or 'affinity' between the beautiful and the good such that the 'feeling of the beautiful conceals an interest precisely in realizing what moral law describes' (Lyotard 1991, pp.164-71). The sublime, on the other hand, is a more 'pure' reflective judgment 'in regard to subjective purposiveness' (Lyotard 1991, p.185). Critical to the analytic of the beautiful is its communicability. Taste, he affirms, 'is a sanction that immediately demands to be communicated.' It is this which provides the 'basis for its universal validity'. Taste is a 'singular subjective judgment' which 'lays claim' to universality. Judgment is not itself universal, but it 'awaits' universality because its ambition is to realise a 'communicated happiness'. The aesthetic thus provides a 'kind of transcendental pre-logic', and it is here that the origins of an 'ethics' lies. The sublime, in contrast, does not immediately demand to communicate itself aesthetically. The sublime exists only in thought. It is not an object itself. It is instead 'mediated' by 'moral feeling'. Unlike the beautiful, therefore, there is no question of *sensus communis* emanating from the sublime. The *sensus communis* is, rather, the claim for universality made by the beautiful (Lyotard 1991, pp.16-19, 191-239).

The kind of politics which Lyotard espouses is precisely the kind which would be expected from someone steeped in the later Kant. Most immediately, there is the familiar rejection of the metanarrative of modern universalism. More precisely, Lyotard attacks the textualism of twentieth century technology and capital. A postmodern politics will be 'participatory', and built upon an 'open-ness' of language. It will be a kind of new 'post-humanism', which he describes as a kind of a self-determinative Kantian moral humanism complementary to a theory of rights (Lyotard 1993, pp.108-11). A number of commentators have been willing to extrapolate a more overt postmodern politics from Lyotard's often obtuse writings. Bill Readings has suggested that Lyotard is a fundamentally 'political thinker' who seeks to reintroduce a critical ethics to contemporary political philosophy via postmodern textualism (Readings 1991, pp.137-9). A number of commentators have noted the affinity between Lyotard and Arendt. Both recognise that the postmodern crisis is unavoidably a 'crisis of judgment' (Ingrams 1992). Anne Barron has suggested a related affinity between the postmodern ambitions of Lyotard and John Rawls, who have both recognised the virtue in a political philosophy of the 'fragmented self' and the ever-pressing need to be alert to the exclusion of this self. Of course, in contrast to Rawls, Lyotard is content to merely articulate the difference (Barron 1992). But then, a postmodern Kantianism can do little else.

Deconstruction and Postmodernism

It has been suggested that Derrida's critique of the Heidegger-Kant exchange might be the most important development in contemporary philosophy (Hoy 1979). Derrida himself acknowledges that his debt to Heidegger is perhaps greater than to anyone else, and his writings have been recently characterized as an 'ongoing dialogue' with Heidegger (Rapaport 1989, p.7). Heidegger lies at the heart of Derrida's project because Heidegger lies at the heart of deconstruction. Not that deconstructionism is a precise idea or concept. The refusal to admit the validity of such a determination is in many ways the essence of the concept itself. Derrida's own suggestion, in a 1991 interview, is perhaps one of the simplest; deconstruction is the recognition that there is always more to the text than what the author has written (Mortley 1991, pp.96-7, 107). It is the acknowledgement that text cannot close off possibilities, because the reader will always introduce a particular context. At the same time, there is only the text, because what the reader brings to the text is, itself, text. The (re)turn to text is the heart of deconstruction. The ambition of *Of Grammatology* is to impress that philosophy was writing. In *Phaedrus* Derrida suggested that philosophy since Plato had deliberately sought to insulate itself from writing. The purpose of *Margins*, in turn, establishes 'limits' which lie beyond the reappropriative grasp of philosophy. The inspiration for this evolving critique is Kant. Derrida's *Of an Apocalyptic Tone Recently Adopted in Philosophy* is a conscious echo of Kant's *Of an Overlordly Tone Recently Adopted in Philosophy*. Both make common cause in the need to keep philosophy open through its continual critique. According to Derrida, what Kant bequeathed to future generations was a belief in 'philosophy's finally open and unveiled future.' We are, he adds, the '*Aufklaerer* of modern times' (Derrida 1984).

Derrida's association with philosophy must be seen through his association with Kant, and more particularly the third *Critique*. According to Christopher Norris, the 'activity of deconstruction is strictly inconceivable outside the tradition of enlightened rational critique' found in Kant. There is, for Derrida, 'no opting out' of the Kantian critique (Norris 1987, pp.236-7, Norris 1990, pp.194-207). Derrida's affinity with the third *Critique* is clearest in *Parergon*, in which he seeks to explore the 'supplement' of judgment. Judgment, he asserted, cannot be divided from the whole Kantian project. Thus judgment becomes a supplement to the first two *Critiques*, just as they are supplements to it. Aesthetics is a supplement to, and supplemented by, ethics. Thus judgment can be deconstructed. But the veracity of it, as a constitutive part of critical philosophy, cannot be denied. Any subsequent critique will be a supplement to it.

In *Before the Law*, he reaffirmed judgment to be a 'human' faculty, which lies 'beyond' the law alone. Judgment is a literary and a liberating faculty. Kafka's parable, which provides the impulse for the essay, is interpreted by Derrida to imply the 'supplementing' of the moral law, with the faculty of reflective judgment. It is, accordingly, a parable about supplementing the Kantian critique, and above all, about 'responsibility' and self-assertion (Derrida 1992a, Beardsworth 1996, p.26). The essential problem for both Kant and Derrida is that of establishing the 'limits' of reason (Gasche 1986). Ultimately, both seek to determine reason and, in Derrida's case, move 'beyond' it by means of invoking a critique of aesthetics, and the technology of the text (Beardsworth 1996, p.2). Derrida's Kantian orientation is, thus, precisely the same as that of Lyotard. Kant presented the question of reason and its limits, and then teasingly, suggested the (im)possibility of an answer.

The accusations of negativism which deconstruction has so often attracted, can be deflected if it is appreciated that deconstructionism suggests, not that philosophy is ended per se, but that it has served to close off certain things. Appreciation that certain possibilities defy closing off, because the text itself can never fully close off meaning, is a positive and creative force. Derrida made this clear in his famous encounter with Hans-Georg Gadamer in 1981. Whereas Gadamer sought to establish meaning through recourse to a hermeneutic circularity, Derrida insisted that there was only text, and thus any 'closing off' could only be textual and thus incomplete. The engagement between the two was a struggle for Heidegger's soul, with both claiming to be taking the thrust of Heidegger's linguistic turn to its inevitable conclusion. It has been suggested that Gadamer developed the early Heidegger, whilst Derrida developed the later (Michelfelder and Palmer 1989, pp.3-4). Heidegger, Derrida suggests, was the first deconstructionist of the twentieth century. Hermeneutics, not deconstruction, is the denial of ethical possibilities, and it was Heidegger, if unwittingly, who kept open the door for a reconstituted, deconstructed ethics. A critical ethics requires openness. Derrida thought himself to be going 'beyond' Heidegger, and thus avoiding the metaphysical humanism which trapped both Heidegger and now Gadamer (Michelfelder and Palmer 1989, pp.94-5).

The text in which Derrida most immediately approaches Heidegger is *Of Spirit: Heidegger and the Question*, written as a deconstruction of the *Rektorat*. According to David Krell, *Of Spirit* is the most important book on Heidegger 'in our time' (Krell 1993, p.11). What interests Derrida is Heidegger's use of *Geist*, a concept conspicuous in its 'absence' in *Being and Time*, but which emerges onto centre 'stage' in the *Rektorat*. It 'marks a line along the edge of the Heideggerian enterprise' (Silverman 1989, p.164). It is at the margins of Heidegger's philosophy, because beyond it Heidegger did not want to go. *Geist*, it seems to Derrida, not only describes the political, but determines it also. *Geist* 'seems to designate, beyond a deconstruction, the very resource for any deconstruction and the possibility of any evaluation.' (Derrida 1989, pp.1-6, 14-5) What *Geist* symbolises is a recourse to metaphysics which Heidegger felt that he had to make in his approach to the question of ethics in 1933-34.

The use of quotation marks, to 'guard' *Geist* in its pre-1933 invocations, is suggestive of a 'deconstructed' *Geist* which 'designates something other which resembles it'; the 'spirit of another spirit'. The quotation marks defend it in space and time. This, of course, seems to be akin to the kind of transcendental deconstruction for which Derrida is himself now so regularly criticized. In the *Rektorat*, however, *Geist* emerges triumphant and unguarded, to lead the self-assertion of the German university and the German people. Self-assertion is a 'spiritual exaltation' (Derrida 1989, pp.23-5, 31-44). The central concept, as Derrida impresses, is 'responsibility'. It is this which *Geist* is to unlock. In Heidegger's immediately subsequent writings, Derrida notes, 'responsibility' emerges as the alternative to 'resignation'. *Geist*, moreover, consolidates its position as the central Heideggerian construct. Heidegger, having once invoked *Geist* can never escape its humanist temptations (Derrida 1989, pp.60-7, 79-82). The question which Heidegger is asking, and answering, according to Derrida, is 'what is humanism?' The ultimate realisation is that anti-humanism is itself a humanism. It is this which has entrapped Heidegger (Derrida 1989, pp.47-55).

It is clear from both *Of Spirit* and the engagement with Gadamer that Derrida situates his 'deconstruction' as the offspring of Heidegger's 'destruction' of philosophy. The former could only be understood in 'remembrance of the latter' (Bernasconi 1989). 'Difference', Derrida has repeatedly emphasised, is the object of the 'entire' Heideggerian project. Heidegger's was the 'first deconstruction'. Thus, what trapped Heidegger in 1933-34 awaits to trap Derrida today. According to Geoffrey Bennington, *Of Spirit* merely confirms that Derrida has slipped into precisely the same 'quasi-transcendental' trap as Heidegger (Bennington 1993). Derrida, however, remains committed to deconstruction. In *Of Grammatology*, he deconstructed Heidegger's 'destruction' of Nietzsche in order to refine a 'second' deconstruction which was intended to avoid the hermeneutics into which Heidegger's linguistic turn had developed. In *Of Spirit*, Derrida had suggested that a deconstruction 'beyond' Heidegger was one which grasped the 'difference' which could not be arbitrated by any (non)humanism; an idea strikingly resonant of Lyotard's 'differend'. (Derrida 1989, p.109) The precise nature of the Heidegger-Derrida affinity has emerged as one of the most tendentious questions in contemporary philosophy. According to Renaut and Ferry, Derrida's writing is simply '*l'heideggerianisme francais*' (Mortley 1991, p.4). Lyotard, as we have already seen, makes the same suggestion, and condemns Derrida precisely for remaining a Heideggerian. Robert Cummings suggests that Derrida's deconstruction is irreducibly 'modelled' on Heidegger's 'destruction' of philosophy. Both Heidegger and Derrida ultimately saw text as the space from which a radically indeterminate anti-humanist 'ethics' could be brought forth. Derrida cited the reconstruction that Heidegger's deconstruction logically and unavoidably demanded, but which Heidegger could not bring himself to acknowledge (Cummings 1981). The question of Heidegger and Derrida is, then, a question of whether or not Derrida's attempt to move 'beyond' Heidegger, can really effect a move 'beyond' humanism.

The engagement with Heidegger, or more precisely the deconstruction of Heidegger, the move 'beyond', leads Derrida unavoidably into the terrain of ethics and politics. According to Richard Bernstein, any attempt to see 'an ethical-political horizon' of Derrida necessitates a Heideggerian perspective (Bernstein 1987). In a 1991 interview, Derrida himself suggested that his immediate research was directed towards the complementary study of Heidegger and of the application of deconstruction to issues of political nationalism (Derrida 1991, pp.96-7). Heidegger, according to Derrida, possesses the 'deconstructing strength' which is necessary for a postmodern politics (Derrida 1987a, p.179). The central message of *Of Spirit* is the unavoidability of the political-ethical dimension of the deconstruction enterprise (Krell 1993, p.13). Simon Critchley has strongly asserted that Derrida's engagement with Heidegger necessitates a Derridean ethics, which takes essentially the same form as Heidegger's because it concentrates upon the same central concept, 'the thought of responsibility of language as a response to the other.' (Critchley 1993) In *GeschlechtII*, Derrida reaffirmed that his recent interest in political thought, and particularly nationalism, has served to underline the centrality of Heidegger to his thinking. The problem of politics is the problem of 'we', of humanism. It is the 'we' which Heidegger cited as *Volk* and *Geist*.

Paradoxically, as time has progressed, the call for Derrida to 'write' an ethics has grown louder and louder. It is a curious request because, as Derrida has repeatedly implied, deconstruction is a positively political activity. Because it seeks to reveal the politics of philosophy, by emphasising that the writing of philosophy, like any textual enterprise, deconstruction is innately political. The attempt of western philosophy since Plato, to insulate itself against writing, is a conscious attempt to deny the politics of any philosophical enterprise. Deconstruction, however, denies political neutrality. The exercise is always ethical-political because it assumed the existence, and presence, of the 'other'. This 'other' is, of course, determined by the 'we'. 'Difference' is ultimately determined as the difference between the 'we' and the 'other', those with voice (and text) and those silenced and powerless. Because deconstruction is politics, so too is justice.

In *The Force of Law*, Derrida stresses that the 'force' of law is the product of the necessary 'difference' in relations between self and other. It is, thus, a 'differential force'. In aligning textual deconstruction with political power 'differentials', Derrida explicitly approves the textual turn in critical legal studies (Derrda 1990, pp.925-33). His concentration on the 'deconstructibility' of justice, as opposed to the undeconstructibility of law, serves to emphasise still further its ethical component. Law is insufficient, an act of violence and power. Using a metaphor which consciously echoes Heidegger's humanistic *Geist*, Derrida suggests that the story of law's ambitions is a 'ghost story'. Law has nothing to do with justice, which is itself an 'obligation' owed to the 'other' (Derrida 1990, pp.1007-15). Postmodern jurisprudence is a jurisprudence which forever deconstructs the pretended universalism of any philosophy of law. A properly critical jurisprudence is the championing of the particular, and a complementary openness to the textually determined justice which lies 'beyond', and which has yet to be realized (Derrida 1990, pp.945-7, 959-73). Such a deconstructionism, according to Michel Rosenfeld, creates a tangible affinity with the contemporary Kantian formalism (Rosenfeld 1990). Barbara Smith suggests that Derrida's deconstruction of justice is an invocation of the Kantian critique of judgment, whilst Stephen Watson asserts that Derrida's deconstruction of justice, finally effects the postmodern return to Kant (Smith 1990, Watson 1990).

There is, thus, no need to 'write' a Derridean ethics, or for that matter, a Derridean jurisprudence. Indeed, deconstruction is precisely against any 'demand' for an ethics. It is not, however, against ethics. It cannot be. Ethics is already written, and it is a jurisprudence. However, there are more obviously political texts, with we which can 'supplement' our understanding of a Derridean ethics. The central philosophical conceptions which gear these political essays are precisely the same as those which are determined in the more abstract texts. Most immediately there is the concept of 'limit' and exclusion. At the same time as it tried to marginalise the writing of philosophy, western philosophy has also consistently attempted to silence those at the margins of political philosophy. The ambition of a Derridean postmodern ethics is to reinvest the other in contemporary political philosophy. His recent essay on the direction in European politics and culture, *The Other Heading*, describes the weakness in contemporary European politics brought about by technology and its exclusion of the 'other'. Europe, in failing to identify itself, excludes the 'other' by negating the 'discourse' of the other. Only a deconstructionist Europe can effect a genuine participatory democractic Europe (Derrida 1992b). According to Nancy Fraser, such a politics can be most readily aligned with that of Hannah Arendt. The purpose of critical philosophy is to identify the 'margins' of politics and philosophy, and give voice to the silenced. It seeks ultimately to reform a revolutionary participatory democracy (Fraser 1984).

In *Violence and Metaphysics*, Derrida suggests that a postmodern, or post-Heideggerian, ethics will be the product of a revolution of reason from within. It will be a Kantian 'supplement' to Heidegger. It will also be an ethics which will remain inaccessible, in the sense that it will remain a questioning ethics. It will remain undetermined because any postmodern ethics, indeed any ethics, is a textual ethics. The text preserves ethics, and the freedom of ethics, in a precisely Kantian sense of free-will. Ethics is thus deconstruction because ethics is text (Derrida 1978, p.109). The fact that a deep engagement with Heidegger should lead to an engagement with ethics, and ultimately with Kant, is no suprise. It is precisely the same movement as was made by Heidegger himself. As we have already noted, Derrida's debate with Foucault, at the outset of his career, was about the nature of a post-modern 'Kantian ethics'. The Kantian nature of Derrida's postmodern ethics comes over strongly in *The Laws of Reflection: Nelson Mandela, in Admiration*. The core ethical and political concepts are freedom and equality. Presented as the approbation of Mandela's own ethical vision they emerge as irreducibly transcendental principles. What has made Mandela so 'admirable' is his allegiance to the 'institution of jurisprudence', and the authority of a 'moral law' which can transcend various positive laws, such as those of apartheid. Like Heidegger before him, in 1933, Derrida, in his critique of apartheid, seeks recourse to Kant. Mandela's jurisprudence, to which Derrida assigns his own fidelity, prescribes revolutionary participatory 'democracy', based on the 'principles of justice' and 'respect' for the person. This, Derrida suggests, is the core of a postmodern 'reflective' jurisprudence. Derrida, it seems, like Mandela, is a good critical legal scholar in the best Kantian tradition (Derrida 1987b).

Progress, political or otherwise, is an ethical endeavour. The deconstructive 'beyond' is an indeterminable progression. Derrida's awareness of this comes across in *The Principle of Reason: The University in the Eyes of its Pupils*, an essay written as a conscious echo of Kant's *The Contest of the Faculties* and Heidegger's *Rektorat*. The university, Derrida acknowledges, is founded upon a 'principle of reason'. But the post-Heideggerian ethic demands that the adherents must go beyond the 'limits' of reason, where Kant refused to go. Echoing Foucault, Derrida suggests that this requires a conscious breaking down of the universalistic pretensions of 'specialized' knowledges and discourses. The university must remain consciously self-reflective and determinative. That is its 'responsibility' (Derrida 1983). The Heideggerian-Foucaultian critique of techno-languages was repeated in his *Onto-Theology of National Humanism*. Nationalism, Derrida suggests, whilst seeking to self-determine, always does so by establishing itself as a universal philosophy. It thus denies the particularity which it needs (Derrida 1992c). In *The Other Heading* he suggests that this is precisely the trap into which contemporary Europe has fallen. In each case, that of Europe, of the university, and of nationalism, only a post-modern textual ethics effects a means of moving 'beyond' the universalist ambitions of metaphysics.

The Heidegger-Kant strain in Derrida's ethics is very apparent, once again, in *The Politics of Friendship*. Jurisprudence, he suggests, is the 'assignation of responsibility' by the 'other'. The genus is Heideggerian and involves a 'rigorous rereading' of the Kantian idea of respect, which is inseparable from the 'moral law'. What Derrida seeks to achieve is an opening up of law which can move 'beyond' the one-dimensional Kantian plane, and can reintroduce the 'other' as the 'third party' to a jurisprudential-ethical dialogue. This is the 'responsibility' of a postmodern ethics (Derrida 1988). This thesis is repeated in *The Force of Law*, where Derrida suggests that deconstruction is the 'responsibility' of the self-assertive postmodern jurist. A postmodern jurisprudence in the final analysis is one which must be asserted by us. Derrida referred to the jurisprudential lesson of any holocaust, which 'defines a task and a responsibility' which 'is the thought of difference between these destructions on the one hand and a deconstructive affirmation on the other' (Derrida 1990, pp.953-7). Ethical responsibility, as Geoffrey Bennington has emphasised, lies at the heart of Derrida's project, or, more accurately, at its margins where the limits of self and other are 'interrupted' (Bennington 1993, p.310). As Richard Bernstein has recently noted, it is this concept of 'responsibility' which ultimately determines the ethical-political thought of both Heidegger and now Derrida, and in both cases its origins lie with Kant and the responsibility incumbent upon the reflective moral person. The Derridean postmodern move 'beyond' humanism and beyond Heidegger is, ultimately, a (re)turn to a reflective Kantian ethics (Bernstein 1987, pp.93-117).

CHAPTER 4

POSTMODERN BOURGEOIS LIBERALISM

1 Continuing the Conversation

Rorty's Mirror

Richard Rorty, it has been recently asserted, is the most influential thinker in contemporary Anglo-American philosophy (Haber 1994, p.7). Richard Rorty is also an imperialist. He claims dominion for a new postmodern bourgeois liberalism. According to Rorty, postmodern bourgeois liberalism represents another generation in a genealogy which begins with Kant and then moves through Heidegger, sprouts illegitimate offspring in the likes of Foucault and Derrida, and then comes to rest with the liberal ironist like himself. More than this, Rorty claims dominion for postmodern bourgeois liberalism over a number of other political philosophers including John Rawls and Roberto Unger. The purpose of this chapter is to investigate the nature of this particular genealogy and to assess the validity of Rorty's dominion.

The investigation must being with *Philosophy and the Mirror of Nature*; a critique of the representationalist tendencies which Rorty perceives as lying at the heart of the Enlightenment project. In one sense, Rorty's own sympathies lie at the most extreme edge of anti-foundationalist thinking. Yet, at the same time, Rorty is thoroughly immersed in the Heidegger-Kant dialogue. *Philosophy and the Mirror of Nature* is a careful and systematic critique of Kantian foundationalism, culminating in the work of Rorty's three heroes, Dewey, Heidegger and Wittgenstein. Heidegger, in particular, is the genie awaiting to be released from the bottle.

What makes Dewey, Heidegger and Wittgenstein so important in contemporary philosophy is the fact that each engaged with Kant, and attempted to develop the Kantian critique to its immanent conclusion; a philosophy without foundations. It is Kant's mirror which Rorty wants to break. The anti-technological later Heidegger, with which Rorty expresses a particular affinity, made the particular contribution of emphasising that philosophy is always history, and always a discursive history; both constituted as and constitutive of, history (Rorty 1980, pp.7-13). Whilst wholly approving the spirit of Kant's critical enterprise, his mistake, Rorty suggests, was the failure to move beyond the pervasive reality-appearance problem, and its various associated dualisms. Kant realised that, since Aristotle, philosophy had been the history of an idea of self-delusion, but in searching for foundations within the individual, and most damagingly within the individual mind, he merely presented another metaphysics of mirrors. Any attempt to describe 'how things are', will unavoidably be a creative act of 'how things are' (Rorty 1980, p.114).

If the Enlightenment philosophy of mind was determined by its dualisms, its epistemology was similarly beset, and flawed, by the cause-effect 'myth'. And again the chief villain was Kant, because, although he first suggested non-foundational knowledge of philosophy as politics, by distinguishing science from philosophy, he represented a philosophy of transcendental ambition. With regard to the Truth Problematic, which following Heidegger Rorty places at the heart of the problem of metaphysics, Kant's most dangerous mistake was to distinguish the 'contingent' truth from the 'necessary'. Rorty's ambition, in his denial of this distinction, is to present an anti-necessitarian theory of knowledge (Rorty 1980, pp.157-8).

If Kant made the first crucial critique of Enlightenment philosophy, and then the first reconstructive defence, his neo-Kantian apprentices have sought to continue the reconstructive enterprise. Rorty identifies and critiques three particular types of neo-Kantianism, each of which he characterizes as positivist; analytical philosophy, empirical psychology, and the foundational philosophy of language. The most dangerous of these positivist variants is certainly the analytical. Analytical philosophy emerged as an instinctive reaction to the perceived anti-philosophical undertones of the 'spirit of playfulness' which had caught the imagination of Cassirer and the Kantian pluralists. It was, in other words, the product of an internecine Kantian dispute (Rorty 1980, pp.166-79). If there is a flaw in Rorty's treatment of Kant, it is, as Thomas MacCarthy has emphasised, a failure to appreciate the depth of Kant's own anti-foundationalism; a failure to appreciate Kant's own playfulness (MacCarthy 1991, pp.16-7).

The hermeneutic alternative which Rorty presents in the final chapters of *Philosophy and the Mirror of Nature* is thus cast in this Kantian image. At this time, Rorty is less perturbed by the foundational tendencies of hermeneutics; in some of his subsequent essays, as we shall see, he is more circumspect. Richard Bernstein has suggested that in adopting the hermeneutic alternative, Rorty has fallen in the same foundational trap which snared both Heidegger and then Gadamer. The reason is that neither Heidegger nor Gadamer nor Rorty can bring themselves to abandon the transcendental subjectivism of Kant's third *Critique* (Bernstein 1983, pp.110-69). However, for Rorty, hermeneutics offers a constructive non-foundational alternative to epistemology. It is not some sort of replacement; hermeneutics is the 'hope' that we can do without replacements, so 'that our culture should become one in which the demand for constraint and confrontation is no longer felt.' It is thus, above all, an anti-necessitarian concept: 'Hermeneutics sees the relations between various discourses as those of strands of a possible conversation, a conversation which presupposes no disciplinary matrix which unites the speakers, but where hope of agreement is never lost so long as the conversation lasts.' (Rorty 1980, pp.315-8).

Any philosophical 'constraints' are thus merely the constraints of 'normal discourse', and instead of a 'way of knowing' there is merely a 'way of coping' (Rorty 1980, pp.320, 356). Hermeneutics, in its determination to describe our self-expression, rather than to attempt to construct it, is, to use Rorty's term, an 'edifying', as opposed to a 'systematic', philosophy. Such a philosophy is 'poetry'; a theme which will be intensified in his subsequent essays. In proto-postmodern language, Rorty adds that a poet edifies by opening rather than by effecting 'closure' (Rorty 1980, 370). The three great 'edifying' philosophers are, of course, Dewey, Heidegger and Wittgenstein. They recognised the exlusionary power of language, and sought to keep it open by effecting 'abnormal discourse'. This will emerge as the central theme in Rorty's own later linguistic writings. The discussion of the self-assertive qualities of our existence, and our particular 'responsibility for choice'.

The Heideggerian Conversation

Rorty's particular conversation with Heidegger is a conversation with Heidegger's conversation with Kant. According to Rorty, Heidegger, along with Dewey, was the first of the 'conversationalist' philosophers; both fully aware of the import of our historical selves, and the possibilities offered by a poetic release (Rorty 1982, pp.37-59). In Rorty's own historical account of American philosophy, he suggests that the anti-foundationalism which Dewey 'predicted' in American philosophy, actually appeared, in its purest and most effective form, in the literary philosophy of Heideggerians such as Sartre, Foucault and Derrida. Indeed, it is clear that Rorty sees one of his most important functions as that of revitalizing the Deweyan spirit in American philosophy, by effecting an alignment with the Heideggerian tradition. His essay on Dewey's metaphysics is perhaps Rorty's most explicit early engagement with the full import of the Heidegger-Kant dialogue (Rorty 1982, pp.86-7).

Rorty's sympathy with Heideggerians is perhaps most explicit at this stage in his essay on Derrida, who, he suggests, is the latest to continue the assault on the Kantian tradition. Whereas Heidegger thought that he was the first to break away from the Kantian constraint, Derrida suggests that Heidegger himself was in the same way constrained, and that he is the first to achieve the break. It is, however, Rorty's thesis that Derrida's ambition to overcome Heidegger is in fact innately Heideggerian, and in its attempt to finalize philosophy, overtly Kantian. What Derrida must avoid, according to Rorty, is this finalizing and exclusionary tendency. There is no philosophy of language to be written; there is just writing. Derrida is, of course, as we have seen, aware of the danger, and in his later writings emphasises the 'lived experience' of writing.

A revitalized textualized pragmatism, a conjoining of Dewey with the Heidegger-Derrida line, can itself revitalize American philosophy. What Dewey did, and what Heidegger did not, is write in a 'spirit of social hope'. What Rorty ultimately wants to do is to take the deconstructive tendencies of the Heideggerian inheritance, and the reconstructive tendencies of the American pragmatic liberal tradition, and together present a radical transformative theory of democratic liberalism. The great value of pragmatic liberalism is its 'vocabulary of practice rather than of theory, of action rather than contemplation, in which one can say something useful about truth'; in other words that it is contingent. Its other great value is that the only practical constraints it recognises are conversational. A reconstructed democratic liberalism would be a society of conversationalists, aware of the contingency of every truth, but *contra* 'relativism', willing to 'self-assert' each particular truth, in the spirit of democratic pluralism. The concessions which Rorty makes, towards some sort of reconstructive rationalism, are of course those necessary to any liberal democratic political vision; a plural discourse must still be a communicatively rational discourse (Rorty 1982, pp.160-75). It was, of course, this unavoidability which led Rorty towards Gadamer, and thus back to Kant, in *Philosophy and the Mirror of Nature*. However, it is clear that Rorty becomes ever less comfortable with the foundational tendencies of the hermeneutical alternative, and it is noticeable that the more he engages with the French Heideggerians, the less comfortable Rorty becomes with hermeneutics. Hermeneutics is a tool, not a philosophy.

The turn towards Heidegger and the complementary anti-foundationalism is Rorty's essential concern. The marrying of the two is most explicit in his 'Contingency' essays in *Contingency, Irony and Solidarity*. The whole tone is more overtly political. Rorty suggests that the driving concern for any liberal philosophy is that of achieving justice. In its overriding concern to effect the accommodation of 'private' and 'public', postmodernism is an innate jurisprudence. The echoes of Hannah Arendt are striking, and, as the essays unfold, those of the later Rawls and Unger become equally resonant. Developing the division of the pessimistic and optimistic, Rorty suggests that the Heidegger-Foucault-Derrida line is that of 'private irony', whilst the Dewey-Rawls line is that of 'public hope'. The later Rawls is the later Kant. Rorty acknowledges as much in acknowledging that the key to the new post-philosophical philosophy is freedom and truth, not freedom or truth. The marrying of these dualities, freedom and truth, private and public, irony and solidarity, will realise the liberal utopia, which will be a narrative rather than a theoretical utopia, meaning a created, self-asserted, rather than discovered, utopia (Rorty 1989, pp.xiii-iv). The three 'Contingency' essays attempt to achieve this private irony-public solidarity synthesis, through 'language', 'selfhood', and 'community'. The realisation that truth is created not found was Kant's greatest contribution to philosoohy. It was how he 'created' it, within the morally driven individual, that Rorty disputes. The determination of truth is defeated by the contingency of language. This is not, however, a necessarily nihilistic or pessimistic fact. On the contrary, it empowers us, as the creators of our discourse: 'The world does not speak. Only we do.' (Rorty 1989, pp.5-6) Such a language is a shared intersubjective language, created by a never-ending sequence of contingencies. It is, thus, an open language; in Derrida's terms, forever seeking its horizon.

The 'contingency of selfhood' is the complement to that of language, because the self is a conversationalist, and is defined as such. Thus Nietzsche's 'mobile army of metaphors' is central to the self-assertive capacity of the liberal ironist. Life is itself a narrative, and we, as self-assertive liberals, are 'poets' of our own contingencies and indeterminacies. Again, though nihilistic in a Nietzschean sense, and pessimistic in the Heideggerian and Foucaultian sense, for Rorty this very fact is the key to unlocking a postmodern conception of freedom. It provides 'social hope'. The original 'turn' towards the self, Rorty again acknowledges, was Kant's. It was this which made Kant a liberal philosopher. It is the philosophy, not the liberalism, which Rorty wishes to address, and it is precisely addressed by a turn from philosophy as philosophy, to philosophy as text (Rorty 1989, pp.23-43). The synthesis of language and self is effected in the 'Contingency of Community'. Freedom in the contingent community is the freedom to converse and to persuade. It is the freedom to access 'public space'; the same freedom which Arendt had sought. What distinguishes Rorty's notion of public space is that it is discursively constructive. Language is lived. It is not something we can stand outside of, and use merely in the public sphere. Language is at once private and public. The language of philosophy is thus the language of politics and of literature. The liberal 'polity' is the community in which the 'strong poets' are the heroes. Poets describe and redescribe, aware that any truth is their truth, and a merely textual truth (Rorty 1989, pp.43-4).

A postmodern liberal politics must pursue the poetic model. Moreover, it is the politics pursued, not just by Dewey, but also by the later Rawls. This Rawls, Rorty perceptively notes, is a different, more critical, more ironic Rawls, and his thesis is that of a 'mature... Enlightenment liberalism'. Such an ironic politics recognises that moral principles are only of value in relation to specific institutional and practical situations, and can only be determined as a communicative morality (Rorty 1989, pp.57-60). This is public freedom. Although Rorty sees the Rawlsian as the most immediately political model, it is towards the private ironist in the Heidegger-Kant dialogue that he suggests that we should turn in order to further effect the poetic community. We must privatise the Nietzsche-Heidegger-Foucault line, by concentrating on the situation of the ironic individual (Rorty 1989, pp.61-5). Therein lies philosophical freedom. If the politics is Rawls's and the philosophy is Foucault's, the spirit is Kant's:

> A liberal society is one whose ideal can be fulfilled by persuasion rather than by force, by reform rather than revolution, by the free and open encounters of present linguistic and other practices with suggestions for new practices. But this is to say that an ideal liberal society is one which has no purpose except freedom, no goal except a willingness to see how such encounters go and to abide by the outcome. It has no purpose except to make life easier for poets and revolutionaries while seeing to it that they make life harder for others only by words, and not by deeds. It is a society whose hero is the strong poet and the revolutionary because it recognizes that it is what it is, has the morality it has, speaks the language it does, not because it approximates the will of God or the nature of man but because certain poets and revolutionaries of the past spoke as they did. To see one's language, one's conscience, one's morality, and one's highest hopes as contingent products, as literalizations of what once were accidently produced metaphors, is to adopt a self-identity which suits one for citizenship in such an ideally liberal state. (Rorty 1989, pp.60-1)

The extent to which this liberal politics depends upon a Heideggerian philosophy is brought out both by three supplementary essays on the nature of 'private irony' in *Contingency*, and by a series of further essays collected in *Essays on Heidegger and Others*. All converse directly with the Heidegger-Kant dialogue. The conversation with Heidegger is the most animate. Heidegger is the great champion of the non-foundationalist stance, and the great advocate of the poetic alternative. In an essay allying Heidegger with Proust and Nietzsche, Rorty suggests that Heidegger is a 'paradigm of ironist theory' in that, as an ironist, a Heideggerian philosopher is always first a historian and second a philosopher. The inspiration is Kant's, but the ironist wants to take the Kantian canon and redescribe it in such a way that it loses its historicist constraint over him. Thus, Heidegger, like Proust and Nietzsche, effected a replacement of inherited 'dead' contingencies with a living history of self-made contingencies. Above all, he effected our re-empowerment as self-redescriptive beings. However, despite the endeavour, in Rorty's opinion, Heidegger was never able to shake off the Kantian canon, first trying to present a transcendental ontology, and then, following his encounter with Nietzsche, a transcendental vocabulary, of 'elementary words'. Heidegger's failure was the attempt to produce a public vocabulary; exactly the same failure as that ascribed by Unger. It has been left to the French Heideggerians in particular, most notably Foucault and Derrida, to attempt to detranscendentalize the Heideggerian vocabulary, and return irony to its natural, private, habitat.

The aim of a Heideggerian ironist philosophy, Rorty suggests, is to acknowledge the ever-openness of discourse, as the residuum of freedom, both public and private. It is, he suggests, a matter of taking Kant on and conceptualizing, not just beauty, but sublimity in our conversation. The attempt to retrieve such a humanism from within Heidegger is, of course, precisely what Heidegger so fiercely resisted, but also very much what Derrida has tried to do (Rorty 1989, pp.96-120). What Rorty wants to do, he repeatedly emphasises, is take Heidegger's philosophical-linguistic insights, desacrilize them, and 'yoke' them to a Deweyan-Rawlsian political theory. He specifically approves of the description of *Being and Time* as a potentially pragmatic text, at least in its political import. Being-in-the-World is an unavoidably pragmatic conception. The later Heidegger attempted to refine this conception linguistically, stressing that our contingencies are linguistic contingencies, and that, foreshadowing Derrida, Being is nothing other than linguistic contingency. It was Heidegger who, realizing our historical condition of 'forgetfulness', first recaptured the 'space' of 'social practice' for the thinkers and 'poets' who are now left to inhabit it (Rorty 1991b, pp.45-6). Whilst becoming aware that philosophy was language, Heidegger's failure was his inability, perhaps coloured by the events of 1933-1945, to believe that philosophy was also politics. It is this final synthesis which can be achieved by a Rawlsian reading of Heidegger (Rorty 1991b, pp.27-49).

The affinity with Michel Foucault is at once an affinity with Heidegger. Foucault, he suggested as early as 1979, 'caught a glimpse' of a 'culture' of acute 'contingency and chance', a culture of 'genealogy but not eschatology' (Rorty 1986, pp.41-9). It is not Foucault's pessimistic 'anarchic' politics which Rorty wants to defend, but rather his understanding of the separate spheres of private and public morality. Rorty effects a rereading of Heidegger to retrieve a Foucault that can be used for social theory. There are, he suggests, two Foucaults, the American, anti-universal and Deweyan-Rawlsian, and the French, Nietzschean, and anarchist. It is the accommodation of the two which can be achieved by a translation of the thesis of private autonomy into a public liberal politics. Whilst approving Foucault's archaeology of discourses, Rorty disapproves his more prescriptive analysis of power. In making this analysis, Rorty suggests that Foucault himself slipped into a transcendental trap by trying to stand apart from humanity. A liberal politics which makes use of the discursive nature of private irony must, on the contrary, embrace its existential reality. It must work out a 'banal moral vocabulary' which it can use to 'make it as easy as possible for people to achieve their wildly different private ends without hurting each other.' We must take Foucault's truth, shared with Dewey and Heidegger, that 'human subjectivity' is a 'centreless bundle of contingencies', and translate it into a pragmatic discourse (Rorty 1991b, pp.193-8).

Rorty's engagement with Foucault and Heidegger has led unavoidably to an engagement with Derrida (MacCarthy 1991, p.22). The constructive role for deconstruction, according to Rorty, is that which teaches us to read, and which teaches us that philosophy is always read. Derrida's great contribution to critical philosophy is his particular concentration on the beyond; that beyond every text is another text. Rorty sees Derrida as Heidegger's natural heir, and as his most effective critic (Rorty 1991b, pp.85-6, 95). The effectiveness of his critique is played out in his determination to undercut any attempt to sacralize language. As with Heidegger, Rorty sees a turn from the early to the late Derrida, from an almost obsessive concern with the metaphysics of Heidegger to an interest in the intensely private 'fantasy' of 'anti-theory'. The early Derrida, in particular, in his determination to argue, tends towards metaphysics. Rorty is particularly suspicious of *difference*, suggesting that Derrida invocation of it is conceptual rather than merely descriptive (Rorty 1991b, pp.101-6).

Reviewing Gasche's work on Derrida, and his suggestion that Derrida is ultimately himself a neo-Kantian, Rorty has reaffirmed his earlier suspicion that Derrida himself comes close to a metaphysics of language. In the end, Rorty acquits Derrida of any transcendental leanings, but acknowledges the force in the alternative reading of Derrida, and admits that at times Derrida seems dangerously attracted by the lure of a 'public' conception of language (Rorty 1991b, pp.119-28). Despite these early tendencies, the virtue of the later private and ironic Derrida, for Rorty at least, is far more important. Moreover, in his refusal to present any 'model', deconstructive or otherwise, but instead merely to stress the 'recontextualizing' heart of philosophy, Rorty is fulsome in his support (Rorty 1989, pp.122-37).

The engagement with deconstruction has lead to a refining, or perhaps redefining, of Rorty's own political philosophy, which has increasingly taken the appearance of an optimistic variant of postmodernism; the translation of the private irony into the social hope. It is not, thus, the postmodernism familiar from such as Lyotard. Whilst wholly approving the critique of metanarratives which Lyotard presents, Rorty is critical of Lyotard's dismissal of consensus. Again, it is the involuntary and thus irreducibly pessimistic politics of Heideggerian postmodernism which Rorty cannot accept. In the pragmatist world, institutions cannot be escaped from. What we need is a postmodernist form of social life, not a postmodernist philosophy. More precisely, what Rorty advocates is a postmodern liberalism, for which the models should be those of Rawls and Unger, not Foucault and Lyotard. Though postmodern, this optimistic liberal variant will take a quite different shape from the pessimistic variant which, he suggests, has been familiarised in America by the 'Cultural Left'. The pessimists, inspired by Foucault and Lyotard, have given up hope because their ambition, which Rorty stresses is irreducibly Kantian, of discovering a new vocabulary, has failed. But the failure is the very strength of private irony, and thus of social hope. Rorty is particularly critical of what he perceives to be Lyotard's Kantian leanings. Yet in his own presentation of the possibility of an international humanist order, possible if we want to effect it, Rorty himself consciously adopts a Kantian 'idea' of tolerance (Rorty 1991a, pp.211-22). What is clear here is the ultimate division within Rorty's own thinking, between the private ironist, the engager in the Heidegger-Kant dialogue, and the public liberal democratic champion of solidarity, driven by the same humanism as other Kantian constructivists, such as the early Sartre and the later Rawls.

In a striking dismissal of such Foucaultian political pessimism, Rorty makes a strong play for the pluralist pragmatist polity of the type which he perceives as being presented by the later Rawls and by Roberto Unger. Unger, Rorty suggests, offers the optimistic pragmatic alternative to Foucaultian Heideggerianism. Unger's vision, as we shall see shortly, is that of a pluralist solidarity. In his critique of Lyotard, Rorty spelled out in more detail his own intensely plural localised and decentralized idea of a postmodern liberal polity (Rorty 1991a, pp.211-22). The further Rorty develops his idea of liberal solidarity, the more he becomes embroiled in ethics, and the more open he becomes to the criticism - which he has levelled, in turn at Heidegger, Foucault, Derrida, and Lyotard - that in his political vision, he finds it impossible to avoid the lure of constructive transcendentalism. The most striking example of this is his tortuous attempt to distinguish a pragmatic ethics from a relativist ethics, which comes out almost indistinguishable from the kind of neo-Kantian relativism more familiar in the writings of such as Ernst Cassirer.

Rorty's proclaimed 'alternative' to pure relativism, is 'ethnocentrism'; which has itself attracted a flood of criticism (MacCarthy 1991, pp.34, 38-9). In his fleshing out of ethnocentrism as the complement of pragmatism, the priviliging of localised group beliefs, Rorty suggests that what he is doing is merely presenting a pragmatic variant of the more 'traditional Kantian' constructions of such as Rawls (Rorty 1991a, pp.21-34). Subsequently, Rorty refines his discussion of relativism, by distinguishing 'silly relativism' from the relativism which seems closer to that advocated by the 'traditional Kantians'. At the same time, when it comes to defining the postmodern liberal polity, in place of the French Heideggerianism Rorty quickly returns to his flirtation with hermeneutics, and its constructive qualities, as a kind of interpretive complement to ethnocenterism (Rorty 1991a, pp.89-92). In a specific response to Clifford Geertz's doubts regarding the compatibility of such a seemingly non-universal concept with liberalism, Rorty has asserted that his 'liberalism' is akin to that of such as Unger, in that it is directed towards a subversion of the 'psychological problem' of Enlightenment liberalism, and its mythical complements such as 'rights'. Liberals need not engage in such metaphysical pursuits. All a postmodern liberalism need do is point towards the practical benefits of liberal institutions. Here Rorty again associates himself with the later Rawls in suggesting that postmodern liberalism can now do nothing other than make a commitment to a Rawlsian procedural justice, as a 'connoisseurship of diversity'; a pluralist jurisprudence of variable content (Rorty 1991a, pp.203-10).

In *Postmodern Bourgeois Liberalism*, Rorty makes the comparison between the Deweyan-Rawlsian commitment to rights and the Dworkinian which, he suggests, is a paradigmatic example of the 'strong' or 'naturalized Kantian'. The alternative to the Dworkinian is the ethnocentric polity; the historical as opposed to the ahistorical, the narrative as opposed to the philosophical (Rorty 1991a, pp.197-202). Again, in *The Priority of Democracy to Philosophy*, Rorty has used Dworkin as the most dangerous type of Kantian, because the Dworkinian variety of freedom reduces it to a mere philosophical ideal. The Rawlsian and Ungerian alternatives offer the best hope for a postmodern liberalism, because they redefine freedom as 'interdependence' and as a constituent of 'solidarity'. In his defence of Rawls against Dworkin's critique, Rorty specifically approves Rawls's support for Kantian 'justice' as opposed to Kantian 'philosophy'. What he is doing, of course, is supporting the later Kant against the earlier Kant, and the later Rawls against the earlier Rawls. What he is also doing is making a plea for choice as the core of a liberal politics, and in doing this he is led inevitably to a philosophy of individual responsibility, and thus back to the private irony of Heidegger. The two are, as ever, a complement. The 'intersubjective reflective equilibrium' which Rorty thus takes from Rawls (and from the later Kant), is precisely that which he can also find, on a private ironic level, in Derrida, and Heidegger and Unger and so on. Indeed, he suggests in the final passages of the essay that the time has now come for Unger to 'come out' and acknowledge the liberalism of his project. The synthesis of the two is that of 'light-minded aestheticism' on a postmodern philosophical level, together with a similarly light-minded postmodern politics of transformative pluralist 'experiments in cooperation' (Rorty 1991a, pp.195-96).

In its most recent guises, solidarity remains very much a Rawlsian and a humanist politics. Indeed, Rorty is sufficiently confident that he uses it as a means to describe a non-foundational human rights. Such a human rights, he suggests, is a human rights of consciousness, a response to hearing 'sad and sentimental stories', rather than a human rights founded on moral knowledge. It is, Rorty adds, a human rights in the spirit of Kant, but situated beyond Kant's residual transcendentalism (Rorty 1993, pp.111-34). In the absence of any universal foundations, Rorty remains committed to a localized, tranformative, pluralist postmodern politics. Rorty reaffirms that 'belief', what makes people do what they do, is 'nothing deeper than contingent historical circumstance'. It is a radically anti-philosophical philosophy, and though still Rawlsian as a politics, is equally very much a philosophy of irony, that is a poetry of irony:

> I want to distinguish human solidarity as the identification with 'humanity as such' and as self-doubt which has gradually, over the last few centuries, been inculcated into inhabitants of the democratic states - doubt about their own sensitivity to the pain and humiliation of others, doubt that present institutional arrangements are adequate to deal with this pain and humiliation, curiosity about possible alternatives... Distinguishing these questions makes it possible to distinguish public from private, questions about pain from questions about the point of human life, the domain of the liberal from the domain of the ironist. It thus makes it possible for a single person to be both. (Rorty 1989, p.198)

It is here, with the coming to consciousness of public solidarity, as a synthetic complement of private irony, that literature can inform us. Just as it did most strikingly for Sartre, literature can reveal our irreducible contingency as political liberals and private creative interpretive readers. A reading of Nabokov and Orwell can better inform us about our private and our public existences, and most particularly our relationship between the two, than can Kant or Rawls or Heidegger or, of course, Rorty himself. By turning to literature, as the logic of his own argument demands, Rorty thus achieves his own marginalization. Orwell is the hopeful ironist, the embodiment of Rawlsian politics and Heideggerian philosophy as literature. So, it is perhaps fitting that a study of Rorty should close with a quotation from an essay on Orwell, and a reading of an Orwellian jurisprudence: 'I take Orwell to be telling us that whether our future rulers are more like O'Brien or more like JS.Mill does not depend... on deep facts about human nature... What our future rulers will be like will not be determined by any large necessary truths about human nature and its relation to truth and justice, but by a lot of small contingent facts.' (Rorty 1989, pp.187-8)

Conversational Partners

As is so eminently suitable in Rorty's particular case, his plea for conversation has been taken up with an increasing vengeance. Conversational partners fall, generally, into two camps. There are those who suggest that Rorty falls into precisely the transcendentalism which he decries, whilst, on the other hand, there are those who take exception to what they perceive to be a dangerous and destructive anti-foundationalism. In the end, as we shall see, the critiques are closely related. The assertion that difference is itself a universal serves to relativize Rorty's entire project. Roy Bhaskar suggests the Rorty is trapped by Kant, because the pervasive problem of freedom, which lies at the heart of his thesis, is rooted in the self, and the determination of the material from the free discursive self. Thus Rorty is trapped in precisely the same way as are Heidegger and Derrida. Rorty follows Kant's thesis of the free-will, in acknowledging people as empirical selves, and as moral agents. The tension that this creates in Rorty's thesis, Bhaskar suggests, is best seen in the final part of *Philosophy and the Mirror of Nature* and Rorty's tentative alignment with Gadamer. As Rorty has shown himself to be increasingly aware, a thesis which suggests that discourse is essential is dangerously foundational. But this, Bhaskar suggests, is unavoidable. The later Rorty moves ever further towards the Derridean position, without fully acknowledging the Kantian import of this reorientation. As Bhaskar perceptively notes, the trail is that which was laid by Kant's third *Critique*. The real weaknesses come to the fore in Rorty's attempt to translate ironism into a postmodern politics with an ethnocentrism which seems to defeat his own rigorous public-private dichotomy, and verge instead upon the transcendental (Bhaskar 1991).

The Kantian and anti-foundational critiques converge here in the accusations of relativism and ethnocentrism, and the concomitant doubts about the viability of the public-private dichotomy. Hilary Putnam accuses Rorty of 'cultural relativism' (Putnam 1987, p.228). Thomas MacCarthy condemns an ethnocentrism which articulates the 'desperate hope' to which anti-foundationalism inevitably leads. At the same time, he adds, an idea of solidarity, based on ethnocentrism, is a 'moral universalism' anyway. Like Bhaskar, MacCarthy suggests that Rorty is trapped by his continuing flirtation with Kantian free-will, and his desire to somehow effect a neo-romantic design

(MacCarthy 1991, pp.34-9). The related accusation, that Rorty makes fundamental universalist assumptions about the nature of humanity and difference, is a common one. Fern Haber suggests that Rorty's failure to extricate himself from the constraints of free-will signals the limitations of any post-modernism. The idea of a solidarity founded on the public-private divide similarly fails to appreciate that, just as the free-will is never unconstrainedly free, so the private is never fully insulated from the public (Haber 1994, pp.44-70).

The enduring Kantianism of Rorty's project has been noted by a number of other commentators. Comparing Rorty with the more familiar neo-Kantian reading of Rawls, Martin Hollis has questioned whether there is any real difference between their respective 'relativisms', suggesting perceptively that any self-assertion thesis such as Rorty advocates is a constructivist Kantian thesis at root (Hollis 1990). Jo Burrows has similarly wondered if Rorty's contingency thesis can be really distinguished from ordinary 'everyday relativism' (Burrows 1990). From the perspective of the Heidegger-Kant dialogue, Charles Taylor has suggested that Rorty is 'still partly trapped in the old model' precisely because he follows Heidegger so closely. All the 'good' deconstructionists, he adds, such as Heidegger, to some extent have 'espoused' a Kantian doctrine (Taylor 1990). Michael Fischer has made the same observation; conversation is deconstruction, and so is a Kantian critique (Fischer 1990). So have Charles Guignon and David Hiley, suggesting that Rorty's allegiance to the Heideggerian project of 'decentring' the self necessarily commits him to the 'quasi-Kantianism' of the Heidegger-Gadamer hermeneutic. Moreover the attempted translation of ironic postmodernism subverts his underlying communitarian ambition. The hermeneutic Rorty, they conclude, is viable, the pragmatic is not (Guignon and Hiley 1990).

Perhaps the most perceptive conversationalist of all is Richard Bernstein. In his recent *The New Constellation*, Bernstein seeks to present contemporary critical theory in the context of the Heidegger-Kant dialogue. The dialogue which generated Heidegger's 'obsessive' concern with ethics (Bernstein 1991, pp.82, 86-9). *The Question Concerning Technology* was a question concerning ethics and 'ethical responsibility', an essay about the threat of instrumentality and the self-assertive potential of the individual to secure a 'free relation' with technology. The self-assertion of anything and the idea of free relations is, as Bernstein again acknowledges, a Kantian idea. Freedom, as Heidegger understood it, is a 'revealing', between man and the thing with which he is in relation. So ethics is our 'keeping watch over the unconcealment'; a 'reflecting on man's dwelling'. The discovery that the route to an ethics lies in discourse has been continued by the French Heideggerians as a determination to keep the 'beyond' of current discourse open, assigning its proper complementary, as opposed to foundational, role (Bernstein 1991, pp.33-52, 90-98, 106-14, 120-5). It is this concern with the 'beyond' which represents the postmodern 'rage', and betrays the ethical-political ambitions which lie at the heart of postmodernism. But it also betrays the transcendentalism of postmodernism. Deconstruction is a way of taking a 'position', and taking a position is always a transcendental move, whether it be external or internal. A textual position is still an ethical position; indeed, it can only be an ethical position (Bernstein 1991, pp.172-91).

It is in the appreciation of this transcendentalism in postmodernism that Bernstein distinguishes himself from Rorty. Whereas Rorty wants to keep the private and the public as quite distinct realms, and simply import the insights of private postmodern irony and then translate them into a postmodern polity, Bernstein sees a political ethics emerging from within ironic discourse. One of Bernstein's most pertinent observations is that Rorty's later 'aestheticized pragmatism' owes far more to Heidegger than it does to Deweyan pragmatism. The later Rorty, Bernstein suggests, is characterised by a Kantian aesthetic inclination, together with an acute sense of history, and an urge to refine a postmodern polity (Bernstein 1991, pp.233-4, 259-64). The overriding ambition, particularly with regard to the later Rorty, is the hope of sequestering Rawls, and placing him at the apex of a postmodern constructive liberalism; an ambition of extraordinary bravery, if not recklessness. But in his attempt to capture Rawls, Rorty flirts with an ethnocentrism which is only barely separable from a constructive foundationalism. Its dependence on rational communication and persuasion lends further fuel to the accusation that Rorty's entire contingency thesis is at best constructivist, and at worst, in its 'darkest side', a simple relativism, as comfortable with a rationally argued fascism as with a rationally argued liberalism. Indeed, Bernstein finds Rorty's very language, of 'philosophical foundations' and 'philosophical groundings' disconcerting. The assertion of a liberal 'consensus' is fine for Rawls, who explicitly assigns it constructive foundations. It sits less comfortably with Rorty's Heideggerian aesthetics. Ultimately, Bernstein suggests, despite the wizardry of his efforts, Rorty is unable to produce a Heideggerian Rawls, and simply ends with a soft 'apologia' for cold-war liberalism, which makes fundamental and untenable assumptions about the nature of consensus and democratic institutions. Paradoxically, what Rorty does not do, in his increasingly passionate liberal rhetoric, is keep the conversation open (Bernstein 1991, pp.233-53).

2 The Politics of Liberalism

A Theory of Justice

John Rawls's *A Theory of Justice* is one of the seminal works of contemporary political philosophy. The keystone of Rawls's *Theory of Justice* is the principle of justice as fairness. Rawls acknowledges this and proceeds, principally though the 'original position', to construct a justification for its acceptance. Justice, Rawls suggests, is a self-evident concept, in the same way as truth is. It is the central conception in Rawls's architectonic, and is one, in the final analysis, of 'intuitive conviction'. Rawls goes on to suggest that the centrality of the concept of justice must be 'shared' by all 'communities' or 'well-ordered societies', even though particular 'conceptions' of justice may be various (Rawls 1971, pp.3-10). In other words, justice is a formal concept.

The 'free and rational person' who enjoys an 'original position of equality' reveals the essence of a Kantian political theory founded on autonomy and equality. It is these two conceptions which occupy a reflective position between the *a priori* and the *a posteriori* of Kant's synthetic structure; innate qualities, developed in the moral philosophy, applied to the political (Rawls 1971, pp.11-2). Rawls's awareness of the ever-presence of the synthesis is revealed most sharply in the introduction of his principle of 'reflective equilibrium', as describing the process of reaching a consensus of judgment and principle. What a Kantian 'model' actually provides is a mechanism for deciding 'principles' of ethical and political philosophy. The theory of justice is inextricably part of 'a theory of rational choice' (Rawls 1971, pp.4-5, 16-20). The alternative to utilitarian 'intuitionism' is 'constructivism', a term which Rawls increasingly uses as the descriptive label for the nature of his Kantianism. Constructivism recognises the creative potential of the 'reflective equilibrium'. Only a 'contract theory', by its very nature an accommodation of interests, offers a valid 'constructive' alternative (Rawls 1971, pp.39-53).

The most overtly neo-Kantian construct in *A Theory of Justice* is the 'original position'; introduced as a means of grounding the process of 'reflective equilibrium'. This equilibrium is one constructed internally, by the individual in the 'well-ordered society'. The 'original position' is, thus, a model which performs precisely the same function as Kant's synthetic model. It represents a 'state of affairs in which the parties are equally represented as moral persons and the outcome is not conditioned by arbitrary contingencies or the relative balance of social forces.' (Rawls 1971, pp.120-1) It is, therefore, immanently rational. The infinite potential variety of theories of substantive justice in no way challenges this rationality. This society is, however, constrained by one thing; the conception of individual right. It has been suggested by some that this is a natural right. But Rawls is quite adamant, and quite explicit. This conception of rights is a Kantian conception, derived from the immanent moral law of the discrete individual.

The only constraints in the 'original position' are thus internal constraints. Rawls proceeds by suggesting that a 'veil of ignorance', by which he intends to validate his principles as constructively rational, is 'implicit' in any Kantian ethics, because only it can preserve the possibility of universality. He further adds that the preservation of the possibility of universality is achieved by a communicative constructive ethics. This initial agreement by the morally driven individuals is absolutely crucial to his architectonic, as it was to Kant's. The original position accordingly provides the conditions for the evolution of principles of justice (Rawls 1971, pp.140-1, 149). The assertion of the moral law in the political situation validates the rule of law and, moreover, introduces another conception, responsiblity. The 'principle of liberty' leads directly to the 'principle of responsibility'. Thus, indirectly, the notion of the rule of law, as Rawls suggests, appeals to and depends upon, a 'sense' of community (Rawls 1971, pp.241-3).

In placing the concepts of liberty and equality at the heart of his own moral philosophy, Rawls expressly invokes Kantian authority:

> Kant held, I believe, that a person is acting autonomously when the principles of his action are chosen by him as the most adequate possible expression of his nature as a free and equal rational being. The principles he acts upon are not adopted because of his social position or natural endowments, or in view of the particular kind of society in which he lives or the specific things that he happens to want. Now the veil of ignorance deprives the persons in the orginal position of the knowledge that would enable them to choose heteronomous principles. The parties arrive at their choice together as free and equal rational persons knowing only that those circumstances obtain which give rise to the need for principles of justice. (Rawls 1971, pp.251-2)

The categorical imperative, Rawls emphasises, is constructed around the free and equal rational being. These two principles, developed from the 'original position', 'add' to, or develop, a Kantian ethics, because they ground what might otherwise be perceived as free-floating decisions. The original position thus continues Kant's own determination to ground the ethical decision within the constructive community. The decision is thus always collective and, moreover, and here Rawls particularly emphasises the Kantian origins of the idea, such a law is a law that is given to oneself (Rawls 1971, pp.255-7).

It is in the final part of *A Theory of Justice* that the emanently critical nature of Rawls's Kantianism is brought into sharpest focus. Here Rawls is concerned with the substantive principles of justice, or 'ends', and it was, of course, 'ends' which geared Kant's third *Critique*. The 'good', Rawls suggests, is an end to which we can aspire, and perhaps one to which we should aspire. At the same time, goodness is a judgmental concept. Of course, it can still be rational (Rawls 1971, pp.395-8, 404). Its rationality is derived from it being a purposive concept. Here, of course, Rawls is making an explicitly relativist gesture. Invoking the Aristotelian 'principle of motivation', Rawls suggests that every person has a rational plan, a determination to pursue something, even if that something amounts to a nothing. The person's rational plan determines the person's contingent good. It makes that individual purposeful and responsible to himself. The contingent good is that constructed by the deliberative rationality of the community. A community constructs what it perceives to be virtuous, and does so by internal communication. Thus whilst individual good must be contingent, the communal good will always be constructively rational; goodness will always be 'relative' (Rawls 1971, pp.408-9, 416-41).

The development of the idea of a 'sense' of justice takes Rawls ever closer to the spirit of Kant's third *Critique*. The position of the community in determining the principles of substantive justice becomes ever more important. These are 'basic structures of well-ordered societies' which correspond to 'the different conceptions of justice'. The community shapes individual desire, and thus creates a 'sense' of justice (Rawls 1971, pp.457-8). A society's morality is founded upon a 'common allegiance to justice'. At the same time, because of the creative role of the individual in constructing that morality, it becomes a 'morality of self-command'. Substantive principles of justice thus evolve experientially, as a means of determining 'relations' between members of that society; precisely the purpose of a contract (Rawls 1971, pp.472-9, 495-6). The final chapter of *A Theory of Justice* is reminiscent both in style and substance, of Kant's final 'chapter', the *Critique of Judgement*; its theme being the process of agreement between different individuals in a community. The community itself develops through a shared conception of judgment; through the creative activity of individuals, who are always 'historical beings'. The 'community sense' which these individuals construct, is always a historical sense, and a historical rationality. This 'sense' is thus itself a synthetic modelling of the 'well-ordered society', which itself becomes a 'social union of social unions' (Rawls 1971, pp.523-9). Ultimately this realizes the self-assertion of the moral self. The self must assert, and must construct, with fellow individuals, a rationality; there is 'no way to get beyond deliberative rationality.' (Rawls 1971, pp.561-5)

Variations on a Theme

A Theory of Justice immediately engaged the attention of numerous moral and political philosophers. Perhaps the sharpest criticism was articulated by communitarians who refused to sanction any apparent divorce of the self from community. In response to these criticisms, Rawls has redefined the nature of his Kantianism, in order to stress the constructivist nature of the relationship of self and community. It is this development which has led such as Rorty to suggest that Rawls has turned towards the anti-foundationalist camp and adopted a postmodern liberal stance. As early as 1975 Rawls conceded that the 'motivations' of the 'persons in the well-ordered society' would always be socially and historically contingent, but at the same time would be grounded in the rationally purposive existence of the morally driven individual. This 'society' would thus be established as a 'framework' or 'background scheme' for 'communitarian aims' (Rawls 1975, pp.539-54).

A series of essays entitled *Kantian Constructivism in Moral Theory*, published in 1980, further emphasised Rawls's turn to the later Kant; setting out 'more clearly the Kantian roots' of the central conception of justice as fairness (Rawls 1980, p.515). One of the more striking features of *Constructivism* is Rawls's determination to present a more 'practicable' theory of justice. He is not looking for a universal formula, but one which can work for the 'basic institutions within democratic society' (Rawls 1980, p.518). The first essay concentrated on autonomy; by comparing full autonomy with rational autonomy. The two central constructs or 'models' in this essay are the 'moral person' and the 'well-ordered society', and Rawls's ultimate aim is that of any Kantian constructivist model: 'to connect definite principles with a particular conception of the person' (Rawls 1980, p.520). Kantian constructivism, Rawls noted, is 'distinguished' by its placing the morally driven individual at the centre of the 'reasonable procedure of construction' (Rawls 1980, p.525). It is this construction which 'determines the content of the first principles of justice', and which in the Kantian pluralist vision will be responsive to the established social and political conditions. This conception overcomes indeterminacy by trying to identify fundamental shared values between free and equal persons who are thus 'capable' of acting rationally. Such individuals are constrained by an immanent 'rational autonomy', but nothing else: 'Kantian constructivism holds that moral objectivity is to be understood in terms of a suitably constructed social point of view that all can accept. Apart from the procedure of constructing the principles of justice, there are no moral facts' (Rawls 1980, pp.516-9).

This describes the 'formal condition' of a 'well-ordered society'; a community of communicative individuals constructing their own morality, constrained only by their own rational autonomy and the immanent rationality of the construction. Substantively, of course, this carries with it all the collateral baggage of a relativist thesis, principally historical and social contingency, and the ability to create and to alter the 'ends' that the rational persons have in mind as 'reasonable'. The constraints of the 'reasonable' are the 'formal conditions implicit in the moral powers of the members of a well-ordered society... the way in which the Reasonable frames the Rational in the original position represents a feature of the unity of practical reason. In Kant's terms, empirical practical reason is represented by the rational deliberations of the parties; pure practical reason is represented by the constraints within which these deliberations take place.' (Rawls 1980, p.532)

Rawls continued to flesh out his perception of a Kantian constructivist model by developing the fundamental Kantian conceptions, of freedom and of equality, which had been so central in *A Theory of Justice*, and placing them at the heart of his 'well-ordered society'. A 'precondition of freedom', he suggests, is that individuals should know the 'background conditions', in other words the social and historical circumstances, which shape their 'conception of their good'. Thus, although 'a well-ordered society is divided and pluralistic, its citizens have nevertheless reached an understanding on principles to regulate their basic institutions (Rawls 1980, pp.537-40). This understanding will frame what can only be a necessarily contingent conception of substantive justice: 'There is no alternative, then, to founding a conception of justice suitable for a well-ordered democratic society on but a part of the truth, and not the whole, or, more specifically, on our present commonly based and shared beliefs' (Rawls 1980, p.542).

This is not 'skepticism or indifference'; it is an inevitability of history: 'Justice as fairness tries to construct a conception of justice that takes deep and unresolvable differences on matters of fundamental significances as a permanent condition of human life.' (Rawls 1980, p.542) He continues by stressing the role of the creative and 'self-originating' individual, who is at all times capable of 'revising and changing' his conception of the good. Indeed, according to Rawls this capability is the hallmark of the Kantian moral person, who thus, and most importantly, has an immanent 'responsibility' for 'his ends' (Rawls 1980, pp.543-5). In his concluding comments to this second essay, Rawls notes that his conception of fairness as justice diverges from Kant, in that whereas he moves from collective agreement to the particular, Kant moves precisely the other way. At the same time, he acknowledges that in the establishment of synthetic model, from which the notion of the moral person can be 'reflected' in the reasonable and the rational, he is using a specifically Kantian model of construction (Rawls 1980, p.552).

In the final of the three essays, Rawls returns to the central Kantian problem of pluralism. A multitude of various social and historical forces can impact upon and form substantive principles of justice:

> The constructionist view accepts from the start that a moral conception can establish but a loose framework for deliberation which must rely very considerably on our powers of reflection and judgement. These powers are not fixed once and for all, but are developed by a shared public culture and hence shaped by that culture... The essential point is that a conception of justice fulfills its social role provided that citizens equally conscientious and sharing roughly the same beliefs find that, by affirming the framework of deliberation set up by it, they are normally led to a sufficient convergence of opinion. Thus a conception of justice is framed to meet the practical requirements of social life and to yield a public basis in the light of which citizens can justify to one another their common institutions. Such a conception need only be precise enough to achieve this result. (Rawls 1980, pp.560-1)

In contrast with other theories of justice, such as natural law or utilitarianism, a Kantian conception of justice as fairness 'as a constructivist view, holds that not all the moral questions we are prompted to ask in everyday life have answers' (Rawls 1980, p.563). In his final concluding comments, Rawls stresses that the construction is everything. It constructs its own rationality. It is this which distinguishes it from what he terms the 'radical choice' of existentialism. Kantian constructivism places 'constraints' on choice, derived from the first principles of justice. Above all, there is the 'central place of the conception of person'; a centrality ensured by Kant. The very centrality of the person makes any theory of justice, at root, a relativist one (Rawls 1980, pp.570-2).

In his subsequent *Justice as Fairness*, Rawls again stressed the synthetic nature of his construction; the discretion of the political (Rawls 1985, p.230). What he wished to do more than anything was to 'avoid... claims to universal truth' (Rawls 1985, p.223). The particular conception of justice as fairness is a constructed conception, developed through the rationality of the political circumstances of a democratic society: 'Justice as fairness is a political conception in part because it starts from within a certain political tradition. We hope that this political conception of justice may at least be supported by what we may call an overlapping consensus, that is, by a consensus that includes all the opposing philosophical and religious doctrines likely to persist and to gain adherents in a more or les just constitutional democratic society.' (Rawls 1985, pp.225-6) This 'overlapping consensus' is inherently political and historicist. It is developed from a society's 'shared fund of implicitly recognized basic ideas and principles', by the means of 'reflective equilibrium'. The purpose is to 'shape... into a coherent view the deeper bases of agreement embedded in the public political culture of a constitutional regime', and this can only be achieved if people can be persuaded from the basis of some shared 'consensus'. Political indeterminacy makes such accommodation a requisite for any 'well-ordered society'. The pervasive tenor of the argument is one of describing political accommodation. It is, he stresses, a further development of Kantian constructivism, which again very much depends upon the centrality of the Kantian moral person, free and equal, and the resultant assumption of 'responsibility for ends' (Rawls 1985, pp.229-33). It is, he concludes, in the nature of political liberalism for there to be fundamental indeterminacy, and thus the need for a rational constructivist theory of politics as the only alternative to skepticism (Rawls 1985, pp.245-51).

The idea of the 'overlapping consensus' was refined further in 1987. The components of the idea were much the same as they were two years earlier; the irreducibly historical and indeterminate nature of politics, and the need to construct a community rationality grounded on the Kantian conception of the morally driven person: 'The idea of an overlapping consensus enables us to understand how a constitutional regime characterized by the fact of pluralism might, despite its deep divisions achieve stability and social unity by the public recognition of a reasonable conception of justice'. (Rawls 1987, p.2) Democracy, Rawls suggests, is about indeterminacy. Power thus remains with the individual. The idea of an overlapping consensus leaves 'citizens' with the freedom, and of course, responsiblity, for creating a substantive politics 'in accordance with their own general and comprehensive views.' (Rawls 1987, p.15) Democracy thus needs an overlapping consensus because it 'forces political philosophy to be, so far as possible, independent of and autonomous from other parts of philosophy, especially from philosophy's long-standing problems and controversies.' The overlapping consensus is an expression of Kantian formalism as constructivism (Rawls 1987, pp.24-5).

The transmission from a 'Theory' of Justice to a 'Political' Liberalism is reinforced and completed in Rawls's most recent essays. *Political Liberalism* reaffirms Rawls's ambition now to develop the previously 'unrealistic idea' of the 'well-ordered society' into the 'overlapping consensus' (Rawls 1993, pp.xv-xvi). The pervasive problem in contemporary political theory is that of pluralism and 'stability'. It is this problem, together with a re-awakening interest in the position of the liberal individual which lies at the heart of modern democratic politics. In response, the central principle of 'justice as fairness' must become a 'political conception of justice' based on the principles of practical reason. What modern democratic politics must address, he re-emphasises, is 'the fact of reasonable pluralism', and it can only do so my maintaining a rigid distinction between the political and the metaphysical. The 'elements' and the 'basic arguments for them', freedom and equality, remain as in 1972, but the key now lies in understanding them as political concepts. The collateral component of the 'basic structure' of this tradition is the 'well-ordered society', which must be defined in terms of an 'overlapping consensus'. This 'consensus' is derived notionally from the 'idea of social cooperation'. This is more than simple coordination, but is formal in structure and immanently rational in purpose: 'The aim is specify any idea of reciprocity between free and equal citizens in a well-ordered society.' (Rawls 1993, pp.15-7) The development of Rawls's position, through the 1980s, can be strikingly seen in his preliminary statements on the 'political conceptions of the person', a person capable of, indeed defined, by rational change, politically committed, self-assertive and responsible for his ends (Rawls 1993, pp.30-3). All these conceptions, at root pluralist neo-Kantian conceptions, develop what Rawls terms a 'freestanding view' of political theory. What they construct ultimately is not just a sense of 'community association', determined by an accommodation of ends, but a society defined by 'deep conflict' and its ability to resolve dispute by 'continuing public discussion'.

Rawls also readdresses the nature of citizenship in democratic society, as determined by the demands of a 'reasonable pluralism'. Reasonableness is the practical and purposive preparedness to communicate and the accommodate in the political situation. The 'reasonable' is thus inherently public, and inherently a Kantian idea of practical reason. Related to the Kantian moral person, 'reasonableness' connotes the willingness to accept responsibility for judgment; the spirit of the third *Critique*. More explicitly, Rawls concentrates on the nature of judgment, which, he suggests, can be determined as the balancing of rational desires with reasonable concern for the interest of others, both internal and external. The 'sources' of judgment, he adds, are experiential, social, political and historical. Judgment is always contingent (Rawls 1993, pp.56-7). Rawls is keen to stress again the distinction between political and Kantian moral constructivism. The moral agent, he emphasises, is never 'in general', but always 'in society'. In other words, the morality of jurisprudence is always to some degree political, even if the structure of jurisprudence is not. The conceptions of the person and of society are conceptions of practical reason, from which can be derived conceptions of political right and ethical good. There is a constructed political objectivity, which is 'an account of agreement in judgment amongst reasonable agents' (Rawls 1993, pp.107-10). Rawls description here is very much akin to Arendt's idea of the practical purposive morality which she drew explicitly from the third *Critique*. And like Arendt, and of course Kant, Rawls is quick to appreciate that this objectivity is always an historically contingent objectivity. As he emphasised in 1980, political constructivism is not just an idea, but a fact which can provide a practical 'framework of reasoning' (Rawls 1993, p.128).

Interestingly, Rawls has felt less need to revise the later 1980s essays, although he is keen to stress time and again the communicative nature of deep consensus which, he repeats, can be deepened by the active participation of the legal order. If communication 'deepens' the overlapping consensus, democratic politics can 'broaden' it. There is thus a 'totality' of reasonable views, not merely a 'compromise' which many of his critics have alleged (Rawls 1993, pp.164-72). In *The Idea of Public Reason*, which serves primarily to emphasize the ever-presence of a conception of public reason in democratic society, he emphasises that only articulation can lead to a 'collective' cognition and acceptance of political doctrine. The keystone of democratic politics is 'public discourse' (Rawls 1993, pp.213-5). The role of a 'public reason' is to provide guidelines of form which can specify the means of reasoning. Liberalism is not thus a philosophy; it is a 'kind of view', a way of thinking, something in which the morally driven individual and the morally driven community participate to the full. Thus, 'public reason' provides a 'framework' for 'fundamental discussions', which can then determine the 'constitutional essentials' in a political structure. This discursive process of reasoning leads Rawls to reintroduce and to further refine his idea of an 'overlapping consensus', which can be situated in the 'leeway' between the various 'comprehensive' doctrines which construct it.

The final comments in *Political Liberalism* provide a fitting conclusion to Rawls's reorientated Kantian vision. As Kant realised two hundred years before, the key to a political philosophy lay with the individual and the individual's capacity for judgment. Only it can overcome the ravages of ethical and political indeterminacy:

> The conception of justice to which these principles belong is not to be regarded as a method of answering the jurist's questions, but as a guiding framework, which if jurists find it convincing, may orient their reflections, complement their knowledge, and assist their judgement. We must not ask too much of a philosophical view. A conception of justice fulfills its social role provided that persons equally conscientious and sharing roughly the same beliefs find that, by affirming the framework of deliberation set up by it, they are normally led to a sufficient convergence of judgement necessary to achieve effective and fair social cooperation. (Rawls 1993, p.368)

The conception of justice that Rawls presents is an empowering conception, just as is Heidegger's, Arendt's or Unger's. The consistent theme in Rawls's writings lies in its concentration on the creative and constructive individual. For each it is a matter of constructing a rationality from the individual, not for the individual.

Rawls the Postmodern Liberal?

So, is Rawls now a postmodern liberal? Rorty thinks so. As we have seen, Rorty sequesters Rawls as the postmodern champion against the 'strong' textualism of such as Dworkin. He specifically approves Rawls's switch to Kantian 'justice' over Kantian 'philosophy'. Rawls's political liberalism is a postmodern liberalism, founded upon a theory of public solidarity which can complement the private irony of the Heideggerians. It is a thesis of 'mature... Enlightenment liberalism' (Rorty 1989, pp.60-5, Rorty 1991a, pp.197-202). This attempted sequestration has certainly attracted much criticism. Bernstein suggests that Rorty's ethnocentrism precisely lacks Rawls's model of constructive justice complemented by a theory of democratic public institutions (Bernstein 1991, pp.230-92). In similar vein, Martin Hollis suggests that Rorty fails to detect the continuing foundationalism in Rawls's later constructivism, necessitated by his retention of the twin concepts of freedom and equality (Hollis 1990, pp.244-57). Nonetheless, the turn in Rawls's writings, from the early Kant to the later, is widely acknowledged (Yack 1993, pp.224-31, Arneson 1989). At the same time, the perceived abandonment of a comprehensive theory has also generated much disappointment in some quarters (Kukathas and Pettit 1990, pp.120-45). Yet the extent to which Rawls has abandoned foundationalism remains a matter of contention. Thomas Hill applauds Rawls's constructivism precisely because he perceives it as remaining shackled to the Kantian idea of the autonomy of the moral self (Hill 1989). Jean Hampton, on the other hand, suggests that Rawls has abandoned Kant precisely because he has removed comprehensive theory from politics, and thus divorced the politics from the ethics. She deplores the 'abandonment of metaphysics' (Hampton 1989).

Others have been more supportive of Rawls's political turn. William Galston approves Rawls's recognition that modern liberalism is 'characterized by an irreversible pluralism', but suggests that liberalism cannot rest completely upon social agreement, and that Rawls maintains, in his constructive thesis, a necessary residual ethical constructivism. Articulating the communitarian criticism of Rorty, Galston casts doubt upon the possibility of any political thesis which seeks to divorce the private from the public. What distinguishes the later Rawls from the earlier, and implicitly from Rorty, is the appreciation that the individual is socially determined (Galston 1989). Communitarians remain critical of Rawls's continuing determination of the liberal individual as constructive of society. In Rawls's defence, it must be noted that the accuracy of this accusation is itself a matter of some contention (Kymlicka 1989). In a defence of Rawls's political turn, against the communitarian critique, Gerald Doppelt argues that it is precisely the re-reading of the Kantian moral self which lies behind his abandonment of comprehensive moral theory. The key to understanding Rawls's political turn, his postmodern liberalism, is an appreciation of the complementary roles of self-determination and responsiblity. It is here that Rawls's new liberalism is grounded. It is an ontological, even existential, foundation which finds its cutting edge in Rawls's adoption of 'reflective equilibrium'. Rawls's 'identification of Kantian self-determination' provides the mechanism by which to determine the private and the public (Doppelt 1988, 1989). Rorty's attempt to sequester Rawls remains a bold and adventurous one; and not one that is widely approved. Yet, there can be little doubt with regard to the change of emphasis in Rawls's writings, from the early Kant to the later Kant, and there can be little doubting its veracity. There does not need to be a precise congruence between Rawls's vision, and that of Rorty. Both are postmodern in their approach to Kant and the Kantian inheritance, and both are liberal. To this extent, Rorty is right. Differences apart, both are indeed postmodern liberals, and it is precisely this engagement with Kant which defines their postmodern liberal ambitions.

3 The Politics of Solidarity

Politics and Personality

In the introduction to *Knowledge and Politics*, Unger repeatedly stresses that any critique of politics or law, or whatever, must be both a political deconstruction and a philosophical-political reconstruction. It is the 'practice of total criticism', and an eminently jurisprudential actvity. It was, Unger admits, in the particular process of making jurisprudential investigations that he realised the limitations of uncritical philosophy, and the need to engage in critique. He expressed the sentiment which first led Kant to destroy the possibility of a pure metaphysics: 'the house of reason in which I was working proved to be a prison-house of paradox whose rooms did not connect and whose passageways led nowhere.' (Unger 1975, p.3)

The reconstructive nature of Unger's enterprise is emphasised, even at this early stage of the first section of his first book, in his introductory commentary on the nature of liberalism. Liberalism, he acknowledges, is the pervasive theory in modern social sciences, and has been since Kant; it enshrines the liberal concept of pyschology, the 'idea of personality', as a relation of self-other. This dynamic, pivotal to the Heidegger-Kant dialogue, is the one which ties Unger irrevocably to a liberal thesis.

Unger does not wish to destroy liberalism, rather he wishes to discover 'the deep structure' of it; to reveal the creative potential of its antinomies and finally to reconstruct it. In later works, he refers to his reconstruction as 'superliberalism'. The reconstructive project, he stresses, is thus a dual 'positive program', to develop 'correct ideas' of both 'personality and society' (Unger 1975, pp.4-18). It is this ambition which gears the development of his later writings, and is realised in *Passion* and *Politics*, published nearly a decade later.

The process will be a dialectic one. The first step is to grasp that liberalism is not just an idea, but an inevitablity of life, and so it is that way of life which must be reformed, so that in the place of extreme individualism, there is an alternative vision of society as one of 'communities of shared purpose', rather than as an association of conflicting and irreducibly alienated individuals. The complementary second step of this 'positive doctrine', as distinguished from the negative of pure criticism, is to reveal a new theory of self which can accommodate and improve the human condition in a relative fashion. It is here, as Unger admits, that he is thrown unavoidably into the territory of moral philosophy. A reconstructive theory cannot be just a political philosophy. It must also be an ethical philosophy. The first two steps will realise a third and ultimate ambition; the introduction of a new 'theory of organic groups' based on a new 'moral sentiment', itself a new ethics of respect, both for the self and the community (Unger 1975, pp.18-25). Unger's ambition for *Knowledge and Politics*, and indeed for his subsequent writings, is precisely that which lay behind Kant's construction of the *Metaphysics of Morals*.

In the first chapter of *Knowledge and Politics*, Unger acknowledged that the key player in liberal philosophy is Kant. The liberal rejection of the received 'doctrine of intelligible essences', as epitomised by Kant, was the first critical step. Kantian liberalism doubted, crucially, the idea of predetermination, and sought to accommodate the universal and the particular in a revised theory of form and substance. It was, in Unger's words, the 'genius of Kant's answer to the question of theory and fact' (Unger 1975, p.32). In acknowledging an irreducible contingency in the concept of the free-will, Kant, in Unger's opinion, opened the door to a critical theory, not only of the mind, but also of social and political theory. Like Arendt, Unger recognised that the key to understanding the critical nature of Kant's political philosophy lay not in just reading the political essays, but in understanding the nature of Kant's philosophy of the individual and individual judgment. A truly reconstructive theory of personality and judgment must move beyond the logic of form and substance, and into the nature of 'reflective judgment'. A morality of pure reason alone, he emphasises, can never 'serve as the foundation for moral judgment'. A philosophy of personality must 'revitalise' judgment. The new Ungerian 'self' must accept right and duty as a control and a determination of community, must accept the contingency of ends, and finally, must accept the indeterminacy of individualism. Unger emphasises that such a revision must now concentrate upon a better appreciation of 'difference' (Unger 1975, pp.38-58).

Unger's refutation of positivist formalism is itself reliant upon the conceptions introduced in a Kantian critical theory. As in the revised liberal psychology, a revised liberal politics must first of all develop a 'reflective' mien. It must not be merely immanently rational, but, at the same time, immanently critical and self-revising. Such a political visage is demanded by the Kantian conception of 'respect', which was itself articulated by Kant in the second part of the *Metaphysics*. The key to presenting a new and 'reflective' political theory lies, as it did in the presentation of a revised philosophy of mind, with the Kantian rejection of 'intelligible essences'. It was this which opened the door to a critical 'principle of subjective value' (Unger 1975, p.79). According to Unger the substantive liberal theory of freedom, whilst introducing critical possibilities, 'breaks down' because it cannot mediate subjective values. Thus, like both Rorty and Rawls, Unger centres the need to develop a theory of consensus at the very heart of his political ambitions. It is the failure to effectively mould a theory of consensus which condemns 'collectivist' theories, such as Marxism, and to a certain extent liberal compromises, such as 'representative democracy' (Unger 1975, pp.82-7).

The advocacy of an alternative form of 'participatory democracy' emerges as one of the strongest themes in Unger's writings. Orthodox liberal theories of both law and politics are thus irretrievably incoherent because they fail to accommodate the particular of substantive value. Liberal theories of adjudication and interpretation are likewise condemned, because both are ultimately matters of purely subjective value judgment. What we need, then, is a new theory of judgment, which we can then apply to political and legal thought; a theory of constrained subjective judgment. In essence what we need is a theory of judgment based around a fundamental principle of integrity with regard to constructive principles. The constructive alternative which must be developed is to overlay individual subjective value with a conception of 'communal' value, and to thus construct the possibility of a communal theory of judgment which is itself derived from a 'conception of shared values'. The most important factor here, and one which explains the striking similarity between Unger's rhetoric and that of such as Dworkin, is the retention of a value-system as an alternative constructive ethics (Unger 1975, pp.97-102).

The seeds of a reconstructed liberal theory are then found within orthodox liberalism, and the most important of all is the possibility of a reconstructed ethics from a revised conception of judgment. Unger continues this revision by suggesting that the core for a new complementary theory of personality and of society lies with a new philosophy of 'being'. In doing so, Unger places what he terms his 'total criticism' squarely in the Heidegger-Kant tradition. The new conception of 'being' must emphasise the 'reflective' nature of being, and its potential for overcoming the universal-particular antithesis. Whereas liberal theory suggests that the universal is the whole as a sum of its particulars, Unger wants to suggest that everything is whole and everything is particular. Thus, he hopes, a reconstructive theory can proceed by transcending this familiar dichotomy. A revised political morality will recognise that both the universal and the particular are internal, as Kant acknowledged, in the very real sense that they are precisely universal and particular to the individual. The example of such a concept which Unger introduces, a 'morality of sympathy', is an important one, because over the ensuing years, it emerges not only as a central construct in

Unger's theory of political morality, but also because it increasingly comes to resemble Kant's own conception of respect (Unger 1975, pp.117, 136-43).

Before presenting his revision of liberalism, based essentially on this fundamental reconception of personality, Unger briefly introduces the 'theory of the welfare-state', as a preliminary stage. The idea of the welfare-state is important because it understood the nature of solidarity, and attempted to overcome the alienation of the self implicit in orthodox positivist liberalism. The liberal state entrenched structures which, unavoidably, determined a liberal and individualist theory of personality. The negative freedoms around which liberalism was constructed could do nothing else than alienate the individual. Unger's development of this thesis is, of course, familiar as that also presented by such as Arendt and Rorty (Unger 1975, pp.151-74).

Unger contrasts the positive effect of developing a sense of solidarity with the idea of 'communities of shared purpose'. The association of work with personality and identity, which Unger employs, is precisely that used by Arendt in her description of the alienated condition in unreconstructed liberal politics. Instead of the centralised bureaucratic reality of contemporary welfare-corporate states, Unger posits the notion of an 'open community' which, although feeding on the same basic idea, effects a strategic 'reorientation' (Unger 1975, p.184). Unger's own reconstructive blueprint is presented in the final chapters of *Knowledge and Politics*, which present a revised philosophy of the self together with a revised theory of society. In making this complementary presentation, Unger is establishing a dual precedent which continues throughout his subsequent writings, and is finally realised most effectively in the publication of *Passion* and *Politics*. The revision of a philosophy of the self, one which is not trapped by the historicism of contemporary social science, he quickly acknowledges, must entail a return to metaphysics. The key to understanding the metaphysics of personality lies in understanding the indeterminacy of the self, and at the same time, the drive in the individual to objectivise by gaining knowledge of external objects (Unger 1975, p.202).

This tension describes man's invariably troubled relation to society, of which he is a constitutive part, or, as Unger calls it, the 'paradox of sociability' (Unger 1975, p.217). As a classic piece of synthetic modelling, Unger suggests that 'sympathy', or as he later terms it, love, as an extension of the Kantian concept of respect, serves as an 'analogue' to the politics of community:

> The elements of the idea of community are the same as those of love... Community is held together by an allegiance to common purposes. The more these shared ends express the nature of humanity rather than simply the preferences of particular individuals and groups, the more would one's acceptance of them become an affirmation of one's own nature; the less would it have to represent the abandonment of individuality in favor of assent and recogntion. Thus, it would be possible to view others as complementary rather than opposing wills; furtherance of their ends would mean advancement of one's own. The conflict between the demands of individuality and of sociability would disappear. Each person, secure in his individuality, would be able to recognize his humanity in other persons. Moreover, in this community individuals would have to live together in a situation sufficiently varied, intimate, and stable to allow them to know and treat each other as concrete persons rather than as role occupants. To the extent that a community acquired these features, it would become a political realization of the idea of sympathy. (Unger 1975, pp.220-1)

This relationship of the abstract with the concrete self is the relationship between self and world. It is an existential problem. Orthodox liberalism, Unger suggests, has tried to separate the two. In a passage reminiscent of Rorty's 'mirror of nature' argument, Unger suggests that it is the existential response which has revealed the fallacy of this approach. The 'theory of self' can provide an alternative to a 'mode of union' based on 'hierarchic communitarianism', because it 'contains the elements of a possible synthesis of transcendence and immanence in consciousness, and of autonomy and community in organization', which alone 'holds the promise of political solution to the problem of the self.' The theory of the self allows the self to develop in relation to society, and thus maintains the autonomy of self, as a strength derived from indeterminacy, not a weakness.

The reconstruction of the community ideal upon a conception of sympathy will transcend and overcome the idea of government by institution (Unger 1975, p.262). Unger suggests that such a process will effect an alternative participatory form of democracy. Government will be from within each individual, and each individual's responsibility, because government will become an expression of sympathetic relations, rather than a prescription for them. Government will truly become a government of consensus, and democracy a 'democracy of ends' (Unger 1975, p.267). Such a form of self-government will be effected only through this democratization of institutions. In an effective restatement of the Heideggerian ambition, he suggests that it will be, the realisation of a pro-active, self-assertive idea of freedom. It is an expressly internal Kantian idea of freedom, as opposed to the external liberal orthodoxy, and will effect a 'constitutional charter of freedom' which will encapsulate a political philosophy which shies way from neither the universal nor the particular, but which seeks to express freedom precisely within the tension between the two. The universal is the 'premise' of 'the plurality of groups'. Participatory democracy will be effected by the self-assertive participation in such groups. The role of a democratized institutional government of consensus is to provide the participatory opportunity (Unger 1975, pp.274, 277-83).

Unger's *Law in Modern Society* was published immediately after *Knowledge and Politics* and was intended to be read in conjunction with it. As in *Knowledge and Politics*, Unger states that his own ambition is to present a revised theory of judgment and a revised theory of consensus, as opposed to the established liberal orthodoxy which seeks to invoke rules where consensus is perceived to absent. The conclusions which Unger draws from a series of comparative analyses of various legal orders is employed in the study of the relation of law and modernity. This relation is, for Unger, the essential problem in contemporary jurisprudence, just as for Arendt the relation of politics and modernity is the essential problem in contemporary political theory, and for Heidegger, of course, the essential problem of philosophy is the relation between being and modernity. Unger immediately stresses that the story of modernity's relation to man and to legal and political theory is the story of the rise of positivism. The allegiance to specialized groups went hand in hand with the 'carving up' of personality. Individualism became the pervasive ethic, as opposed to 'communal solidarity' which had been suggested by customary law, but which had been quickly suppressed by bureaucratic law (Unger 1976, p.168). As he suggested in *Knowledge and Politics*, this was accompanied by the emergence of a 'dominance-dependence ethic' which could realise a complementary control of consciousness. Law, he suggests, at least the liberal conception of law, replete with its rights thesis and the 'myth' of the independent judiciary become the keystone of the liberal counterattack.

The ambition of any critical legal response to positive liberalism is thus a critique of the idea of the 'rule of law'. It is the 'quest for substantive justice' as opposed to formal justice. In an eloquent passage, Unger describes the critical alternative to the rights thesis as solidarity:

> What accounts for our seeming inability to devise a set of prescriptions that adequately reflects the subtlety and richness of our moral ideas?.. The kernel of solidarity is our feeling of responsibility for those whose lives touch in some way upon our own and our greater or lesser willingness to share their fate. Solidarity is the social face of love; it is concern with another as a person rather than just respect for him as bearer of formally equal rights and duties or admiration for his gifts and achievements... But solidarity means that one takes no entitlements for granted. A powerholder who acts out of a sense of solidarity will always have to ask himself whether the exercise of his power in a particular situation would be consistent with the aim of sharing the burden of the people with whom he is dealing. To this question, there can never be a general answer, laid down in advance. Everything will depend on issues like the degree to which the other person has acted wrongly in the particular relationship and his ability to bear the loss that would result from the exercise of power. These are not factors which can be made the basis of rules; instead they are elements of decision that bear on how one uses the rights allocated by existing rules... Neither the individualist or the collectivist side of formality satisfies the demands of solidarity. For the ideal of solidarity implies that one is never permitted to take advantage of his legal rights so as to pursue his own ends without regard to the effects he may have on others. And this ideal holds that the overriding collective interest is the interest in maintaining a system of social relations in which men are bound to act, if not compassionately, at least as if they had compassion for each other. (Unger 1976, pp.206-9)

It is this sort of rhetoric which has so impressed Rorty. The description highlights the derivation of the solidarity, not only from a new theory of society, but also from a new theory of personality, itself clearly a perceived elaboration upon the Kantian conception of 'respect'. Unger wishes to represent this as sympathy, the personal correlate of solidarity. The passage also emphasises the irreducibly relativist underpinnings to any reconstituted theory of liberal solidarity. The 'post-liberal society' in which we live today, and which Unger describes as the 'contemporary form of liberalism', is the first step because it is a resolution of the extremes of 'traditionalistic' and 'revolutionary socialist' ideology. The next step is to develop this post-liberalism from within the tensions provided by the political extremes. Such a conflict is to be treasured because within it lie the origins of a social pluralist consensus determined by solidarity. What, ultimately, will emerge, Unger reassures us, as opposed to the bureaucratic law of liberal orthodoxy, is the 'latent and living law' of 'human interaction' (Unger 1976, pp.241-2).

The demand for 'common meaning' in law, as an alternative to pure formalism, must be developed into an 'interpretive method' and a communicative method. The importance of communication as the mechanism by which to reconstruct alternative legal method is vital. The law must be appreciated as the law of the people who live it. Critical legal thought is accordingly a phenomenological enterprise, which seeks to provide an alternative way of 'doing' law (Unger 1976, pp.249-54).

Communication is vital to the construction and is essential to any reconstructive enterprise, because it is the sole expression of personality. Ultimately Unger concludes as he did in *Knowledge and Politics*, by demanding firstly, a return to a critique of metaphysics, because in its revised philosophy of personality lies the key to a reconstructed theory of consensus, which seeks not to resolve dispute, but to create from it, and secondly the need to revise our method of thinking by redefining the nature of judgment as a mechanism for self-revision (Unger 1976, pp.262-7). It is a revised theory of value-judgment which can unlock the door to a critical theory of law. The crisis of law and modernity can be resolved only by appreciating the contingency of the personality constrained only by the Kantian limits of freedom. A political philosophy must appreciate this:

> A society resolves the crisis of order insofar as it manages to reconcile individual freedom with community cohesion, and the sense of immanent order with the possibility of transcendent criticism. The more perfect this reconciliation becomes, the more does society's emergent interactional law reveal the requirements of human nature and social coexistence. Thus, people find a criteria with which to evaluate agreement and to define equality. The availability of these standards to everyone makes cohesion and stability possible. At the same time, such a society acknowledges that the requirements of association change as nature itself is transformed. Thus, it provides for dissidence and change. (Unger 1976, p.264)

Passion, Politics and Law

The Critical Legal Studies Movement, published in 1983, signalled the emergence of a second phase in Unger's writings. The habit of legal positivists and formalists, to attempt to 'sanctify' the 'actual', to staticize it through a 'background conception of right', Unger asserted, is a prime example of the consciously 'unreflective'. It denies the creative potential of reflective judgment. Adopting a methodology which has become particularly popular amongst critical legal scholars, Unger revealed the incoherence of liberal positivism by means of illustrations of inconsistencies in liberal law. The critique is of course one directed against a legal tradition which makes a claim of formal and substantive coherence. The example which Unger is most fond of citing is the contradictions which lie within the idea of freedom of contract, which is itself both constrained and a constraining force (Unger 1983, pp.5-14).

Unger suggests that the spirit of critique is to reveal the dangers of 'necessitarian theories' which make a claim to permanence. A static rights theory is just such a theory. It is Unger's thesis that a legal system, like any other social construct, must triumph the quality of change above all else. This is 'enlarged doctrine'. There are three virtues in such a doctrine. First, it attempts to cross the frontier between the empirical and the normative (the is-ought distinction). Second, it seeks to create through conflict. This he terms the 'transformative conflict', and subsequently becomes the centrepiece of his critical strategy. Third, it wishes to reveal the limitations of law as a pure science by revealing the politics and sociology of law. Three ambitions, therefore, as essential to the critical legal project as they were to the *Metaphysics of Morals*. This is not a pure external criticism, as so many critics of critical legal studies suppose. Such an exercise, as Unger is only too well aware, as a properly critical exercise, is an 'internal argument' (Unger 1983, pp.16-9).

It is an argument, moreover, which can only be enjoined by participation in its process; the Rortian ambition. Unger calls this process 'deviationist doctrine'; it deviates from the jurisprudential norm which lays claim to a 'rightful order of society'. The reality of reconstructive 'transformative practice', as revealed by 'deviationist doctrine', is to present effective decentralizing processes and institutions. This thesis is worked out in much greater depth in *Politics*, published four years later. Such a seemingly radical alternative does not in fact require the abandonment of the liberal ethic; it needs the liberal ethic, but a revised version of it, and not the staticizing positivist variant. Rights are thus vital to the emancipation of the individual, but they must be rights which are commensurate with the critical spirit. Unger suggests four complementary 'kinds of rights'; 'immunity rights', which are absolute rights against all others, 'destabilizing rights', which destablize centres of power, 'market rights', which preserve a right of access to capital, and 'solidarity rights', which offer a legal entitlement to a communal life. With the arguable exception of the second of these, 'destabilizing rights', Unger's reconstructed rights thesis presents precisely the same reconstructive vision as advocated by Kant. Even 'destabization rights', which played around the edges of not only Kant's, but also Rousseau's and Locke's contractual model, might be defensible in the Kantian social contract. As Unger stresses, this model is not a rejection of the Kantian model of rights, or of liberalism. Rather it is an intensification of liberalism, a 'superliberalism' (Unger 1983, p.41).

Such an exercise fully embraces the critical enterprise, deconstruction and normative reconstruction. The 'entire argument' he stresses, 'amounts to an exercise in imagining internal development'. It is an alternative 'formative context' which seeks to stress the power of self-assertion, or 'negative capability' (Unger 1983, p.93). Negative capability is a complement to a fluid conception of critical ethics, which Unger terms 'normative judgments'. Such a constructive skepticism does not deny the 'possibilities of prescriptive judgment', rather it enhances them by undermining the entrenchment of the already prescribed. The key conception for Unger, the whole purpose of the critical legal project, is freedom and its redefinition. Anything that wishes to staticise the conception of freedom must by deconstructed, if the idea of freedom is to be preserved. It is this which places Unger squarely within the Heidegger-Kant dialogue (Unger 1983, p.103). The project is a 'qualification' of existentialism in that it concentrates on the sociology, rather than just the philosophy and the psychology, of freedom (Unger 1983, pp.104-5). In following this methodology, and in broadening the 'sense of collective possibility' and participation in the concept, as well as the idea, of freedom, critical legal studies can be presented as an exemplification of 'transformative action'. Freedom properly becomes the property of pluralism, and thus of the individual (Unger 1983, pp.109, 116, 119).

Before we turn to discuss what is undoubtedly the most pertinent of Unger's texts, *Passion*, we should briefly consider its contextual complement, the three volume *Politics*. Volume one, *Social Theory*, is characterised by the repeated call for self-assertion and the awareness that society is neither static nor an inevitability, but something that is created, and thus something that can be continually 'revised'. Echoing Arendt, Unger stresses that it is an 'artifact'. Turning ever more towards a Kantian conceptualisation of the problem, Unger urges that the one factor which validates this thesis is the presence of the free-will (Unger 1987a, p.17). The 'context-breaking' which executes the experience of freedom is a defiance of 'nature', and represents a state of 'endless quarrels within contexts' (Unger 1987a, pp.18-25). Unger identifies four 'points of departure' for a reconstructive and 'context-breaking' thesis. The first point of departure, transformative 'vocation', places precisely the same stress as Hannah Arendt on the liberating potential of labour. Transformation must be 'worked' and thus, unavoidably, experienced. It is in this way that the politics of transformative action will complement the 'internal world of passion', and the 'antinaturalistic conception of self and society can inform the life projects of the individual.' (Unger 1987a, pp.26-35)

The critical project has revealed the possibilities of a new normative vision, but because of a determination to found this vision there has to date been only 'partial freedom from false necessity' (Unger 1987a, p.52). The ambition of *Politics*, in comparison, is to present a leftist political project which embraces the potentials of a radically indeterminate social science. It is the only means to total 'emancipation from false necessity' (Unger 1987a, pp.135-7). *Politics* is thus a 'super-theory' which provides a 'research agenda' for emancipation. It provides the political edge to the possibilities presented by the critical return to the passions and the subjectivities of judgment. As Arendt suggested, such an approach provides the impetus for a new theory of revolution which seeks to reconstruct society, rather than merely transfer power between hierarchies (Unger 1987a, pp.155-6)

This is the essence of 'negative capability'. It is the practical expression of 'contingency' in personal relations, and represents the 'key' to his reconstructive vision. It is the fundamental appreciation, across all personal and social sciences, 'that all things or some things might be otherwise than they are' (Unger 1987a, p.173). In a classically existential and Kantian expression of this situation, Unger stresses that 'contexts' are always in reality 'our relations' to contexts, and our perceptions of them. The power of such perception or imagination is always greater then the structures which hope to define and to determine them; therefore we can break them. Ultimately every 'truth' is contingent and, as Kant realised, this fact alone necessitates our emancipation as free-wills (Unger 1987a, pp.192-9). To this extent, the criticism, although external to the object, is internal to the critic. Emphasising once again that such a critique is reconstructive as well as deconstructive, Unger finds 'encouragement not only in the constructive work that modern social thought has silently begun to accomplish but also in the emergence in many areas of thought of an image of man that emphasizes both his context-bound predicament and his context-smashing capabilities.' (Unger 1987a, p.204) Such an approach 'frees' liberalism from the constraints of its 'institutional fetishism', presents a view of consensus which evades the lures of foundationalism, and 'dispels the illusions... of false necessity.' (Unger 1987a, pp.209, 211, 214-5)

The fleshing out of this thesis, in the second volume, *False Necessity*, affirms the key concepts as being 'free-will' and 'determinism'. The task of modern social theory is ameliorate the two; the personal and the social. It is thus a continuation of the Heidegger-Sartre project to realise emancipation through a new theory of personality and politics (Unger 1987b, pp.32-7). The pretended rationalism of modernist politics has 'frozen' the 'social order', as can be illustrated by the 'cycles of reform and retrenchment' which Unger first noted in *Knowledge and Politics* and *Law in Modern Society*. The modernist response to this entrenchments has been one of 'negative existentialism'. Unger's alternative is to positivise existentialism; to reconstruct 'models of human association' from the individual, rather than to perceive the individual as forever alienated (Unger 1987b, pp.64-75, 98-105).

The core chapters apply the principles of transformative action, and present Unger's 'program for empowered democracy'. In a real sense this represents the realization of the ambition Unger first acknowledged a decade before; to marry the politics and the passion. It is thus, above all, another existential project, which seeks to develop the critical question which Kant left hanging with the third *Critique*: 'A vision of human empowerment and its conditions describes a form of life rather than a discrete value. But what is its relation to the ideal of love - the acceptance of the concrete other - and to the many forms of commitment and concern that often seems to represent the diluted counterparts of love?.. The answer will not have been formulated until the program for institutional reconstruction extends into a vision of the transformed relations among individuals.' (Unger 1987b, p.355) The key is to revise and reconstruct society, so that it more closely reflects the lived experience of law and politics. As a reconstructive argument, furthermore, it must be an argument from within, which can seek to reexamine the nature of human relations from the position of personality and individual empowerment (Unger 1987b, pp.363-4). We can thus reform our own 'norms' as expressions of 'democratic pluralism' and 'economic destablization'. An important stage in this practice of 'destablization' is an appreciation of the need to disempower linguistic hierarchies and thus empower communication (Unger 1987b, pp.430-2).

The central political ambition remains the reconstitution of institutions; firstly, of constitution and government, secondly, of the economy, and thirdly, of rights. At present the 'constitutional and legal order' is a 'disharmonious conversation between controverted ideals of human association and the practical arrangements supposed to embody them in different domains of social existence.' (Unger 1987b, p.437) Constitutional and governmental reconstruction is the most important and the most pressing. The fundamental reconstruction is thus a reconstruction of constitutional norms which can multiply centres of power. A new body of norms must be more 'expressive of ideals of human association'. Most of all, there must be a reorganisation which can empower an 'overlapping consensus'. It is an overlapping consensus which can realise the transformative extension of orthodox consensualism. In practice this must effect a more thorough system of 'checks and balances' that, rather than stabilizing society, are continually destablizing, and inhere 'a principle of permanent self-revision'. This does not 'paralyze' the 'decisional centre', but by better effecting a principle of 'collective deliberation', it does empower participatory decision-making (Unger 1987b, pp.452-9).

The ultimate ambition is to reconstruct a participatory, as opposed to representative, concept of democracy. It is a matter of institutions determined by personalities. These practical reforms will effect, not only an institutional reconstruction, but also a 'cultural revolution', because they will realise the 'transformation of personal relations'. This will be a culture of 'responsibility' and 'self-assertion' because participation demands responsibility. Ultimately, Unger concludes, the reconstruction of society will engender a 'spirit' or 'attitude' of a constitution. We must think, then, in terms of 'attitudes' rather than 'structures', because attitudes 'emphasise... an ideal of personality and a psychological dynamic'. Attitude is indeed itself the 'ideal of empowerment'. Ultimately, it is the ideal of 'superliberalism' (Unger 1987b, pp.572-90).

The theory of personality is the necessary correlate for a postmodern politics. *Passion: An Essay on Personality* provided this complement, and as a rewriting of the Heidegger-Kant dialogue, takes Unger firmly into a postmodern embrace. The purpose of *Passion* is to develop the conception of sympathy which had emerged in Unger's earlier writings as a possible mechanism for binding the newly reconstructed social order in a non-positivist way. It is again an attempt to reconstruct a 'normative' basis for society; a radically skeptical methodology, but with a reconstructed normative resolution. In Unger's words: 'the opportunity for discovery and self-expression outreaches at any given time all the frameworks for thought or conversation that we can make explicit prospectively.' (Unger 1984, p.8) The idea of freedom is the ability to transcend context in order to change it. The key concept is 'self-assertion'; the empowerment, which 'solidarity' effects, to seize the idea of freedom, and to conceptualise it. The ambition of critical theory is to realise and facilitate self-assertion. It alone can retrieve the individual from the abyss of alienation (Unger 1984, p.13-4, Ball 1987, p.627). It is, Unger explicitly states, the project of Heidegger and Sartre, Kafka and Proust. The development which Unger wishes to contribute is the reconcentration upon 'solidarity' as a means to empowerment. In his opinion the failure of the Heidegger-Kant dialogue was the failure to present a 'vision of a reconstructed society'. Unger's ambition is thus to furnish the final chapter. The concept which will allow him to do so is 'personality'. Ultimately the critical project will be an advance on the existential project, and *Passion* is thus given over to reconciling an existential conception of personality. Such a conception will be a 'normative' Kantian expression of self-affirmation; an expression of the immanently moral person (Unger 1984, pp.25-6, 33-9, 46-8).

The essay itself continues this theme; the development of an alternative human ethics derived from within the moral person and expressed as a theory of personality. The opening passages, in their concentration upon the acute existential condition, the threat of the other, and the emancipatory potential of self-assertion are overtly Heideggerian, and absolutely pivotal to the development of his thesis (Ball 1987, p.644,

Sunstein 1987, 882, Smolin 1986, p.427). The 'transformative forces' which can be retrieved from Sartre's analysis, and which constitute 'passion', are faith, hope and love. Passion does not replace reason, but it does modify it. It contributes the lived experience so popular amongst critical legal scholars, and in doing so provides a 'supplement' to the 'effort of much moral teaching'. 'Participation' in such a 'consensus' does not disempower the individual, but rather complements him (Unger 1984, pp.95-104). Social science, Unger thus concludes, is always a science of relativism, so that consensus is always the science of accommodation.

It is not, however, as he stressed in *Knowledge and Politics*, a consensus which seeks to transcend conflict, but one which cherishes the empowering potential of conflict and difference. Conflict heightens the sense of 'participation', so that from conflict comes an unconstrained conception of freedom and a new 'morality of freedom'. The indeterminacy of freedom is the 'idyll of moral success' (Unger 1984, pp.106-12). Passion alone prevents subjugation, because it alone resolves 'the problem posed by the relation between the enabling conditions of self-assertion' (Unger 1984, p.115). In his *Program for Late Twentieth Century Psychiatry*, Unger suggests that the 'life of passion is the school of freedom' (Unger 1984, pp.289-91). In other words this redefinition of personality defined by solidarity rather than by alienation resolves the fundamental Heideggerian threat of the 'other': 'Under the terms of this resolution the other person's existence is experienced as confirming you in yours; your relation to him exemplifies the experience of freedom that comes from engagements or attachments without dependence or depersonalization, the reconciliation of the enabling circumstances of self-assertion'. (Unger 1984, p.117) Solidarity is thus the key which unlocks Unger's reconstructed vision of society or, more precisely, it is the immanent relationship of solidarity and personality. In a passage strikingly reminiscent of Kant's definition of the 'virtue of respect', Unger determines this relationship as one of respect and trust, culminating in the 'ideal of reciprocity'. Even more strikingly, ultimately, the new reconstructed ethics of society must be an aesthetics of judgment (Unger 1984, pp.126-8, 133-5).

The 'personality' that lives out 'passion' is the personality that is capable of self-judgment and 'self-reflection' (Unger 1984, p.146). Such a person is reconciled to the 'utter contingency of his own being and of the world', and appreciative of the fact that this alone preserved the possibility of a self-assertive sense of freedom. Echoing a generation of fellow Heideggerians, Unger stresses that this reconciliation is a reconciliation to a constant state of unsettledness and instability. Reconciliation, however, precludes despair. Irreconcilable antinomies are to be cherished. The only thing which can advance despair is the concretization of social and personal contexts (Unger 1984, pp.156-7, 191-3). An appreciation of the ever changing life of the mind, to know consensus from sense, will release the liberating potentials of reflection and judgment. Such liberation can only be realised by active participation in society. Judgment is always a relative conception:

By one movement you throw yourself into transformative action and reflection about the way unjustified inequality corrupts community and collaboration. Through your participation in conflict and controversy over inequality and diversity, you begin to pull apart, in yourself, envy and indignation. By another movement - the movement of love - you have, in the here and now, an experience of association in which no disparity of advantage holds you to the descending spiral of hatred. Through the twofold effort of this response to inequality, the facts that might have led to the self-reinforcing cycle of envy, with its narrowing acquiescence in established constraints on action and vision, become instead goals to the discovery of possibilities that these constraints close off. (Unger 1984, p.220)

From such a sense of 'communal affection' comes a sense of 'allegiance'. This positive constructive relation of personality and solidarity realises the cherished Heideggerian dream of 'openness': 'It is the acknowledgement of more openness in a situation than the situation easily reveals: openness above all to the possibility of attachments that are also opportunities for self-assertion, openness to our chances of resolving the problem of solidarity in a way more promising to our freedom.' (Unger 1984, p.244). It is also with the reality of solidarity that the Dworkinian dream of 'integrity' can be realised. 'Integrity' is the thoroughly indeterminate and contingent construct of the 'character of relations among people'. It is the manifestation of their reconstructive rationality, as realised by the creative possibilities of 'transforming passions' (Unger 1984, pp.246, 250). Transformative passion leads directly to transformative action. It is, for Unger, the purpose of transformative passion to do so. The 'brio and panache, the sheer vibrant life, of a personality', heightens 'the sense of experienced human power' (Unger 1984, pp.260-1). It convinces us to embrace the potentials and possibilities of indeterminacy. We thus find ourselves 'set down in particular social and mental worlds', whilst the 'modes of discourse and explanation available' to us 'never exhaust the possibilities of understanding and communication' (Unger 1984, p.261).

Unger the Postmodern Liberal?

Unger's most recent writings have leant ever further towards a theory of imagination and legal consciousness. Imagination is the key to effecting transformation, and remains the essence of his declared neo-romantic ambition (Unger 1996). It is this neo-romantic interest in personality as constitutive of public and participatory democracy which so attracts Rorty. In contrast with what he calls the 'School of Resentment', Unger's thesis, he suggests, 'does not give the last word to the time he lives in. He also lives in an imaginary lightly sketched future. That is the sort of world romantics should live in.' (Rorty 1991b, pp.183, 186). Ultimately, the radical political and jurisprudential alternative which Unger presents may well have a greater chance of implementation in the third world, but there is no doubt with regard to Rorty's respect for it as a universal potential. No single book, of course, no single social vocabulary 'will do the trick', but Unger's writings are 'shot through with a romanticism for which we Alexandrians no longer have the strength' (Rorty 1991b, p.192).

Aside from Rorty's enthusiasm, Unger's writings have encountered wide-ranging responses. John Finnis and Denise Meyerson have taken issue with Unger's suggestion that the liberal legal order is pervasively inconsistent. The accompanying suggestion that he fails to provide a reconstructive alternative, though mistaken, is a common one (Meyerson 1991, Finnis, 1985). Andrew Halpin has articulated a common concern that Unger's revised theory of rights leaves everything to 'individual discretion' (Halpin, 1994). On the other hand, Unger's attempt to refound politics through an alternative vision of personality and thus to revitalize liberalism has provoked critical commentary from within the Critical Legal Studies movement. Whilst applauding Unger's achievement in turning passion into a 'bridge' between 'politics' and 'personal life', James Boyle has suggested that Unger's thesis is 'quintessentially modernist', and thus dismisses it as another kind of foundational liberalism (Boyle 1985).

Hutchinson and Monaghan have been particularly censorial of Unger's liberal and reconstructive ambitions. Whilst applauding Unger's unremitting critique of existing liberal rights-talk, they dismiss his 'deviationist' doctrine and its putative reconstruction of a rights thesis. It is, at root, another constructivist thesis, not so different, and certainly not in ambition, from that presented by John Rawls. Thus although, he might share the same philosophical origins as Sartre, Unger is trapped by his own attempt to escape alienation by impressing the sanctity of individual autonomy (Hutchinson and Monahan, 1984). This association of Unger with Rawls, and with Sartre, is precisely Rorty's. As we have already seen, in Rorty's opinion, Unger presents the jurisprudence of a Heideggerian pragmatism. Significantly, Hutchinson repeated his critique of Unger's foundational vision of personality in a 1989 essay directed against what he perceived to be the same failings in Richard Rorty's most recent writings (Hutchinson 1989).

An alternative approach has been taken by Ernest Weinrib who applauds *Passion*'s anti-positivistism, but suggests that his reading of human nature would be better recast in a more explicitly Kantian mould. Ultimately Weinrib's critique is that Unger's optimism makes him too metaphysical, and too little critically aware of the nature of practical reason. Weinrib doubts our ability to ever transcend context, and suggests that Unger's conception of 'solidarity' is precisely metaphysical, and that its concurrent championing of the 'good' over the 'right' finally removes the thesis from firm relativist grounding. The observation, however, that the logic of Unger's ambition leads irreducibly back to a critical Kantian ethics, makes Weinrib's critique amongst the most perceptive of all. Ultimately, Weinrib suggests, Unger uses 'passion' just as Kant used 'morality', as a foundation for a critical political theory (Weinrib 1985). An incipient foundationalism is similarly detected by William Galston, who suggests that, in this, Unger falls into the same trap as Rawls. Unger's 'utopia' is one premised upon an incessant 'proferring' of 'universal truths' (Galston 1987). The idea that Unger's project represents a progressive variant of Rawls's is taken on by Geoffrey Hawthorn, who redefines neo-romanticism as generically Kantian (Hawthorn 1987).

The suggestion that Unger's 'passion' entraps him in a comprehensive theory is, of course, immediately reminiscent of similar critiques of Rawls's more recent work, and its presentation of the moral self as a determination of 'reflective equilibrium'. It is the co-determinative association of some sort of theory of personality or moral self with of an idea of liberal solidarity, which ultimately allies the visions of Rorty, Rawls and Unger, and it is the necessary indeterminacy and fluidity of these visions which makes them precisely postmodern. This is certainly Drucilla Cornell's conclusion. Society as an 'artifact', something made rather than given, is an acknowledgment of the postmodern project. Unger, she suggests, writes the 'language of postmodernism' because he writes to 'protect and institutional space for difference'. Such a space is essential to the postmodern idea of 'a dialogic communitarian program of collective self-governance' (Cornell 1987, pp.693-8). The concentration in Unger's theory of personality and politics around the 'good of self-assertion' and 'self-governance' places it squarely in the Heideggerian project, adding a theory of passion to Arendt's established theory of self-governance and participatory democracy. What Unger does is force is us to 'confront the significance of post-modern de-centring of the subject' (Cornell 1987, pp.711-7). It is, as Rorty suggests, a thoroughly postmodern liberal idea.

CHAPTER 5

CRITICAL LEGAL STUDIES AND BEYOND

1 A Brief History of Critical Legal Thinking

Critical Legal Studies

The Critical Legal Studies movement has emerged as the *bete noire* of contemporary legal scholarship. The response to CLS has been often vitriolic, and too often hysterical (Carrington 1984, Price 1989). Radical pluralism has been perceived as threatening the very foundations of liberal legalism. Yet, as Andrew Altman has emphasised, CLS cannot be singularly determined. The alternative 'radical' and 'moderate' variants of CLS present very different visions, and the hallmark of the 'moderate' variant, as epitomised by such as Unger, is its affinity with a reconstructive liberal counter-critique. Pluralism provides the fuel for liberalism, and as we saw in the previous chapter, the ability of a consensus theory to ameliorate the pluralist critique is an explicit recognition that the Rawlsian thesis complements the Ungerian (Altman 1990).

But what precisely is Critical Legal Studies or, more pertinently, what does it think it is? For such a relatively recent phenomenon, CLS enjoys a number of self-proclaimed historians. One of the greater virtues of CLS is that it has awakened legal scholarship once more to the nature of historicity and historical 'relativism' (Gordon 1981). In the case of one of more ardent historians, Mark Tushnet, this is a particularly apposite observation, for own sympathies lie very much with the original socio-political wing of CLS, and his 'histories' thus tend to rather minimalise the recent moves towards textuality and the critical postmodern tradition (Tushnet 1991). The empirical basis to much of the early CLS scholarship can be explained, in part, by the lingering influence of realism, not just doctrinally, but in its concern with legal education. The practical impulse for CLS was not just the demise of certain scholers in individual tenure disputes with various universities, but more generally, a deep-seated feeling that the established orthodoxy of legal education was wholly uncritical, both socially and politically. According to Jay Feinman, legal education actively alienated the lawyer and reified the legal process, training students in a particular 'cognitive method called thinking like a lawyer'. The alternative, he suggested, again developing one of Unger's key themes, is to transform 'the classroom into a participatory learning community in which critical values can be applied and tested.' (Feinman 1985)

The desire to facilitate a more participatory democracy is one of the centrepieces of CLS. Karl Klare advocates a Marxist instrumentalization of the legal process. Klare combines this inevitably determinist analysis with a discussion of the creation of legal consciousness, individual alienation and the need to readdress the human condition (Klare 1978, p.265, Klare 1979). His historiography of collective bargaining law is underpinned by analysis of its alienating and disempowering effects. One of the problems with 'liberal rights-consciousness', he suggests, 'is that it excludes the possibility of conceiving of human freedom as self-expression and growth in and through community.' (Klare 1981, p.479) The evolution of labour law consciousness corresponds with evolution of civil rights law. Both, he suggested, were entrapped by the image of the 'public/private' dichotomy, and liberation could only be realized by a transendence 'beyond' the 'restrictive confines of a bureaucratized, process oriented industrial governance system'. The fate of both industrial and civil democracy lay in the 'convergence' of economics and justice (Klare 1982).

Gerry Frug has consistently advocated the democratization and decentralization of power. The expressly historical methodology is complemented by a particular concentration on the public/private distinction. The model Frug advocates is Arendt's phenomenological redefinition of participatory freedom; her political articulation of Heidegger's engagement with Kant's conception of free-will. The reconstructed participatory democracy should 'respond to what Hannah Arendt has called the need for public freedom - the ability to participate actively in the basic societal decisions that affect one's life.' (Frug 1980, p.1068) What Arendt had done, above all, is show how the exercise of freedom is not a specialized task but something which can be self-asserted by all of us. The liberal overtones to Arendt's message was not lost on Frug: 'The liberal image of law as mediating between the need to protect the individual from communal coercion and the need to achieve communal goals could thus be retained even in the model of participatory democracy.' (Frug 1980, p.1072)

It is the Arendtian programme which, according to Frug, has been taken up by Unger, who has thus by implication engaged in the Kantian dialogue (Frug 1980, p.1074). The desire to reconstruct from within liberalism is a striking facet of Frug's programme. Advocating a Rortian conversation, Frug suggests that the 'radical' strategy, which will encompass not just reform of local government and administrative bodies in general, but also the workplace, will be that constructed by 'debate' between interested parties, and the consensus thereby achieved. The central plank to this programme is the effecting of administrative democracy through radical decentralization of power to 'units small enough to make popular participation in government decision-making feasible'. The ultimate triumph will be the overcoming of the 'bureaucratic consciousness' which always accompanies undemocratic administrative government (Frug 1990).

The empirical impulse behind early CLS writing can be exemplified in the writings of Duncan Kennedy and Mark Tushnet. Kennedy's famous debate with Peter Gabel will be considered shortly. Suffice to say for the present, whilst Gabel wanted to engage with Sartre, Kennedy wanted to campaign in supermarkets. Similarly Mark Tushnet condemned liberal scholarship for its recourse to 'moral philosophy'. Law, for Tushnet, can never be about philosophy, critical or not. More particularly, Tushnet's central concern lies with constitutional theory and the rights-discourse and the inconsistencies and implicit politics of the liberal rights discourse (Tushnet 1981, Tushnet 1984). There is no doubt that the critique of rights lies at the heart of CLS scholarship. Yet much of the more reconstructive critique bears striking comparison with Unger's superliberalism. Paul Brest advocates an alternative 'participatory public dialogue', against liberalism as utilitarian positivism (Brest 1981). As Frank Michelman observed, what rights-critics like Brest advocate is simply a restructured rights thesis in the same 'liberal' tradition as Kant and Arendt (Michelman 1981). Similarly, whilst Tushnet is right to emphasise the centrality of the indeterminacy thesis, the real bite of indeterminacy now lies, not so much in political as in textual indeterminacy, and this does not necessarily weigh against liberalism, merely liberal positivism. Indeed Ken Kress suggests that the indeterminacy critique triumphed by CLS against utilitarian liberalism is, in fact, a wholly Kantian critique (Kress 1989).

A more perceptive contemporary historian is Peter Goodrich, who emphasises the 'turn' in CLS to 'continental traditions and disciplines, ranging from literary criticism to psychoanalysis and aesthetics'. More perceptively still, Goodrich notes the natural affinity between critical legal thought as a textual exercise with the Kantian aesthetic (Goodrich 1992). There has been an increasing awareness in recent years of the need to reorientate critical legal scholarship towards a deeper more substantive and more textually aware alternative. Stephen Diamond's history of the new CLS, 'more conciliatory, less critical, more troubled', charts the development of a greater textual awareness and an increasing interest in continental critical philosophy (Diamond 1985). This might be seen, by some, as a return to liberalism, but that rather begs the question of whether early CLS, despite all its huff and puff, was ever really anything else. It is of course the thesis of this book that the origins of CLS are precisely those of the liberal critique, and that the engagement with the Heidegger-Kant tradition of neo-Kantianism is simply the natural progression of a critical impulse seeking a critical theory.

Relatedly, it is suggested that, just as CLS was itself an 'inevitability' so too is the developing engagement with the Heidegger-Kant tradition of critical philosophy (Hermann 1982). From the earliest days the sociological import of Michel Foucault was considerable. Mark Kelman used it as the theoretical foundation for his 'trashing' (Kelman 1984). It was also a key component of Thomas Heller's influential *Structuralism and Critique*, which first suggested that there might be more to CLS than a mere reworking of realist empiricism (Heller 1984). Robert Gordon, too, has stressed the central role that Foucault and, on a wider scale the French Heideggerian tradition, is having on the development of the CLS critique (Gordon 1982). Frug invokes Derrida's 'dangerous supplement' as the law itself, presenting itself as something of virtue to be added to our existence, and emphasising the essentially rhetorical nature of this supplement (Frug 1984). Thus the cherished 'ideal' of 'participatory democracy' would be approached as much through a rewriting of the language of 'democracy', as by empirical reform. It was an explicit appeal, not only to Derrida, but also to Richard Rorty, and in particular his idea of the conversationally created context: 'In our daily encounters with others, we recognize that we help create each other through our interactions. It is because these interactions are both necessary and threatening that all of them must continuously be open to reconstruction and revision. In the everyday world of human interdependence, there can be no such thing as a foundation that could render (even part of) social life noncontroversial.' (Frug 1984, pp.1385-6)

Legal language, Frug suggests, is the primary cause of closure in legal theory. As Derrida affirms, silence effects otherness and exclusion. Frug cites Heidegger as his explicit authority and acknowledges the now unarguable case for engaging in the textual critique of the Heideggerians. Despite the apparent radical indeterminacy of language, rhetoric is in fact a means of providing a 'place of relative stability' upon which a critical dialogue can be established. Rhetoric is the means by which critical legal scholars can effect value consensus and agreement in the manner of developing corporate character. It is, of course, both a communicatively constructive and self-asserted rationality (Frug 1988).

Joan Williams emphasises the textual and literary influences of such as Barthes and Derrida, as well as Foucault. Ultimately, she suggests that the aligment of the more moderate CLSers, such as Unger or Boyle, with the structuralist and post-structuralist impulses makes them 'neo-Kantian' in both ambition and methodology (Williams 1987). Boyle has suggested that all critical legal scholarship made a critical assumption about the constructive nature of 'apparently rational discourse'. Anti-formalism is more accurately anti-positivism, rather than anti-Kantianism or anti-liberalism. He used Unger as a particular example of a discursive rationalist, along with Peter Gabel, whom he suggested has emerged as Unger apprentice, and with Gary Peller, whom he suggested, was 'carrying on the rationalistic project that has been neglected since Kant' (Boyle 1985, pp.736-45). Peller firmly placed Unger in the Heideggerian tradition. From here it is inevitable that CLS must encounter, indeed embrace, the textual critique of knowledge, as represented by Sartre, Foucault and Derrida amongst many. Rather than representing a fundamental turn from the realist empiricism to textuality, the redirection of CLS was merely the redirection from a less obvious to a more obvious, social to textual 'deconstruction'. For Peller, it is a need to reinvestigate theories of the self, rather than of society, which necessitates a turn to textuality and the processes of self-determination (Peller 1985).

CLS textualists have shown an increasing interest in Rorty's non-foundational conversationalism. Specifically applying Rorty's description of the 'edifiying' philosopher as one who appreciates the ever-presence, and the ever-present threat of 'loneliness', and who thus devotes himself to describing a fluid non-foundational morality, Joseph Singer suggests:

> Theory expresses our values; it does not create them... Legal theory cannot tell us what to value, but it can help us (judges, scholars, citizens) make choices by helping us to articulate what we value... Like law, consensus must be made, not found. Emphasis on the creative, communal nature of common understanding creates an appropriate relationship between thought and action... Once we have envisioned how we would like to do things, we can then use the principles and counterprinciples in legal discourse to describe what we value about these alternative arrangements. (Singer 1984, pp.60-5)

Michael Moore seeks to critique Rorty on the assumption that to destroy Rorty's theory of language is to destroy CLS textualism. For Moore, the underlying threat is of Heideggerian nihilism (Moore 1989). Stephen Feldman has replied to Moore by specifically advocating the desirability of a critical return to Heidegger, because the Heideggerian hermeneutic can provide critical legal theory with a new 'ethics of Being'

(Feldman 1991). With Heidegger has come a renewed interest in hermeneutics. Thus when David Couzens Hoy, like Feldman, advocates Gadamerian hermeneutics as a method of critical legal reasoning, he makes the same explicit appeal as Ronald Dworkin; beyond Heidegger, and beyond Gadamer, to the Kantian tradition (Hoy 1985).

The Approach of the Postmodern

The turn to text is a turn to postmodernism, and if law is approaching postmodernism then law is going forward back to Kant. Alan Hunt presents postmodernism as the natural evolution of critical legal studies, sharing its 'profound disenchantment with modernity' (Hunt 1990, p.516). In his opinion, postmodernism emerged naturally from the deconstructionist and post-structuralist sympathies engendered by encounters with such as Derrida and Foucault in particular. In this sense, it is the logical derivative of the move towards textuality which can be charted in CLS historiography. The key moment, according to Hunt, is Gabel and Kennedy's conversational exchange, *Roll Over Beethoven*, which we shall consider shortly. This text, he suggests, 'marked the moment' of 'reception of postmodernism into the emergent tradition of critical legal studies' (Hunt 1990, p.521). It was Kennedy's refusal to accept the 'possibility of theory' which represented the abandoment of the original Marxist impulse, and instead aligned CLS-postmodernism with the Rortian neo-pragmatist variant of the Heideggerian engagement. 'The Big Fear' is that which follows CLS; the fear of nihilism. In fact, postmodernism offers the only viable possibility for a reconstructed ethics in contemporary post-Kantian scholarship. At the same time, Hunt is keen to emphasise the politics of textuality, and reluctant to leave deconstruction to deconstruction of texts alone. In his opinion:

> As deconstruction migrated from literary criticism to legal theory the context changed, as did the issues and the importance. The question is no longer how to interpret the text; rather it is about the legitimacy of legal discourse as a mechanism for power disguised as the pursuit of interpretive truth. Thus the project of deconstructivist critique is to mount a challenge to the legitimacy of the project of law... The radical inflection of the postmodernist intervention lies not, I suggest, in its interpretive strategy or deconstructive methods, but rather in the way in which the tensions, closures, and contradictions in judicial texts are linked to the wider dynamics of power and dominant interests. (Hunt 1990, pp.513-4)

The underlying ethical ambition of postmodernist jurisprudence is pervasive. Hunt suggests that such a jurisprudence can develop an acute 'cultural relativism': 'Of the different varieties of relativism the one which emphasizes the social construction of reality without any structures outside of linguistic communities being able to impose limits or constraints. Hence culture, in its infinite diversity and irreducibility, ensures the plasticity and relativity of the social.' (Hunt 1990, p.530) The politics of postmodernism, then, is to be a politics of relativism and constructivism, and in particular, in defiance of meta-political theories, it will be an intensely local, decentralized and participatory politics (Hunt 1990, pp.533-40).

There is an increasing literature in support of a postmodern politics and a postmodern ethics. Anna Yeatman talks of a 'postmodern emancipatory politics' located in the 'beyond' of modernism. Such a politics is expressed in a postmodern idea of citizenship determined by active participation in the determination of both self and community. It is a politics of self-assertion. Postmodernism, she suggests, following Derrida, is immanently jurisprudential; it is defined by its concern with the injustice of exclusion. Following Rorty, she espouses a universality of humanity as a universality of difference (Yeatman 1994, pp.86-90, 118). Consciously developing the Heideggerian tradition, as articulated by Hannah Arendt, Heller and Feher concentrate on the concept of self-determination in the radically plural world. Citing Heidegger and Derrida, they suggest that the politics of localism is the politics of postmodernism. Such a politics, whilst denying the metaphilosophies of the Enlightenment, is not an abandonment of ethics, but rather a new 'configuration' or, echoing Richard Bernstein, 'constellation' of localised 'citizen ethics', nourished by 'discursive' relationships (Heller and Feher 1988, pp.1-5, 19-29, 33-43, 76-84).

Aside from the localised participatory democracy and the concept of self-determination, they also approve Unger's idea of false necessity. Unger is a 'pioneer' of postmodernism. Most importantly, they recognise that the postmodern political condition is a Kantian political condition, for it was Kant's 'sophisticated' response to the demise of classical metaphysics which founded both the modern and postmodern possibilities for political morality. Thus the discourse of Rawls, Dworkin and Arendt is essentially the same discourse, generated by a 'particularization' of Kant's 'particular'. It is the reintroduction of Kantian principles in the postmodern critique which can finally effect the critical overcoming of nihilism. More precisely it is the appreciation that 'consensus' politics is the politics of postmodernity (Heller and Feher 1988, pp.44-59, 63-70, 120-31).

Returning to the text, and borrowing consciously from Derrida, Peter Goodrich deliberately employs the tools of deconstruction to effect a postmodern reading of text which can then reflect the deconstruction of the Enlightenment discourse. Goodrich articulates a particular concern with what he calls the 'textual tradition' of western law, the discourse and the rhetoric, the potential indeterminacy of texts and the images and metaphors of the legal discourse. The Social Contract, the centrepiece of Enlightenment political thought, is merely the keystone of a whole series of such images which fashion this discourse. In his *Languages of Law*, Goodrich has charted the development of the 'critique of legal reason to an aesthetics of law' (Goodrich 1990, pp.287-8). More recently he has repeated the thesis that law is at bottom an aesthetic phenomena, a 'poetical sermon', suggesting that 'the text circulates as an image and the power of its effect is largely resident in that aesthetic quality rather than in its supposed rational content, for few ever read the law, none ever read all of it.' (Goodrich 1991).

This conclusion is echoed by Douzinas and Warrington who acknowledge that the key to understanding postmodernism lies in an understanding of the passage of the truth problematic, through the Kant-Heidegger-Derrida line. In *Postmodern Jurisprudence* Derrida and Lyotard emerge as the key figure in their ensuing deconstruction of positivist jurisprudence. It is Lyotard's attempt to represent Kant's theory of judgment which, they perceptively note, is at the very heart of a postmodern ethics. Kant's third *Critique* thus emerges as the key text in postmodern jurisprudence, whilst the Kantian critical project as a whole provides both 'the basis of formalism and aestheticism'. In the specifically legal situation, following Goodrich, they suggest that a judge is always making an aesthetic judgement, subjectively determined but objectively ambitious (Douzinas and Warrington 1991, 5-28, 163-9).

This thesis is continued in their more recent *Justice Miscarried*; postmodern jurisprudence is always about the nature and constituents of judgment. It is, thus, an ethical activity. In particular they emphasise that the deconstructionist origins of postmodernism, as it acknowledges its Heideggerian homage, demands a philosophy of responsibility, more precisely responsibility to self and to other. Echoing Derrida, they suggest that the jurisprudence of the postmodern is a jurisprudence of the unpresenced other, the 'beyond', and that the need to accommodate the 'other' is an appreciation of responsiblity to the 'other'. The move 'beyond' is a move back to Kant and the one 'great intellectual' bequest of Kant; the self-assertion of freewill as realized in the aesthetics of 'Kantian reflective judgement' (Douzinas and Warrington 1994, pp.132-85, 211-41). It is to Kant's third *Critique* that we must look for a postmodern 'ethics of law' and a postmodern 'theory of legality': 'Legality does not belong to the moral but to the aesthetic order. There is a validity to aesthetic judgments, but it is founded upon feeling not upon concepts. It is the legality of the felt which puts into play a subjective attachment to a particular order and organization of experience.' (Douzinas, Goodrich and Hachamovitch 1994, pp.22, 26)

2 Three Studies in Critical Legal Thinking

The Withdrawn Self: Peter Gabel

Peter Gabel is the first of three leading figures in contemporary critical legal thinking who illustrate the critical turn towards the Heidegger-Kant dialogue and the approach of the postmodern. James Boyle suggests that Gabel is Unger's apprentice. He is also most obviously Sartre's (Kramer 1991, pp.205-38). According to Alan Hunt, Gabel's exchange with Duncan Kennedy, and his attempts to introduce Sartre's appropriation of Heidegger into critical legal thought, marks the first step towards a critical legal postmodernism (Hunt 1990, p.521). For Gabel, Sartre, and particularly his use of praxis, as used by other Heideggerians, most notably Hannah Arendt, potentially offers the most suitable way of philosophizing political theory. In a 1977 essay he suggested that a critical reinvestigation of the phenomenology of interpretation of images necessitates a return to Heidegger (Gabel 1977, pp.628-9). It was Heidegger who best appreciated the concretizing tendency of false consciousness. As with Unger, it is the extent to which an alternative approach to contract law might release a 'transformative' political power in the economic and labouring workplace which attracts Gabel. Politics is a lived experience, and so the law of contracts must also become one forever aware of its dangerously concretizing potential.

The publication of *Reification in Legal Reasoning* in 1980 represented the first substantive critical legal application of the Heidegger-Kant dialogue. Again the primary influence was Sartre. The problem of legal imagery was the problem of established 'boundaries of legitimate rationality'. It represented the 'inherently repressive form of interpretive thought' which characterised legal reasoning and, of course, legal discourse. This itself was not particularly new to CLS, but the development of the argument that the repression was in fact a self-repression, which could only be released by as transformative 'self-assertion' was, in its particular Heideggerian colouring, intriguing. This was the nature of Sartrean 'reification'. Importantly, it was also a discursive or communicative reification and repression. So the solution lay with the liberation of language (Gabel 1980, pp.25-7). As it stood, language was a double-edged sword, at once repressing pluralism, but also tantalizingly offering its 'empowerment'. However, it was not merely language which repressed, but also, following the orthodox early Heideggerian line, the phenomenology of legal discourse. In the twentieth century condition of human alienation the experience of legal discourse established a 'collective terror' over its reasoners, and the primary terrorists are the judges, who pretend to value neutral judgments, but in reality import, as the subjectivity of judgment demands, a politics of law (Gabel 1980, p.30).

The key issue, Gabel noted, was the phenomenology of judgment itself; *Reification in Legal Reasoning* developed as a critique of judgment. This process is not however, a purely subjective one, because the judge will often judge in accordance with his subjective reading of an objective image of the law. His perception of judgment as a construction of 'common sense', and his critique of it as concretization of this very construction, is precisely what Kant suggested in his analysis of *sensus communis*. Gabel cites Sartre's application of the same investigation, but his discussion of how law review readers read legal texts, and the relationship between text and reader, is a very precise rendering of the Heideggerian hermeneutic (Gabel 1980, pp.30-43). The hermeneutic 'constraints' on judgment and, more particularly, the particular 'imagined' meaning of words, becomes 'formal and historical', so that ultimately the two key conceptions, freedom and equality, become captured 'signifiers'. It is their necessarily internal liberation which must be secured, and then within the 'delegitimation of law altogether' (Gabel 1980, pp.45-8).

The Phenomenology of Rights-Consciousness and the Pact of the Withdrawn Selves placed the consciousness thesis, as developed specifically through the phenomenology of Heidegger and Sartre, at the centre of critical legal scholarship. Belief in the imagery of rights represented an example of reification, but what was most interesting about the declared ambitions of the essay, was its reconstructive impulse. As with Unger, for Gabel rights were not bad per se; indeed a theory of rights by implication was prerequisite for any just society. It was the liberal imagery of rights which was bad, and particularly its suffocating effects on 'potentially emancipatory social movements' (Gabel 1984, p.1563). The critical feature of the Heideggerian project was the internalization of critique; alienation and reification are characteristics not of law in itself, but of our conscious perception of law. A critical investigation of law demanded first an investigation of the self; a theory of personality. Gabel thus demanded a return of 'desire' to the forefront of jurisprudential discourse, because a denial of desire is a denial of self (Gabel 1984, pp.1565-9). A jurisprudence of the self alone, can better express the law as it is 'lived within consciousness'.

Of course, Gabel recognises that any attempt to articulate this consciousness immediately runs the risk of concretization. But that, as Heidegger pointed out, is a necessary hazard of textual liberation. Rights-consciousness is thus a mechanism by which we 'guard ourselves against the risk of taking existential action against our alienation by repeatedly telling ourselves that our alienation is inevitable, while at the same time denying that this alienation exists.' (Gabel 1984, pp.1574-6, 1581). It is hard to imagine a more expressly Heideggerian commentary on the nature of rights. Gabel's concluding passages on the practical effects of the alienation thesis are striking, not only in their implicit defeat of the often misguided allegation that CLS fails to offer concrete reconstructive alternatives, but also in the echoing of Unger's agenda. The struggle to reconstruct rights, which is itself a notably Ungerian concession, will be achieved by the 'transformation' of 'public space' and by an effecting of 'participatory politics' (Gabel 1984, p.1596).

As we have already noted, according to Alan Hunt, Gabel's notorious engagement with Duncan Kennedy, and his attempt to emphasise the need to reground CLS in the critical tradition against Kennedy's implicit suggestion that to do so is to risk the entrapment of metaphysics, marked the approach of the postmodern. Gabel's contributions effectively repeated the thesis developed in *Phenomenology*. One of the ironies of the Gabel-Kennedy encounter was its immediate portrayal of precisely what Gabel advocated; a communicative rationality employed to effect practical reconceptualizations. For much of the discourse the linguistic and conceptual parameters are those set by Gabel, and so the dialogue continues by considering, first alienation, then 'intersubjective zap', then 'nothingness', and so on. 'Intersubjective zap' as a coming together or, in generic terms, a 'presencing' of consciousness, is one of the more contentious reconceptualizations. More than anything, 'intersubjective zap' articulated a temporal and 'existential' presencing (Gabel and Kennedy 1984, pp.9-19). Its similarity with the Heideggerian hermeneutic of intersubjectivity is striking. The 'consensus' overtones are, of course, precisely those which such a theory of intersubjectivity must always advance. It was perhaps the implicit threat of 'overlapping' consensus which was of greatest concern. The discussion of 'nothingness', in turn, was an explicit discussion of the relevance of Sartrean insights for CLS. For Gabel they were indispensible.

The discussion of 'nothingness' led back, perhaps inevitably, to a rediscussion of alienation, and its particular appropriateness in the legal situation. In an evocative passage, Gabel opened by suggesting that law students are pressed, by their own selves, into expressions of 'bad faith':

because they're going to 'become lawyers', they think they have to somehow transform these feelings into 'good legal arguments' - 'It's not good enough to have good politics; you've got to have good legal argument'. So what happens is people start translating their political feelings into unconscionability arguments or right-to-privacy arguments without realizing that there is a weird dissociation taking place, as if it were inevitable that you had to take your true needs and desires and translate them into one or other of these available arguments. This is the essence of the problem with rights discourse. People don't realize that what they are doing is recasting the real existential feelings that led them to become political people into an ideological framework that coopts them into adopting the very consciousness they want to transform. (Gabel and Kennedy 1984, p.26)

The essential critique is a critique not of politics, but of the politics of language. Only with this critique in place can people exercise their liberated transformative potential:

Exactly what people don't need is their rights. What they need are the actual forms of social life that have to be created through the building of movements that can overcome illusions about the nature of what is political, like the illusion that there is an entity called the state, that people possess rights... So my claim is that the specific aim of lawyers should be not to subordinate their sense of themselves as political actors, not to see themselves as merely representing others, but working with others to build the strength of existing movements in order to realize in a direct language that they believe in, their own political aims - that's the goal. (Gabel and Kennedy 1984, p.33)

However, as the dialogue developed, Gabel made it quite clear, as he had done in his earlier essays, that rights hold the key to liberation. The rights thesis must be deconstructed so that it can be reconstructed. In the final passages, which return more precisely to a discussion of concsciousness and personality, Gabel concentrates on the role of the 'free-will'. Given the constructive impulse, such a recourse is inevitable for Gabel as it was for Kant. Only by somehow accessing a concept of the free-will, whether or not it is discursively reified, can the 'affirmation' or assertion of the self by effected by the 'other' (Gabel and Kennedy 1984, pp.44-54).

From Politics to Text: Allan Hutchinson

What is arresting about the development of Allan Hutchinson's critical legal approach is the development from the political to the textual; so much so that he now aligns himself firmly with the postmodern project. At the same time, he now distances himself from a confessed 'debilitating nihilism' which characterised his earlier writings (Hutchinson 1995a, pp.789-98). In 1984, though describing CLS as a 'philosophical' movement, directed against the positivism of legal 'science', he could only present a 'depressing prognosis' for the future of critical legal thought. The reason for this prognosis is that CLS, at least in 1984, was taken to be a return to realism, and the fear was precisely the same fear of its failures. In an effort to distinguish it from the alluring dangers of neo-realist 'nihilism', Hutchinson suggested that CLS 'passionately believe[s] that some meaningful political theory can be created and defended.' Unfortunately, in 1984 the alternative was far from clear, though he did acknowledge that much would depend on resolving the 'need for a theory of human personality' which could determine the 'ultimate goal' of 'emancipation' (Hutchinson and Monahan 1984a, pp.200-13, 242).

This engagement was a direct engagement with Unger. Whilst supporting Unger's ambition to present a theory of personality as a necessary corollary to a theory of politics, as has already been noted, Hutchinson was critical of what appeared to be a too blatant attempt to reconstruct a theory of rights. It was merely an attempt to replace one consciousness with another: 'Like the liberals he criticizes, Unger projects his own values onto the larger canvas of a new world view. He mistakes private preference for universal insight.' (Hutchinson and Monahan 1984b, p.1479). However, whilst contesting Unger's superliberal, and ultimately constructivist, resolution, Hutchinson's declared ambition was to develop the Ungerian thesis to an alternative conclusion (Hutchinson and Monhan 1984b, p.1539). Whilst sharing Unger's engagement in 'the poetics of transformative politics', Hutchinson is critical of the foundations which he suggests lie at the heart of Unger's attempt to rewrite the discourse of liberalism around a refurbished theory of personality, which is too intensely individualist and too little determined by community. His ultimate criticism is that Unger's revised theory of personality increasingly betrays the influences of his 'philosophical forefathers', namely Aristotle and Kant (Hutchinson 1990).

The same critique has been directed at Richard Rorty. In the enterprise of reconstructing liberalism, Unger is merely 'Rorty's radical sibling'. Hutchinson sees himself as developing, rather than merely abandoning, Rorty's thesis. As such, he is totally in sympathy with Rorty's engagement with the Heideggerian anti-metaphysical project, and wishes to follow the 'radical spirit rather than the liberal letter' of the enterprise (Hutchinson 1989, p.557). He approves the historicity of Rorty's thesis of contingency. Most important is the contingency of language, and Hutchinson expressly approves the central idea of political discourse as 'conversation'. Language is the key to a new politics. However, in his refusal to abandon the possibility of a constructive rationalism, as opposed to a foundationalism, and in his explicit support for Rawls, Rorty betrays his own Kantian roots, and thus remains, unavoidably, within that framework. Rorty, as we already know, is precisely happy with this, and it is his declared ambition to be so. It is not however Hutchinson's ambition. As with Unger, ultimately what Rorty fails to do is 'take seriously his historicist insight.' Thus the theory of personality, which is as important to Rorty as it is to Unger, is equally ahistorical (Hutchinson 1989, pp.560-4, 568).

The better alternative, Hutchinson suggests, is Foucault's 'unrelenting skepticism toward global blueprints for social change', and his particular variety of participatory democracy which uses language, but which is not totally constrained by it. Unlike Foucault, Rorty has taken his existentialism too far and resigned himself to perpetual alienation; the perceived abandonment of the ideal of community, in favour of 'one's own community' (Hutchinson 1989, pp.568-73). Ultimately what Hutchinson is unwilling to accept is any definitive reconstruction of 'democracy', although, perhaps paradoxically, he also suggests that Rorty must effect the transformation of 'the conversation of mankind and not simply continue it.' Suggesting that Rorty 'abandon his flagging enthusiasm for liberal democracy', Hutchinson champions, in its place, an 'unreconstructed democracy because it provides the least worst match with the non-foundationalist project for a truly pluralist polity.' (Hutchinson 1989, p.584)

Perhaps unsurprisingly, the most vitriolic criticism has been saved for Dworkin's vision of liberalism. Dworkin had inherited the neo-Kantian mantle of 'liberal formalism'. Dworkin's rights thesis serves to alienate individuals and deny the role of personality in politics which, correspondingly, determines only the process, and not the meaningful substance of individual rights. Echoing both Unger and Gabel, Hutchinson suggested that the alternative lay in developing a jurisprudence of 'sharing and friendship' (Hutchinson 1984, pp.284-5). Dworkin's liberal vision 'desensitizes the world of personal relations', and the reconstructive alternative lies in in a politics which is 'legitimated by participation and not by principle' (Hutchinson 1988, pp.74-5). The same condemnation of liberalism is directed at James Boyd White, whose attempt to reconstruct participatory possibilities through reading and through the use of literary techniques and literary texts, was condemned once again for the perceived foundational tendencies which haunts such hermeneutical enterprises. The 'search for the hermeneutic grail' inevitably introduces a politics of reading. So too does deconstruction. The critique of the foundationalism of hermeneutics is precisely the same critique which is levelled against Dworkin. The problem with White's approach to literary theory is his ahistoricality; its failure to consider the 'historical situation of particular acts of writing', and to appreciate that language is always necessarily 'lived' (Hutchinson 1988, pp.126-37). It is the same problem which besets Rorty.

Hutchinson's preferred textual engagement is with the French Heideggerian tradition because, unlike the pragmatist, it embraces the full import of textual criticism; historical, social and political. The acknowledgement that critical legal thought must look beyond pragmatism and towards the continental tradition, is an important one:

> Influenced by the French savants, critical theory has dislodged the individual consciousness from its traditional role as the primary source of knowledge and the privileged affixer of meaning. As the significant trends in twentieth century continental theorizing stand in stark contrast to main currents in Anglo-American philosophy, the recent infiltration of continental theory into the Anglo-American tradition has been all the more jarring and perplexing for many. In short, Anglo-American philosophers have preferred positivistic explication to phenomenological critique. Leading continental theorists have been more concerned with evaluating the social dimensions and significance of knowledge, intelligence and rationality... This shift in critical focus has produced a more urgent appreciation of the relation between language and social action. Insofar as the individual consciousness needs to become articulate, it must do so within the social domain of language. Accordingly, we can only express ouselves intelligibly within a pre-existing framework of conceptual relations and social practices. However, although words are silent and need individuals to speak for them, language has a social existence that renders pure intentionality by an individual impossible. Self and other combine and contest in the act of making and remaking meaning. It is in this sense that language must be recognized as both the prize of political conflict and the arena in which the conflict takes place. As language and imagination are inextricably linked, the complex interface between individual consciousness and social systems of meaning is the crucial phase of political engagement. (Hutchinson 1988, p148)

Hutchinson's commitment to a textual approach to critical legal thought is repeatedly emphasised. Thus, whilst disputing the Rortian ambition, the critical textual methodology is overtly conversational; life is itself a story, which defies grand explicatory narratives:

We are never not in a story. History and human action only take on meaning and intelligibility within their narrative context and dramatic settings. There are many stories being imagined and enacted, but we can only listen to them and comprehend them within the vernacular contexts of other stories. Our conversations about these narratives are themselves located and scripted in deeper stories which determine their moral force and epistemological validity... The life of the law is not logic or experience, but a narrative way of world-making... Like all tales, legal stories gain meaning and significance from the selective emphasis of certain features of our always complex and frequently ambiguous experience. As a narrative, legal stories favour some aspects of our experience at the expense of others, thereby empowering some individuals and disenfranchising others. Most importantly, it is the stories themselves that come to comprise the reality of our experience. In this sense, legal stories mediate our engagement in the world and with others: they provide the possibilities the parameters for our own self-definition and understanding. (Hutchinson 1988, pp.13-4)

The textual critique is at once political, and the association of the two is most clearly made in Hutchinson's approach to Michel Foucault. Foucault is deployed as a direct attempt to counter the familiar accusations that deconstruction is inevitably nihilist (Hutchinson 1988, pp.261-93). Ultimately what a Foucaultian critique will realise is 'the constructive possibilities' presented by 'the development of a political theory of discursive practice as the ends and means of a fully democratic polity.' (Hutchinson 1988, pp.266-7) The Foucaultian methodology is to look for points of intersection and transformation in social structures. Hutchinson calls them 'seams'. These are, as Heidegger suggested, at once the strengths and the weaknesses in any power-knowledge arrangements.

The key concept is power. The Foucaultian analysis of power provides a socio-political dimension to the more purely textual critiques. Such power is again both a negative and a potentially positive force. Thus it can subjugate democratic possibilities, as it did in its Marxist appropriation; but at the same time the empowerment of local democratic organs can be a positive force. Along with power, the second key concept in Foucault's analysis is truth. By accepting the Foucaultian variant of the truth problematic as the 'historic complex of power-knowledge relations', he is, of course, acknowledging the later Heideggerian impulse. Thus, again echoing Heidegger, and explicitly citing the similarity of the Arendtian approach, Hutchinson stresses that the key to individual empowerment is temporality (Hutchinson 1988, pp.269-73, 281).

The association of the textual and the political in Hutchinson's critique leads to a reconstructive program not disimilar from those suggested by Unger, Klare or Frug. The critical political challenge is to present an alternative to the 'bureaucratization' of liberal democracy founded upon a revised theory of 'human nature' which 'is not so abstract as to be empty and not so concrete as to be particular':

The essence of human personality is the space between the universal and contingent, the eternal and the ephemeral. It is both within and beyond history. Each person is in part unique and in part representative. The core of humanity lies in each person's capacity for imaginative reconstruction... Democracy is much more than a formal theory of political organization; it is a potent way of daily life. It is not about process, but about action. Democracy means the greatest possible engagement by people in the greatest possible range of communal tasks and public action. Equality, self-determination, individual freedom and personal involvement are the watchwords of a truly democratic culture. (Hutchinson 1984, pp.287. 290)

Ultimately, Hutchinson advocates a radically pluralist approach to intersubjectivity. Accordingly, by 'thinking about and understanding our personal and social lives as complex and overlapping accumulations of such relations, political theory and practice can cut across the traditional organising dichotomies; it can borrow and combine innovatively much from each without succumbing to the excesses and sterile options of either.' Furthermore, an 'acceptance of intersubjectivity helps us to come to terms with our vulnerability to and dependence on others, our commitment to and responsibility for others.' (Hutchinson 1988, p.285) Hutchinson refines his definition of participatory democratic rhetoric accordingly:

> The essence of democracy is that it denies closure or, at least, recognises fully the provisional and historical nature of all judgements and standards for political action; choice and decision-making are necessary, but contingent. In the sense that there cannot be 'a pure and simple landing into a beyond of metaphysics', democracy offers the possibility of accommodating the fact that, while we can never erase or deny the existence of an inside/outside limit, we can be alive to its constructedness and work to keep it on the move... Democracy is the appropriate institutional complement to deconstruction. As deconstruction provides the subversive philosophy to loosen the tenacity of an oppressive culture of rationality, democracy looks to situated interrelationships and represents a form of life that allows the optimal options for transformative politics without losing sight of the sustaining intersubjectivity of social life. Within such a scenario, political knowledge becomes a matter of practical and shared judgment that works to re-cast the world in its own developing and experimental image. (Hutchinson 1988, p.290)

The 'logic of law' is the 'rhetorical experience of life', and lawyers are 'industrial artists'; Rortian poets (Hutchinson 1988, p.290). In his recent analysis of the Canadian Charter of Rights and Freedoms, Hutchinson has applied the textual critique back into the political experience. Approving Unger's idea of solidarity, as the 'social side of love', he appeals for an aesthetic recasting of 'public responsibility' (Hutchinson 1995b, pp.84, 105). There is also explicit approval for Rorty's suggestion that politics can only ever be legitimated by dialogic participation: 'Such a dialectic view of the relations between language, social action, and individual intentionality implies a shift in attention from individuals to the circumstances of their dialogic and constitutive interactions.' Thus, 'conversation and connection' become 'important and valuable in themselves and not simply as a means to the personal end of self-expression: they are the pith and substance of social life.' (Hutchinson 1995b, p.204) Such an 'engaged conversation' can redetermine a politics of solidarity, whilst its implicit 'acceptance of intersubjectivity helps us to come to terms with our vulnerability to and dependence on others as well as our commitment to and responsibility for others.' This, according to Hutchinson, is the politics of postmodernism; a politics of transformative participation and self-assertive conversation. Postmodern citizenship is defined by a 'continuing responsiblity' to self and to others. Ultimately, it is an 'ironic awakening to life's poetic possibilities' (Hutchinson 1988, pp.227-8).

The Philosophy of the Limit: Drucilla Cornell

Drucilla Cornell has taken the deconstructionist and postmodernist teachings of the French tradition and sought to develop from them a new ethics, which she has then applied most immediately to critical legal feminism. Her essential ambition is to counter the idea that not only is critical legal thought nihilist, but that postmodernism is likely to make it even more so. In an essay directed primarily at Unger's idea of personality, Cornell used Derrida to undermine the notion that there can be any 'logic of identity'. It is, she acknowledged, a specifically Kantian critique (Cornell 1985, pp.291-9, 311-4). The use of Derrida is central to all her writings. The critique of Unger is, however, a reconstructive one. Cornell wants to develop the logic of Unger's argument 'beyond' its premature objectivism. The idea of going 'beyond' is, of course, the essence of a Derridean approach. Thus Cornell is in total sympathy with the critique of liberal individualism and formalism, as well as with the hope that the destruction of the ethic of the individual will lead necessarily to a revitalised ethic of the community. Approvingly, she suggests that Unger, in seeking to reroute an ethics from interpersonal relations and the concept of 'passion' is, in fact, developing a neo-Hegelian theory of the subject, but is too 'tentative' in his approach.

It is also, she notes, a Heideggerian interpretation, and an alternative Heideggerian interpretation is also Rortian. Rorty's more pragmatic sympathies help to avoid Unger's objectivism:

> Rorty shares with the French postmodernists a political suspicion of any attempt to say what we are. What is suspected is not only the hypostatization of human life, but also the privileging of one way of being human... One hears echoed in Rorty the call to promote in oneself the compassion for others that develops out of the recognition of our shared experience of finitude... Unger's theory of organic groups in *Knowledge and Politics* is best read in light of this expansive vision, with its emphasis on intersubjectivity and our shared experience of finitude... This reading of Unger also brings to the fore the two central problems we must face in a modern/postmodernist reconstruction of ethics: the redemption of rationality and the situation of the subject. (Cornell 1985, pp.345-8)

Unger's project, read in this Rortian light, is, she rightly adds, an existential one. His 'pragmatism also emerges when he defines an existential project as an individual view that can give meaning to the individual's life'. Unger's 'vision comes close to an existentialism overlaid with a redemptive view of love. Indeed, one can even conceive of Unger as attempting to incorporate what is valid in Sartre's vision while rejecting the bleak implications of the Sartrean conclusion that the divided self can never find its way home.' (Cornell 1985, pp.349, 355) Cornell's alternative is developed from the dialogic reading of Hegel and Heidegger, as presented by Rorty and Bernstein, and by the French 'postmodernists': 'Dialogism involves a commitment to universality: we are all to be recognized as participants in our collective conversation, and we are to hold it out as a possibility that generalizable interests will emerge in the course of that conversation.' (Cornell 1985, p.378) There is thus, following Derrida, a virtue in 'negativity', because it prevents conversational or dialogic closure: 'Negativity, in this context, is a guard against the hypostatization of consensus and a protector of otherness... A dialogic view of the other, by contrast, implies both the negative and positive, as it implies both universality and particularity, both sameness and difference. To privilege either disagreement or agreement is to fail to grasp the dynamic of conversational exchange among equals.' (Cornell 1985, p.369) From such a dialogue can be developed an 'ethic of citizenship', which will radically subjectivize the Kantian ethic of virtue. It is this ethic which, she suggests, was subjugated to the dominant ethic of right, and thus it is this reversal of priorities which can present an alternative Kantian jurisprudence of ethics (Cornell 1985, pp.375-8).

Cornell refines two particular concepts which reveal the influence of temporality from Heidegger and, most immediately, Derrida; 'recollective imagination' and 'transformative legal interpretation'. The development of these ideas, again developed through Derrida's engagement with Heidegger, required an original return to Kant and Hegel, because 'they offer us the most sophisticated starting point from which to begin the task of solving our contemporary legal dilemmas.' (Cornell 1988, p.1136) The postmodern Derridean appropriation of Kant and Hegel is significant in that it rejects the 'favored' contemporary communitarian solution to the reality of political pluralism. It is the adherence to communitarian and objectified consensual solutions which condemns the likes of Dworkin and Rawls to remain within the Kantian metaphysic. In fact, Dworkin fails to see the full Kantian picture, because he fails to appreciate the temporality of the critical project. Continuing the specific critique of Dworkin's integrity and coherence thesis, Cornell cites the locus of postmodern 'principles' in the community where 'institutionalized meaning' resides, and where the past and the future is ever present (Cornell 1988, pp.1145-61, 1170-8). The reconstituted theory of the self, a progression from Kant and Hegel, and from Unger, reveals that 'there is no empirical me that is simply there' and, thus, that desire is not a 'property of the empirical self', but is itself 'an intersubjective relation': 'As a result, this conception of the self as innovative capability does not deny that the subject is a stabilized entity immersed within a field of habits and pre-given linguistic context... It is because of the precedence of the community to the self that the subject can not achieve self-enclosure and, in that sense, create herself as a substantive reality.' (Cornell 1988, pp.1226-7)

The interpretive determination of principles maintains their transformative potential, and it is Dworkin's failure to fully appreciate the deconstructive power of such principles which condemns him to an 'inadequate' socio-political determination of ethics (Cornell 1988, pp.1176-8). The Derridean determination, from which Cornell presents a reconstructed notion of communalism, emphasises the temporality of principle, its past, and moreover its ever present 'beyond'. It is, again, a dialogic ethics; a realization of the 'recollective imagination' and the 'transformative' potential in 'legal interpretation'. The origins of the alternative can be traced through Hegel's and then Heidegger's engagement with Kant, to its contemporary fruition in and then 'beyond' hermeneutic closure, to Derrida's seizure of the later Heidegger. Cornell proceeds by an essentially Heideggerian development of Unger's deviationist doctrine (Cornell 1988, pp.1178-96, 1209). In place of coherence, and as a development of deviationist doctrine, Cornell suggests 'synchronization' as a means of subjectivist determination. This concept becomes ever more important in Cornell's recent writings. Synchronization is the accommodation of temporality.

Cornell's most substantial engagement with postmodernism is presented in *The Philosophy of the Limit*, which represents the application of Derrida in its fullest form to legal and ethical philosophy. It is also, therefore, an application of the 'other'

Kant. The virtue of the term 'the philosophy of the limit' is its immediately Derridean implication of the 'beyond'. From Derrida, Cornell suggests that we can recover a 'new ethical configuration', as an ethics which is not based on duty, but upon respect. The project of postmodernity is an ethical one: 'I will suggest that the entire project of the philosophy of the limit is driven by an ethical desire to enact the ethical relation. Again, by the ethical relation I mean to indicate the aspiration to a nonviolent relationship to the Other, and to otherness more generally, that assumes responsibility to guard the Other against the appropriation that would deny her difference and singularity.' (Cornell 1992a, p.62)

Again the Kantian parallel is marked, and it is certainly no coincidence. In a revealing discussion of Rawls's Kantianism, Cornell suggests that Rawls misused the Kantian division of right and good by objectifying it, and it is this which a Derridean jurisprudence can correct. Indeed, she suggests that there is a inevitable 'affinity' here between Derrida and a post-Kantian jurisprudence. The later Rawls, less foundational, though still objectivist, is more postmodern in his approach. Her definition of ethics, as opposed to morality, as 'the kind of person one must become in order to develop a non-violate relationship with the Other', though more immediately Derridean, is, in fact, the imperative that can be constructed from Kant's second doctrine, of virtue. As Cornell, comments, it is only 'anti-Kantian' in the 'traditional reading of Kant', not in the Derridean engagement. She further acknowledges that the entire critical project revolves around uncovering an alternative locus for the Kantian free-will. This alternative, 'beyond' the internal moral self, lies in 'communicative freedom'. Such a freedom, determined at once by the dialogue of self and community, is thus effected and defined by the 'other'. It is not then, as Gadamer or Rorty suggest, a matter of accessing some sort of notion of 'common sense'. They only pursue the Heideggerian inheritance so far. As the later Heidegger noted, and as Derrida has subsequently acknowledged, communicative freedom cannot be objectified by such metaphysics. Accordingly, any postmodern jurisprudence, from the Kant-Heidegger line, must be an aesthetic jurisprudence (Cornell 1992a, pp.13-5, 30-7).

Derrida's reintroduction of the communal ethic, as effected by an intensely plural, fluid, communicative idea of community is, Cornell admits, 'hesitantly' done (Cornell 1992a, p.60). Though he is keen to impress that it does not have to be the case, Derrida is ever aware of the objectifying lure of community, and the implicit threat of closure. It is this, Cornell again suggests, which serves to entrap Unger. Derrida's awareness is derived from Heidegger's critique of the metaphysics of the Hegelian community and its closing effect. Derrida 'warns us against both the violence of identity that presents the community as a self-contained unit of being and the relegation of the other to a phenomenological relation of asymmetry in which the dance of sameness and difference is forgotten.' (Cornell 1992a, p.40). In the place of the more overtly Hegelian communalism, Derrida suggests 'networks of reciprocally constituted subjects' (Cornell 1992a, p.59). Derrida's hesitancy is derived from his encounter with Heidegger. It is not, however, a hesitancy shared by Cornell who, on the contrary, suggests that we should, in her reading of Heidegger, embrace the 'responsibility' which a pre-contractual postmodern 'community ethic' demands (Cornell 1992a, pp.84-9).

In her more immediately jurisprudential writings, Cornell distinguishes postmodernism from 'strong' neo-Kantianism by developing the notion of the good, as tentatively approached by Rawls but extended by Derrida and Levinas. Thus 'weak' neo-Kantianism is an alternative to more positive neo-Kantian trends, in that it emphasizes that law is never fully enclosed. There is always a 'beyond'. Whereas more radical CLS mistakes non-foundationalism for an impossibility of meaning, and denies the truth of the 'Kantian transcendental ego', more reconstructive critical legal thought must adopt the 'rationalist' counter-position (Cornell 1992a, pp.99-103). A jurisprudence of suitably postmodern principles is a 'necessity'. Indeed the unending 'search for a principle' of legal ethics is what defines a jurisprudence of the 'limit'. Drawing from Derrida's attempt to retrieve a weak neo-Kantian ethic, Cornell suggests:

> In law, reason is a 'practical faith' we are called upon to exercise as an essential aspect of the task of elaborating legal principles. But, of course, if reason cannot ground legal principle in the foundationalist sense through the appeal to the Law of the self-legislating subject, we must be ready to concede to the force of the better interpretation. The exercise of practical reason, in other words, demands that we continually engage in dialogue with one another... The Law of Law calls us to interpretation through an appeal to justice, and this process of interpretation also projects the good of the community, which is itself only an interpretation and not the last word on what the good of the community actually should be. (Cornell 1992a, pp.107, 113)

Ultimately, the philosophy of the limit is, as Heidegger first demanded, a philosophy of responsibility. It is, thus, a philosophy which preserves the 'beyond' in the co-determinative relation of self and community, and with it the ever-present potential of interpretive transformation. Cornell concludes: 'Interpretation is transformation. Thus, we need to remember that we are responsible, as we interpret, for the direction of that transformation. We cannot escape our responsibility implicit in every act of interpretation. The delimitation of ontology reminds us of the positivist fallacy that the legal world is just given to us as a self-perpetuating mechanism. We are left with a reminder of the inescapability of our responsibility for the *nomos* as it is perpetuated and thus transformed.' (Cornell 1992a, p.115)

The call to responsibility is, jurisprudentially, most immediately, a 'call to judicial responsibility'. It is at once a call to acknowledge the ever present juristic 'beyond'. It is a jurisprudential rebellion against 'metaphysics', and against legal positivism. The 'ethical resistance' described by Derrida 'allows us to understand why legal interpretation always involves both discovery and invention'. The judicial 'responsibility' is 'not to an accurate repitition through the recollection of legal norms, but to a refutation that what has been can ever be conflated with Justice'. Accordingly, 'the judge is responsible for his or her projection of the good embodied in the *nomos*.' (Cornell 1992a, p.118) It is not, she again emphasises, a rejection of Kant. Rather it is Derrida's search for the 'other' Kant. Most particularly it is the search for an alternative ethics derived from the premises of judgment:

> this responsibility is connected with the very idea of judgment. Judgment is only judgment and not mere calculation or recollection if it is 'fresh'. The judge is called upon to do just that, judge... The unique Derridean contribution to legal interpretation is to show us why the act of memory in judging involves the seemingly contradictory notion that the judge, in his or her decision, remembers the future, which is why the understanding of the traditional conception of time is relevant to a discussion of interpretation and responsibility. (Cornell 1992a, p.120)

Cornell's discussion of judgment, as suggested by Kant and developed through the writings of Derrida and Lyotard, is the epitome of critical legal thought, and finally brings the 'other' Kant to presence. It at once marries the past, the present and the future, and effects the full import of Heideggerian temporality, and brings into play the full potentiality of an interpretively transformative understanding of jurisprudence. Without the Derridean 'beyond', 'transformation would not be transformation, but only evolution, and in that sense, continuation.' Effecting both the Derridean and the Heideggerian insight, she writes:

> In this sense legal interpretation must be both discovery and invention because there can be no simple origin of legal meaning, whether we call it intent of the founders of the Constitution or some other name... In this sense, interpretation is always an act; moreover, an act for which we cannot escape responsibility... I am using responsibility in the sense that we are accountable for our own actions and our judgments. We are responsible precisely because we cannot be reduced to automatons who cannot choose to do other than what comes naturally... We have to think again about the responsibility to memory that is demanded by deconstruction and the deconstructibility of law. (Cornell 1992a, pp.147-9)

Cornell has applied her jurisprudence of the 'limit' most effectively to feminist issues. In her opinion the philosophy of the limit demands the 'responsibility' to hear the specific 'call' of woman (Cornell 1992b). The ethical possibilities presented by postmodernism have not been lost on other feminist lawyers. Mary Joe Frug championed a very similar thesis, suggesting that, despite its socio-political roots, critical legal feminism must now look across the Atlantic towards the textualism of such as Derrida (Frug 1992, pp.4-20, 125-53). The ambition is to use textuality as a means of rewriting the feminine. The virtue of text is its possession of this 'transformative' potential. Whilst supporting the common search for a feminist ethics, Cornell is unable to accept the phenomenology which accompanies any purely empirical political approach. Phenomenology standing alone, as the later Heidegger recognises, and as deconstruction reveals, positivises. Thus a phenomenological feminism positivises women. Cornell challenges the fixity of a feminist reality, which she suggests, denies transformative possibilities. Thus 'a' feminist voice, as opposed to 'the' feminist voice can replace silence, and effect transformation (Cornell 1991, pp.119-64).

The alternative is a postmodern textuality derived from Heidegger and most immediately from Derrida, but which, at the same time, embraces the Lacanian understanding of the 'Law of the Father'; in other words, that women are the non-Law, the 'other'. The textual strategy is to write the politics of Lyotard's *Differend*; to give voice to that which is shut out, or silenced, or 'beyond'. It is a matter of self-assertion, as the self-assertion of the 'other' (Cornell 1991, pp.21-77). Derrida's deconstruction of

Lacan reveals the 'presence' of the ethics in the 'beyond'. Thus, Cornell asserts that there can be written a feminist 'truth', but that, in obeisance to Derrida's warning, it is a truth which must not be objectified. Such a truth, recoverable from the temporal limits determined by Derrida, must be asserted or 'presenced' in the place of silence. Here she also cites Arendt's metaphor of ethical (wo)man between past and future. But it will never be the objectified truth, because there will always be a 'beyond'. This is the lesson of Derrida's interpretation of *Before the Law* (Cornell 1991, p.109). Justice, as Derrida pointed out, is deconstruction and deconstruction is law, precisely because justice is the ever present and ever future 'other'.

Thus, in turn, justice can only ever be accessed, at least partially, in language. It is within language, and to language, that the feminist 'call' must be directed:

> Deconstruction uncovers this obligation as an obligation, rather than as a paternalistic response to our failure to speak in their discourse... In this way, the alliance of deconstruction and feminism is crucial if we are not to endorse a conception of justice that entraps us in what is as the only basis for a positive definition. We are constantly envisioning what cannot be seen or even imagined, a society in which human beings were not crippled by the hierarchical structure of gender identity. To break our silence we are forced to break up the so-called 'real'. But the *l'avenir* of justice does not mean that we can escape our responsibility to engage in political and judicial battles as they are present to us now... But we must also recognize that as we articulate injustices against justice, we do not presume to define justice once and for all. We are called to work within the law but we should not conflate law with justice. As we work within the law we are also called to 'remember' the disjuncture between law and justice that deconstruction always insists upon. (Cornell 1991, pp.115-6)

The new feminist ethics is a textual ethics, like any and every ethics, and so it is never a merely feminist ethics, but rather an ethics of the limit or the 'beyond'. Deconstruction 'keeps open the threshold to a different destiny' (Cornell 1991, p.202).

The possibilities of the 'beyond' permit Cornell to rewrite a philosophy of right. Echoing Unger, she advocates a 'full program' of transformative rights as a mechanism for effecting the textual empowerment of the feminine voice. In her most recent writings, Cornell has further acknowledged the Kantian nature of the 'philosophy of the limit'. It is Kantian in its essential concern with effecting the reconciliation of freedom with equality. In *The Imaginary Domain*, Cornell rewrites a feminism based on Kantian autonomy as determined explicitly in Rawls's idea of 'self-respect' as a 'primary good', and thus implicitly by Kant's doctrine of virtue. A theory of personality is created only within the domain of free-will. Cornell describes her project as one of 'Kantian constructivism' based on 'minimum conditions of individuation' (Cornell 1995, pp.3-18). Thus issues of abortion, pornography and sexual harassment should be determined with regard to the extent to which the woman's right to self-assertion is constrained. This determination is made as a 'Kantian understanding of freedom under law' (Cornell 1995, pp.173-85). The philosophy of the limit, the articulation of the Derrida-Heidegger engagement in postmodern jurisprudence, is redetermined and returned to the original Kantian idea of autonomy. In this way, the cutting edge of contemporary critical legal thought returns to Kant and to the fundamentals of Kantian critique.

CHAPTER 6

RELATIVISM AND THE RETURN OF THE MORAL SELF

1 Relativism and Formalism

The Neo-Kantian Inheritance: Ernst Cassirer

It was Ernst Cassirer who redefined Kantianism for the contemporary audience. The previous four chapters have sought to trace the genealogy of an alternative Kantianism, developed from the third *Critique*. That which is alternative to is the more orthodox neo-Kantian relativist and formalist variants, as articulated by Cassirer and then by such as Gustav Radbruch and Ernest Weinrib. Whereas the postmodern variants hope to effect a renewed postmodern political ethics, relativist and formalist variants decry such metaphysical ambitions. Cassirer, Radbruch and Weinrib have relatively less to say about ethics, but a great deal to say about the form of Kantian legal thought. The ethics of neo-Kantianism has only re-emerged with a renewed interest in jurisprudential philosophies of the moral self, most recently articulated by Ronald Dworkin. We will turn to Dworkin in the second part of this chapter.

In 1918 Ernst Cassirer published his *Kant's Life and Thought*. It both reflected and enhanced Cassirer's reputation as the most important translator of Kant's ideas from the eighteenth century to the twentieth century audience. As the leading neo-Kantian philosopher he enjoyed a virtually unrivalled position in German intellectual circles (Hamburg 1949). His only challenger was Martin Heidegger, with whom he met at Davos in 1929 to debate the true inheritance of Kant. Where Heidegger suggested that the Kantian inheritance must be drawn from metaphysics, Cassirer countered that it was Kant's theory of science and form which mattered most (Pos 1949, pp.66-7). In his biography of Kant, Cassirer identified three strains in contemporary neo-Kantian philosophy, absolutism, neo-Kantian absolutism, and the most dominant of all, neo-Kantian pluralism. Cassirer very firmly aligned himself with the latter. Relativism and formalism have followed suit. This alignment with neo-Kantian pluralism was in large part due to the considerable influence of Hermann Cohen. In Cohen and the Marburg School Cassirer perceived an authority for the retrieval of German philosophy from the mysticism of the nineteenth century. What Cohen emphasised was the appreciation of the limits of reason, and the unavoidability of experience as an indeterminable factor in human cognition. Above all Cohen stressed the creative power of the historically situated individual and Marburg neo-Kantian pluralism was driven hard in this direction. It was Cohen who convinced Cassirer that any philosophical enterprise had to begin with Kant (Gawronsky 1949, pp.3-37).

Thus at the same time as sharing an obvious admiration for Kant's philosophy, Cassirer's particular interest in Kant was in part a response to his pervasive interest in the history of philosophy. Cassirer was committed to the belief that philosophy was always an historical enterprise. He suggested that the eighteenth century had been the first century which had concentrated on history, and it was this concentration which neo-Kantianism should restore. It was primarily an issue of 'method'. Reason was 'method', and so too was history. It became the 'methodological model' of the eighteenth century. As ever, at the end of a long line of historical Enlightenment thinkers there is Kant, and his critical historical anthropology. In a specific study of Enlightenment theories of law and state, Cassirer stressed its increasing awareness of the contingency of law and politics. The Enlightenment, and Enlightenment philosophers, including Kant, were concerned with law as a component of the unitary whole of philosophy, culture, history and so on. Law could not thus be considered in isolation from any other 'discipline', precisely because it was a component of these disciplines. In Cassirer's perception, the history of Enlightenment legal thought was a history of increasing scepticism. It was only with Rousseau, and then with Kant and the emphasising of the notion of immanent individual right, that philosophy was able to reclaim a concept of justice from the abyss of scepticism (Cassirer 1951, pp.197-201, 262-74).

Thus in the philosophy of law, as in the philosophy of history, Kant lay at the end of the Enlightenment tradition, giving it articulation and structure. Above all, philosophy was an active doing thing; at once political, legal and ethical. It was a realisation of this essential fact which the Enlightenment had bequeathed to future generations, along with an appreciation of the creative power of thought and its interaction with immediate surroundings (Cassirer 1951, pp.18-9). In the final section of *The Philosophy of the Enlightenment*, which investigated the approach of aesthetics, it was again Kant whom Cassirer suggested had given aesthetic philosophy structure. It was Kant who first emphasised the contingency of ethical and aesthetical judgment, and it was the book in which he did so with greatest success, the *Critique of Judgement*, which represented the 'climax' of the entire Enlightenment project (Cassirer 1951, pp.325, 333). Not surprisingly, the centrality of the third *Critique* was the dominant theme of Cassirer's biography of Kant. Moreover, it was the themes of historicity, of the morally driven and creative individual, of language and its constructive potential - the themes which lay at the heart of the *Critique* - which Cassirer used to redefine the nature of neo-Kantian pluralism.

The desire to break the mould, to present a critique of metaphysical method, lay at the very beginning of Kant's writings, and Cassirer's commentary on these 'beginnings' is one of the most important and revealing sections in his biography of Kant. In Cassirer's opinion, Kant's critical 'turn' was more accurately an intensification. Before he attempted to construct the first *Critique*, Kant was already concerned not with the 'what' of objects, but the 'how'; the mind itself, not the object. Although he subsequently concentrated on the third *Critique* as the classic exposition of Kantian critical philosophy, Cassirer was keen to stress the critical in the first *Critique*. The first *Critique* is a critique of reasoning itself, of how we know objects, and thus, according to Cassirer, the central concept in the first *Critique* is precisely the same as it is in the third, 'judgment'.

Its perceived 'preeminence' in 1781 encouraged Cassirer to construct a considerable degree of continuity throughout Kant's critical philosophy, from the first to the third *Critique*. In doing so, he makes much of Kant's increasing interest during the 1780s in ethical and political philosophy. The political writings represented 'the whole foundation of the new conception of the essence of the state of history that Kant had developed', and the historicity which became explicit in these essays was 'momentous'. Kant's reassertion of the historicity of the critical philosophical enterprise presented 'the decisive crisis of the philosophy of the German Enlightenment.' These 'first stirrings of the Kantian philosophy of history' thus lead us to 'encounter a decisive turn that his completely clear'. From then on, according to Cassirer, Kant is at once a historian of philosophy and historicist philosopher (Cassirer 1981, pp.238-41). The encounter with history directs Kant inexorably towards ethics; just as it does with Cassirer. The Kantian philosophy of ethics stresses, above all, the contingent nature of substantive ethics, within the synthetic *a priori* framework. The role of Kantianism is to stress the constructive potential of substantive contingency, guided by a 'universal and overriding ground of determination'. The key to understanding Kant's philosophy of ethics is to appreciate the centrality of the self-determining morally driven individual. Thus the essential concept for any Kantian philosophy of ethics is autonomy (Cassirer 1981, pp.220-7, 238-41).

The *Critique of Judgement* represented a 'revolution' in critical moral and political philosophy, which 'launched a whole new movement of thought' and which 'determined the direction of the entire post-Kantian philosophy'. It was the culmination of an inexorable evolution in Kant's thinking. The *Critique* was not generated by any sudden interest in aesthetics, but was the development dicatated by the logic of Kant's critical project. More than anything, the third *Critique*, as a critique of judgment, 'by definition' concentrated the historicity of Kant's thought most particularly upon the relationship between the individual and the community, the particular and the universal (Cassirer 1981, pp.272-83). The entire *Critique* becomes a 'striving' to accommodate the particular and the universal, within the individual perception. The role of the individual, and individual judgment as a 'doing' thing, leads Kant, and Cassirer, to stress the importance of the idea of 'purposiveness' in human actions, and from there to stress the 'mode of interconnection' between human actions, and then finally to arrive at 'relativism'. Cassirer is keen to stress that 'purposiveness' and 'relativism' are not to be read as divisive or nihilistically indeterminate concepts; but as Kantian concepts and harmonic constructs. 'Purposiveness' thus means 'nothing other than individual creation, which displays a unified form in itself and in its structure' (Cassirer 1981, p.312). The concept of freedom demands that everything should have its own internal structure, and is thus never causally dependent on external nature. Cassirer is particularly keen, throughout his commentary on the third *Critique*, to stress that all the *Critiques* converge on this single point; the position of the immanent end (Cassirer 1981, pp.350-2).

Once Kant has emphasised the power of individual creation, and the relativity of a harmonic perception, or judgment, of this creation, then the next stage is to accommodate judgment with communication. Thus, Cassirer stresses, to say that something is beautiful or good is to say that others may find it beautiful or good. This is the concept of 'subjective universality', which presumes 'universal communicability'. According to Cassirer, 'universal communicability' was the 'principal question' which stood 'at the crossroads of all aesthetic discussions in the eighteenth century'. The 'new route' which it suggested was one of persuasion rather then objective certainty (Cassirer 1981, pp.313-21). Cassirer concluded his study of Kant by considering what he calls the 'last battles', expressed in Kant's political writings. The political writings were an inevitable culmination of Kant's work, because they concentrated solely on the human rather than on nature, and revealed their author's own innate 'humanity'. From Kant onwards, philosophers, certainly neo-Kantian philosophers, would look to the issues of applied ethics and political philosophy, just as Kantian ethical and political theorists would recognise the need to ground their own writings in a coherent moral philosophy. Kant's ultimate achievement was then to effect a harmonic whole in philosophical thinking (Cassirer 1981, pp.414-7).

Cassirer's own philosophical ambitions, unsurprisingly, follow both the spirit and the substance of Kant's. Apart from his historical studies of Kant and the Enlightenment, and his later concentration on political theory, the greater part of Cassirer's career was spent in developing his theory of symbolic form. The inspiration for this project, as he repeatedly acknowledged, lay in the questions raised by Kant's third *Critique* and particularly the communication of knowledge. The idea that thought constructs, and is constructed by, symbols came directly from Kant's 'images', and represented a unity of the sensuous and the intellectual in precisely the same way. At the same time, as with Kant's images, Cassirer's symbols are given meaning solely by man's experience. Symbols are, thus, internally constructive. Cassirer's critical comment, that 'the ethical world is never given; it is forever in the making', articulates the pluralist nature of his Kantianism, and its concentration around the creative subjectivity of the immanently driven individual. His subsequent ethical essays concentrated still further on the creative capacity of the individual, and perhaps most importantly of all, on the resultant relativism of symbolic forms. In his *Essay on Man* Cassirer chose to stress the centrality of the concept of responsibility in human affairs; precisely the same concept was being similarly championed by his great rival Heidegger for precisely the same reason. The individual is ethically responsible on two levels; because the individual creates a community culture and a community ethics, in accordance with universal imperatives, and the individual then creates its manner of communication (Cassirer 1944).

For Cassirer, symbols were both constructively rational and experiential and, thus, also social and mythical in form. They were also inevitably historicist; anything that is creative is historicist. In his influential essay *Language and Myth*, his most famous exposition of the immanent association of language with cultural experience, Cassirer expressly acknowledged once again that the critical influence was Kant's. It was Kant who revealed that reality was always experience, and that human experience was therefore immediately relative, and in turn that language was thus itself an internalised concept, determined by its own immanent rationality. Cassirer was the first in the tradition of neo-Kantians to produce a theory of communicative or discursive rationality; a mode of communication which is both determined by and determines man's experience (Cassirer 1946a, Langer 1949).

Just as Cohen's pluralism had developed Kantianism a step further, so Cassirer's relativism represented another evolutionary stage towards our current understanding of neo-Kantian moral and political philosophy. The concentration on the relativity of symbolic form and language took Cassirer 'beyond' established neo-Kantianism, and led to the development of a particular type of pluralist relativism which accommodated fundamental objective indeterminacy, and which proved to be a major impetus for more sceptical and, at first glance, specifically anti-foundationalist political philosophies. Substantive indeterminacy, according to Cassirer, was an inevitablity of man's creative freedom; creation can only follow a decision between indeterminacies (Cassirer 1949, pp.878-80). Varieties of Kantian constructivism can be traced back to Cassirer's redefinition of pluralism and his acceptance of relative morality. According to Kaufmann, the two strands of neo-Kantianism, that represented by the more immediate Kantian pluralism of Cassirer and that represented by phenomenological existentialism of Heidegger, come together in a shared belief in constructivism and the creative power of the mind, and particularly its discursive creativity (Kaufmann 1949, pp.823-31).

As with Kant, it was later in life that Cassirer became increasingly interested in the more concrete problems of ethics and politics. There were both theoretical and practical reasons for this. On the one hand, the evolution of Cassirer's philosophy had led him to concentrate more and more on the creative capacity of the individual. Philosophy, he realised, more than anything was a 'doing' thing. On the political-cultural level, Cassirer further appreciated and, perhaps to a certain extent, shared the deep spiritual crisis which swept across Europe during the 1920s, and culminated in Germany in the rise of Adolf Hitler. He delved deep into the nature of modern society and the human condition, applying his theory of symbolic forms to the various realms of human culture, and above all emphasising the central role of symbols in creating both culture and history. The individual was indissolubly bound up in language, culture and history (Cassirer 1944, p.191).

In *The Myth of the State* Cassirer expressly addressed the nature of totalitarianism and its reliance on creative symbolic form. Here again, he was keen to emphasise the unity of experience and reason in language and myth. Perhaps more strongly than before, he also reemphasised that the key to understanding politics and ethics lay in understanding communication, both linguistically and symbolically. Language and symbolic form objectify social experience and history. Myths, including the modern myths around which totalitarian philosophies such as Nazism and Stalinism were constructed, were generated by rhetoric; words used as a mechanism for divorcing reason from experience. Totalitarianism, according to Cassirer, in its denial of historicity, was peculiar in its use of communication to destroy morality (Cassirer 1946b, pp.3-49, 189-257).

It is the use of history which defines the neo-Kantian position, and establishes it as the counter to totalitarian political philosophy. It is perhaps fitting that Cassirer should have concluded his final major work by stressing the need to return to a Kantian alternative in order to counter pervasive spiritual pessimism. In the conclusion to *The Myth of the State*, Cassirer emphasised that his neo-Kantianism, as opposed to Heideggerianism, represented the true inheritance. Unlike Heidegger's concentration on the existential individual, Cassirer accommodated the free individual with the morally driven individual. Myth ultimately subjugates the individual; reason liberates. In the final analysis, the neo-Kantian position, inevitably, remained securely founded upon the critical conception of freedom:

> Freedom is one of the most obscure and ambiguous terms not only of philosophical but also of political language... As to political freedom all of us know that it is one of the most used and abused slogans. All political parties have assured us that they are ever the true representatives and guardians of freedom. But they have always defined the term in their own sense and used it for their particular interests. Ethical freedom is, at bottom, a much simpler thing... In the ethical sense a man is a free agent if these motives depend upon his own judgment and own conviction of what moral duty is. According to Kant freedom is equivalent to autonomy. It does not mean indeterminism, it rather means a special kind of determination. It means that the law which we obey in our actions is not imposed from without but that the moral subject gives the law to itself. (Cassirer 1946b, p.287)

The complementary echoes of Kant and Heidegger could not be more striking.

Relativism: Gustav Radbruch

The leading neo-Kantian legal theorist in Germany during the first half of this century was Gustav Radbruch. It was Radbruch who accepted the authority of Cassirer's translation and an investigation of his legal thought reveals precisely how a relativist and pluralist neo-Kantianism translates into the field of legal philosophy (Wolf 1958). Radbruch paid homage to Kant and the 'bright faith of reason' which Kant had infused within him, and his *Philosophy of Law* remains the most impressive presentation of a neo-Kantian relativist jurisprudence.

The fundamental dichotomy in Radbruch's legal thought is that between science and philosophy. It was only in the sphere of juridical science, not legal philosophy, that Radbruch considered the issue of validity and accommodated positivism. Thus, although Radbruch recognised that 'interpretation' was a keystone of the legal science, and stressed that 'juridical interpretation is directed toward the objectively valid meaning of the legal rule', he clung rigidly to a rational basis for interpretation (Radbruch 1950, pp.140-1). His was 'logic interpretation' and 'distinguished from... intuitive forms of interpretation by its utterly rational nature.' The other keystones are 'construction' and 'systemisation': 'the task of legal science is to work out its material in two ways; categorically, to present the law as the realisation of the concept of law and its component legal categories, and teleologically, to depict the law as attempted realisation of the idea of law.' (Radbruch 1950, p.144) The importance of this dichotomy cannot be overemphasised. The influence of Anglo-American jurisprudence was considerable. He cited Bentham and Austin as the pioneers of the science of law (Radbruch 1936). But legal science is strictly limited and quite 'helpless' when 'faced' with more important problems posed by the 'collision of norms' (Radbruch 1950, p.113). It is in philosophy, in the world of norms not the world of science and validity, that Radbruch develops his legal philosophy. In the opening sentance of *Philosophy of Law*, Radbruch asserts that 'legal philosophy is a part of philosophy'.

That legal philosophy is an integral part of general philosophy is a Kantian premise which can only be understood 'in connection with a universal philosophical system' (Chroust 1944, p.25). Apart from the theory of universality and the fundamental Kantian concept of the categorical imperitive, the other pillars of Radbruch's philosophy include the theory of cognition, of reality and value, methodological dualism, the separation of 'is and ought', and reason, both the idea and the practical reality. The most fundamental of these premises is 'distinguishing reality from value'. The distinction is made as an 'achievement of the mind'; what Kant termed the 'theory of Cognition' (Radbruch 1950, p.49). If legal philosophy is 'the evaluating view of law' the method of evaluation is characterised by two features; methodological dualism and relativism: 'Kantian philosophy has taught us that it is impossible from what is to derive what is valuable, what is right, what ought to be.' (Radbruch 1950, p.53) Where 'morals require morality, law requires only legality' (Radbruch 1950, p.85).

Kant's 'categorical imperitave' and the idea of a 'universal moral law' lie at the heart of Radbruch's legal philosophy. The imperative contributes effectiveness as well as universality: 'the very essence of the imperative is not to oblige but to determine, not to be valid, but to be effective.' (Radbruch 1950, p.83) Accordingly: 'Life while it is being lived is subject to the universally valid laws of the good, the true, the beautiful... The only way of a people sure of itself is, not to create a distinct national culture mirroring itself, but to create human values.' (Radbruch 1950, pp.210-3) Although accommodating a humanistic positivism, Radbruch's Kantian sensibilities would have been offended by any absorption of reality and value. Not simply because it would infringe the methodological dualism, but because it would stray from philosophy into the quite separate sphere of legal science (Radbruch 1950, p.61).

The Kantian imperative and universality are critical because they inhere the tripartite qualities of Radbruch's philosophy of law; law must be consistent, effective and just. These are the 'ideas of legal value'; thus once again preserving the distinction between reality and value. Furthermore, they are immanently contradictory, such that 'justice and expediency become contradictory' whilst 'legal certainly demands positivity, yet positive law claims to be valid without regard to its justice or expediency.' This, Radbruch continues, betrays the inherent contradiction within positivism: 'Positivity is a fact, positive law presupposes a power that lays it down... Indeed the demands of legal certainty may ultimately conflict with the conclusions from that very positivity which is required by legal certainty.' (Radbruch 1950, p.110)

A Kantian 'idea of law' serves to reinforce the integration of morality in the philosophy of law, without impinging upon the distinction between reality and value.

Thus 'the idea of law can be none other than justice' (Radbruch 1950, p.73). In his own copy of *Philosophy of Law* Radbruch annotated, 'Justice not expediency, is the ideal of law' (Wolf 1958, p.13). But justice is not an exhaustive principle and, as Radbruch subsequently admitted, 'justice is the specific idea of law...but it does not exhaust the law...justice alone has been found to be insufficient for legal rules of definite contents to be derived from it.' (Radbruch 1950, p.90) Law serves morality, but the integrity of reality and justice is preserved; justice is 'only a value...the law itself, on the other hand, is a definite reality, related to a certain value.' Ultimately then, Radbruch's 'Idea of Law and Justice' is congruent with Kant's 'universal moral law' (Chroust 1944, pp.29-31).

The beauty of Kantian universality lay in the immanence of morality and justice. But so did its problems. Radbruch was afflicted by the indeterminacy that had come to dominate neo-Kantianism. Radbruch was quite aware of the indeterminacy of reason. But that is also something which he was quite prepared to reconcile. Indeterminacy necessitates neither positivism nor natural law; rather it proves the necessity of foundationalist pluralism. The humanistic and the religious combined in Radbruch to produce an ultimate ambition to 'perfect all human justice' (Chroust 1944, p.23). These humanistic influences were pervasive, and determined the nature of Radbruch's pluralism, his cultural relativism, his rationalism, and finally, provided the impetus for the ultimate purpose of his work; social justice.

As with Cassirer, Radbruch's ethical relativism was the inevitable product of the Kantian distinction between reality and value, and the admission of indeterminacy. Radbruch recognised that the key concepts of legal philosophy were all indeterminate or 'abstract'; the individual, equality, justice, even law itself: 'Man's urge toward knowledge will attempt again and again to break through this relativistic self-limitation... Relativism welcomes every such attempt as a clarification of a particular legal philosophical decision... But relativism cannot help rejecting the pretended universality of any such attempt and demonstrating its ties to very definite basic assumptions of world outlook.' (Radbruch 1950, p.69) Thus, positivism is only positivism insofar as it is prescribed by relativism, just as the same is true of natural law. Radbruch repeatedly emphasised the fundamental relativity of values, quoting from Goethe: 'I understand again... that the different ways of thought are founded upon the differences of men, and that for this very reason a general uniform conviction is impossible.' (Radbruch 1950, p.59) The purpose of relativism, according to Radbruch, is thus 'to determine only whether any value judgment is right in relation to a particular supreme value judgment, within the framework of a particular outlook on values and the world, but not whether that value judgment and that outlook on values and the world are right in and of themselves.' (Radbruch 1950, p.57) Radbruch emphasised that 'legal form' was always 'transitory' and, moreover, that interpretation was always 'relative' and indeterminate. As such the evolution of existentialist philosophy nurtured Radbruch's relativism: 'the existential relationship is firmer than an ideal relationship can ever be.' (Radbruch 1950, p.138)

On a more practical level, relativism was a means of facilitating social change. Yet relativism was a double-edged sword; a threat to any ideology, democratic or non-democratic. There was an antinomy within relativism. But antinomy was the very nature of relativism; a fact appreciated by Radbruch himself, who asserted that he had 'no fear of such irreconcilable antinomies, to decide oneself is to live.' At the same time, 'logical Relativism' formed 'the truly philosophical basis of a working democracy', and it was the only effective weapon against 'rational Absolutism' (Chroust 1944, p.28). An acceptance of philosophical relativism in ethical theory opened the question of community and constructive rationality. Radbruch concentrated on stressing the distinction between the constructive capacity of culture, and the wholly destructive capacity of custom. Again the comparison with Cassirer is striking. Custom represented one of the chief threats to democratic society and law; the intersection of a community law with customary law, was one of the dangers which Radbruch, like Cassirer, perceived in Nazism. Culture, not custom, was the catalyst of relativism. Culture was an expression of society, 'as a means to cultivate the person' (Radbruch 1950, p.94). The humanist concept of the individual, though an abstraction, was an important one.

Purpose was of paramount importance to Radbruch, as indeed it was to Kant, and philosophically the purpose of law was 'to serve only... the ethical value of the good.' Although keen to impress 'the independence' of the validity of the law from 'purposes', Radbruch was also aware of the need for expediency rather than abstract justice alone (Radbruch 1950, pp.91, 123, 199). As ever, law necessitated all three antinomies. Thus, although Radbruch's ultimate desire was to make 'perfect all human justice', as Chroust rightly observes, for Radbruch, in the final analysis, 'law is essentially a practical or cultural concept, while morality is only a purely theorectical value-concept.' (Chroust 1944, p.33) Purpose is the vital component of law, 'able to fill the abstract thought of justice with the effective fire of individual life.' (Radbruch 1950, p.136) Again Radbruch coincides justice with the individual, and again the Kantian influence is clear, because, for Kant, the freedom of the individual will was the medium through which reason becomes practical.

Of course, purpose itself is indeterminate and relativism precludes any absolute purpose. Thus, ultimately, the role of any philosopher, and certainly Radbruch's self-perceived role, is not to provide any answers. For Radbruch, 'the task of philosophy is not to take the final practical decision in all relevant matters, that is action, out of our hands. Philosophy like all theory should only make us aware... The final solution of all philosophical questions and problems rests with our work and practical resolves.' (Chroust 1944, p.41) Accordingly, Radbruch is again quite willing to accommodate antinomies within his relativistic scheme: 'A philosophical system is to resemble a Gothic cathedral in which the masses support each other by pressing against each other. How suspect would be a philosophy that did not consider the world a purposeful creation of reason and yet resolved it into a rational system with no contradiction.' (Radbruch 1950, p.112) The reconciliation of fundamental substantive indeterminacy is explicitly Kantian:

Kant's critique of reason has shown that reason is not an arsenal of finished theoretical cognitions, of ethical and aesthetical norms ready to be applied, but rather the mere power to arrive at such cognitions and norms; that is not a complex of anwers, but rather one of questions, of points of view from which what is given is to be appreciated; of forms which need to be filled with a given substance, of categories which need to be applied to a given material, in order to yield statements or judgments of definitive content. These cognitions, or evaluations, which are definite in content are never produced by pure reason, but always only by its application to something definitely given. (Radbruch 1950, p.60)

The combination of purpose, practical reason and humanism came together in Radbruch's concern for social justice and social reform; what Chroust terms his 'slogan' of 'human civilisation and progress' (Chroust 1944, p.37). There can be no doubt that Radbruch's political interests fuelled his determination to make his philosophy of law practical. He certainly believed in the power of ideas which, through the medium of legal philosophy, could lead to social revolution, but emphasised that: 'The ideas do not fight the struggle of the interests all over again in the clouds like the Valkyries above the battlefield; rather, like Homeric gods, they descend to the battlefield and fight, powerful forces themselves, side by side with the other forces... All great political changes were prepared or accompanied by legal philosophy. In the beginning there was legal philosophy; at the end there was revolution.' (Radbruch 1950, p.55) Legal order cannot dominate; it can only command. Only ideas can dominate. Revolution is facilitated of course, by relativism. At the same time: 'Relativism permits a free and tolerant exchange of thought, and therefore, a democratic form of life.' (Radbruch 1950, p.121)

Formalism: Ernest Weinrib

Ernest Weinrib has acknowledged that formalism resembles 'a heresy driven underground' (Weinrib 1988, p.950). Formalism is not, of course, congruent with relativism. Formalism does not seek to provide the substantive complement which relativism adds to the formal analysis of legal norms and structure. But, as an articulation of this normative analysis, legal formalism sits squarely within the neo-Kantian tradition, and Weinrib's affiliation with Kantianism is unambiguous. Formalism cannot be understood outside of Kant. In his opinion all legal and political theorists, at least of liberal leaning, are 'Kant's children', although this truth seems to be more tangible in political ethics than in political science. The distinction between Kantian theories of law and Kantian theories of ethics and the moral self is absolutely fundamental (Weinrib 1987a, pp.501-3).

It was the failure to observe this absolute which served to condemn Unger's attempt to rewrite a Kantian political ethics in *Passion*. Unger's mistake was to proceed without recognising that the moral self is determined by practical reason (Weinrib 1985). This is not to condemn Unger's ambition, for we are all critical legal theorists though perhaps of different kinds: 'we can philosophize with Kant or against Kant, but not without Kant' (Weinrib 1987a, p.474). It was Kant who placed law within the limits of reason, and determined it as an 'idea of reason'. These are the ultimate limits of the law which effect its immanent integral rationality. At the same time, the idea of reason 'refers' in its 'practical reality' to the Kantian conception of free-will. Everything practical 'converges' on the free-will. The idea of reason, as an idea, is determined by the moral personality; as an articulation of moral purposiveness it is self-determined and self-asserted. It finds its expression in the categorical imperative and then, in turn, in the self-asserted 'juridical person'. In modern political thought the idea of reason is translated, via the imperative, into the idea of rational right as the emanation of the 'moral law within', and thus as the determination of free-will and the immanent relation between free-wills. It is this which determines 'duty'. Thus 'we can see how the coherence of law as a Kantian idea of reason is grounded in the will's integration of free choice and practical reason'. It is the 'confirmation' of one's existential autonomy (Weinrib 1987a, pp.481-94).

The essential tenet of Kantian legal formalism is the immanent rationality of legal form or structure. It is not, then, a jurisprudence which troubles itself with the substance of law. In this sense it is positivistic. But it demands a rationality which is nowhere required in legal positivism, and denies the politics which is nowhere denied in positivism. It is also about the autonomy of law; law is autonomous, but autonomous within general philosophical tenets. Most of all, law must be 'differentiated from politics'. The 'political, in contrast to the juridical, refers to considerations whose intelligibility stands outside the interconnecting aspects of juridical form' (Weinrib 1988, pp.951, 964-5, 988). This does not mean that legal formalism is not critical. Weinrib takes particular steps to defend formalism from Unger's criticisms, but only insofar as to deny the relevance of both politics and morality to an account of the formalism of a legal order; not to the nature of a particular law, or indeed, jurisprudential morality. The morality of a law, Weinrib suggests, is a 'matter to be settled by an argument outside rather than inside the law' (Weinrib 1988, p.955).

Legal formalism is determined, then, by an overarching concern with juridical relationships. It is the integrity of these relationships which realises the immanent rationality of law. This integrity can be best illustrated in areas of private law and private law remedies, particularly contract and tort. It is also this relational form which leads Weinrib to repeatedly advocate the virtues of corrective justice over the vices of distributive justice which, he suggests, is the 'home of the political' (Weinrib 1988, pp.966-70, 975-81). Corrective justice enshrines the integrity of the legal relation. In this sense, Weinrib adds, it is the core of a Kantian legal philosophy because it emphasises the 'capacity for self-determination' as an 'abstraction from all particularity'. This acknowledges the Kantian moral self, but does not prescribe its determination: 'In abstracting from the concrete richness of human particularity, corrective justice pays it the supreme compliment of seeing it as conceptually prior to the operation of a self-determining will... Corrective justice's presupposition of moral personality therefore means that implicit in the intelligibility of immediate interaction are the obligations incumbent in Kantian legal theory on free beings under moral laws.' (Weinrib 1988, pp.997-8) It is the emphasis on the autonomy of the Kantian moral self which confirms the 'potentiality of purposiveness' (Weinrib 1988 p.1002). It empowers the self-determining and self-asserting self, whilst acknowledging the creative potential of the self to articulate the demands of substantive justice (Weinrib 1992, p.356). It accommodates the 'unavoidably contingent relation of moral persons within the immanently rational juridical relationship' (Weinrib 1988, pp.1003, 1008). It is interesting that those critical of Weinrib's theory of immanent juridical relationships have levelled precisely the same criticism as that directed towards Rorty and Unger; that the immanently private juridical relation can never be entirely private. Weinrib counters by emphasising that it is precisely this immanence which distinguishes formalism from the ethical relativism demanced by public morality.

This relational, intensely juridical, form renders determinacy; it 'discloses the intelligibility of the thing's content' (Weinrib 1988, p.959). In this sense, law is constituted by thought. In a Kantian sense, it knows itself. In the Heideggerian sense, it comes to know itself. Since 'law is assumed to be intelligible from within, the content of law is regarded as being homogeneous with, and therefore accessible to, thought' (Weinrib 1988, p.962). Weinrib refers to this as the 'dynamic of internal intelligibility': 'The movement is a circle of thought that feeds upon its own unfolding explicitness: from the content of law to the immediate juristic understanding of this content, to the form implicit in this understanding, to the explicit elucidation of the form, to the testing of the content for its inadequacy to the now explicit form.' (Weinrib 1988, p.974)

The content must be rational only to this extent; it must be relationally rational to the form. There is no other prescription for the content of law: 'In this account justice does not... refer to substantive principles; instead, it points to the different structures according to which external interaction can be construed.' (Weinrib 1988, p.981) The determinacy issue is central to dispelling misguided appreciations of neo-Kantianism, both of the formalist and relativist variants. Echoing Radbruch, Weinrib emphasises that 'nothing about formalism precludes indeterminacy... For formalism the possibility of indeterminacy neither can be, nor need be, avoided.' (Weinrib 1988, p.1008) To make a dismissive accusation that formalism might by substantively indeterminate is to entirely misunderstood the nature of the Kantian foundation of the moral self; it is a 'criticism that bites on air' (Weinrib 1988, p.1009). It is primarily a failure to understand the limits of the moral self as formally determined:

> Determinacy relates in different ways to the generality of the forms and to the particularity of external interaction. Formalism comprehends both these ways in their interrelation. The forms of justice are both determinate and indeterminate. They are indeterminate in that they do not predetermine exhaustively the particular results they govern. They are determinate in that they establish the bounds of coherence for the particulars that fall under them, thus making these particulars intelligible as sorts of things that they are. (Weinrib 1988, p.1011)

In essence, in its 'governance of juridical relationships, formalism is universality with a variable content.' (Weinrib 1988, p.1011)

What legal formalism serves to effect, then, is the separation of the form of law from the content of law. It does not deny the importance of content, or the possibility of indeterminacy of content. Indeed, Weinrib recognises that social 'interaction takes place in a world of shared vocabularies and understandings' so that the 'conceptualism of

Kantian right is compatible with cultural diversity' (Weinrib 1987a, pp.504-5). What it denies is the futile 'rummaging around within the law in search of a content' (Weinrib 1987b, p.67). The legal formalist position is here no different from the relativist. Indeed, it has been suggested that, in the final analysis, Weinrib's formalism, centred around the idea of the moral self, lies in a state of perpetual temptation to the snares of relativism. This is not necessarily to its detriment, for it is not something which can be denied (Brencher 1992). Indeterminacy can be cherished. It does not detract from the form of law because it is not relevant to the form of law. Legal formalism has nothing to say on the subject of content or, therefore, of justice, except insofar as a failure to recognise and effect the immanence of legal form might lead to substantive injustice. This does not preclude legal formalism from being complemented by, or indeed complementary to, any of a number of possible theories of legal substance, of the Kantian or non-Kantian variety. In this sense then, there is nothing in Weinrib's account, or indeed in Radbruch's, which is incompatible with the alternative Kantian ethics suggested by such as Unger, Derrida or Cornell, or, as we shall now see, Ronald Dworkin.

2 The Return of the Moral Self: Ronald Dworkin

The Theory of Rights

The starting point for any investigation of Ronald Dworkin's jurisprudence lies with *Taking Rights Seriously*, the ambition of which was precisely that of Rawls's *Theory of Justice*; to recover a principled foundation for legal thought. What *Taking Rights Seriously* did, at the same time as deconstructing the established 'ruling theory of law', was construct an alternative theory of rights which was non-metaphysical. In other words a theory of rights which existed prior to, and conceptually outside, the state; precisely Kant's ambition (Dworkin 1977, pp.vii-xii). The concentration for both Kant and Dworkin lies in the empowerment of the morally driven individual, and as with any other philosopher so engaged, the law lies within the individual.

The basis of Dworkin's critique of positivism lies in its failure to account for the pluralism of modern society. Pluralism necessitates the famous Dworkinian distinction between rules and principles, which is a thoroughly relativist distinction. Principles do not 'decide' cases, rather they 'incline' the decisions. Hart, as Dworkin points out, conceded the relativism of community custom and practice, but did not develop the concession far enough. Dworkin's ambition is to redefine this relativism within a 'constellation of principles' (Dworkin 1977, pp.42-4). Whereas positivists have conceded the idea of 'social rules', Dworkin wishes to develop these rules into principles of community morality, which, of course, makes them something much more foundational than simply 'social rules'. It makes them normative, but normative as derived not from legal statutes, but from forms of 'consistent practice'; conceptual not merely factual (Dworkin 1977, pp.55-7). The real bite in Dworkin's thesis here lies in the famous treatment of 'hard cases', and it is here also that the critical nature of

Dworkin's Kantianism becomes explicit. Whereas positivists use 'discretion' to fill in where the rules do not apply, Dworkin instead presents 'rights' as a kind of Heideggerian 'fore-understanding'; the first of the striking similarities between Dworkin and the Heideggerian position on political and interpretive ethics (Dworkin 1977, p.81).

Rights, because they vest in the individual, are derived from principle and not from policy, which only ever reflects collective goals. The position here is precisely that taken by the early Rawls, and by Kant in his critique of teleological judgment. But whereas Rawls continued by trying to develop the idea of consensus by infusing the morally driven individual, Dworkin concentrates instead on the distinction between 'background' rights and 'institutional' rights, but determined, of course, by precisely the same moral individual (Dworkin 1977, pp.81-3, 90-4). The reason why principles rather that goals should provide the foundation for moral as well as political law, is that arguments of fairness can only be supported by principles. The supreme judge, Hercules, must 'construct a scheme of abstract and concrete principles' which can provide a 'coherent justification' for his judgments. Justification, unlike mere description, invokes principles. In essence then, the judge, in reaching a decision, uses law, either statute or common law, in line with his own philosophical convictions. In so doing, he takes into account the 'community's moral tradition' as articulated within the legal institutional framework. This 'community morality' thus becomes at once a 'political morality' and, being political, is immediately indeterminate and conflictual in substance: 'the conception holds that community is the political morality presupposed by the laws and institutions of the community.' (Dworkin 1977, p.126)

The need to reintroduce philosophy to jurisprudential study is central. On the matter of philosophical justice, Dworkin engages directly with Rawls. Dworkin's chief criticism is of the hypothetical nature of Rawls's contract. In its place he advocates independent arguments for fairness from principle. The same reasons lie behind his critique of the 'original position, which Dworkin similarly sees as weakening the force of principles by preempting them. For Dworkin the principles come first. This distinction, for very obvious reasons, has led some to suggest that Dworkin is more Kantian than Rawls. This suspicion is enhanced by Dworkin's hesitant support for the spirit of Rawls's notion of 'reflective equilibrium', which he clearly describes as a Kantian synthetic model, and it is even more apparent in his support for the 'exciting' possibilities presented by 'constitutive morality'. In both cases, Dworkin takes Rawls's ideas but develops them in an attempt to uncover foundational 'principles'. Dworkin perceives two alternatives for what he terms the 'coherence' theory which founds theories of 'constitutive morality'; the natural and the constructive. It is the 'constructive' model that Dworkin, like Rawls, favours. In fact, Dworkin's description of this model bears as close an affinity with the Kantian formalism of someone such as Weinrib, as it does with Rawls or Radbruch:

This 'constructive' model does not assume, as the natural model does, that principles of justice have some fixed, objective existence, so that descriptions of these principles must be true or false in some standard way. It does not assume that the animal it matches to the bones actually exists. It makes the different, and some ways more complex, assumption that men and women have a responsibility to fit the particular judgments on which they act into a coherent program of action, or, at least that officials who exercise power over other men have that sort of responsibility. (Dworkin 1977, p.160)

Thus, he adds:

The constructive model does not presuppose skepticism or relativism. On the contrary, it assumes that the men and women who reason within the model will each hold sincerely the convictions they bring to it, and that this sincerity will extend to criticizing as unjust political acts or systems that offend the most profound of these... The constructive model requires coherence, then, for independent reasons of political morality; it takes convictions held with the requisite sincerity as given, and seeks to impose conditions on the acts that these intuitions might be said to warrant. If the constructive model is to constitute morality, in either of the scenes I have distinguished, these independent reasons of political morality are at the heart of our political theories. (Dworkin 1977, pp.162-3)

The distinction that Dworkin makes between himself and Rawls, of principles preempting the process of constitutive morality, is perhaps more certainly presented than is warranted. For Rawls, as for any Kantian, the principles of justice are constituted by the morally driven individual, as of course they are for Dworkin. The fact that Rawls rejects the notion of 'comprehensive' theory in no way distinguishes his position on constructive political morality from Dworkin's. Dworkin is keen to retrieve Rawls from any accusations of relativism that might be thought to result from the 'reflective equilibrium'. But if such an equilibrium is understood in its proper Kantian sense, as a synthetic model, then relativism need not detract from the coherence of the constructivist model (Dworkin 1977, pp.163-8). In fact, it might be said that what Dworkin is presenting in *Taking Rights Seriously* is a proto-consensus model akin to that which Rawls was already developing, and which was of course classically pluralist in both spirit and substance.

In Dworkin's opinion there are three alternative 'deep' theories on which a constructive model can be based; either goal based, rights based or duty based. Kant, he suggests, adopted a duty based theory, which is of course true, but only up to a point. Dworkin himself prefers a rights based theory. But of course, Kant's too was a rights based theory. Dworkin assumes that his concentration on the notion of political right is conceptually different from Kant's philosophical moral right, from which political duty was developed. In fact, it is only synthetically different, not conceptually. Rawls, Dworkin suggests, presents a rights based 'deep' theory, because he puts the individual before the universal. Though true, this does not distinguish Rawls from either Kant or the neo-Kantian position, for whom duty was derived from the moral person and not from any metaphysical teleology. Indeed Dworkin implicitly recognises the nature of a critical Kantian theory of right in his description of a Rawlsian 'deep' theory:

But on the constructive model, at least, the assumption of natural rights is not a metaphysically ambitious one. It requires no more that the hypothesis that the best political program, within the sense of that model, is one that takes the protection of certain individual choices as fundamental, and not properly subordinated to any goal or duty or combination of these. This requires no ontology more dubious or controversial than any contrary choice of fundamental concepts would be and, in particular, no more than the hypothesis of a fundamental goal that underlies the various popular utilitarian theories would require. Nor is it disturbing that a Rawlsian deep theory makes these rights natural rather than legal or conventional. Plainly any rights-based theory must presume rights that are not simply the product of deliberate legislation or explicit social custom, but are independent grounds for judging legislation and custom. (Dworkin 1977, pp.176-7)

The basic right in any 'deep' theory must then be an 'abstract' right; one that is not derived from liberty alone, but from equality, so that it is in fact a 'right to equal concern and respect', derived as it is from the position of the 'moral person' as the creative force at the centre of a critical moral and political philosophy. Throughout *Taking Rights Seriously*, Dworkin reasserts the primacy of the individual interest over the collective, the origin of right within the creative individual, and then urges us to 'take seriously' two particularly important ideas, the foundation of human dignity and respect, and the fundamental of political equality. What he is advocating is an overlapping consensus. This is not a free-floating consensus. In responding to such an argument, Dworkin suggests that the conditions of judgment evolve into a kind of constrained relativism (Dworkin 1977, pp.193-205, 279-89).

Following *Taking Rights Seriously* Dworkin's political liberalism has become increasingly 'interpretive', and the overriding need now is to 'identify the constitutive principles of liberalism'. The fundamental interpretive issue is whether words themselves prevent determinacy of meaning. The answer that Dworkin approaches is again the answer that hermeneutic interpretivism presents; that language constructs meaning. The logical next step from this is that the truth of any statement, legal or otherwise, in fact exists quite outside political authority. This process, as Dworkin suggests, represents a transferal of the 'soundest theory', advanced in *Taking Rights Seriously*, to language, and thus makes thinking a narrative enterprise (Dworkin 1985, pp.128-34). The process of legal reasoning is akin to the process of text interpretation:

I shall argue that legal practice is an exercise in interpretation not only when lawyers interpret particular documents or statutes but generally. Law so conceived is deeply and thoroughly political. Lawyers and judges cannot avoid politics in the broad sense of political theory. But law is not a matter of personal or partisan politics, and a critique of law that does not understand the difference will provide poor understanding and even poorer guidance. I propose that we can improve our understanding of law by comparing legal interpretation with interpretation in other fields of knowledge, particularly literature. (Dworkin 1985, p.146)

From here onwards Dworkin is fully engaged in the interpretive and hermeneutic enterprise. Law, because it is interpretive, is political and historical: 'propositions of law are not merely descriptive of legal history... They are interpretive of legal history.' (Dworkin 1985, p.147) A study of literature and literary techniques makes for better lawyers, because it teaches that interpretation is an exercise in what Heideggerian hermeneutics termed 'fidelity'. Interpretation attempts to show a text, not in its objectively true form, but as its 'best work of art'. Such an ambition embraces the potential indeterminacy of interpretation, which is, of course, the central philosophical and interpretive concession shared across the various neo-Kantian positions. In his subsequent dismissal of authorial intent, Dworkin advances the creative role of the interpreter. Interpretation thus empowers, by placing the morally driven individual at the origins of thought. The Kantianism in this process is made even more explicit by the presentation of the 'chain of law' which constrains creativity by the history and by the morality or principles of the text; precisely, of course, what Gadamer suggested were the constraints in any hermeneutic enterprise, and which he acknowledged were taken from Kant's third *Critique* (Dworkin 1985, pp.148-59).

Dworkin is keen to assert the idea of moral interpretivism as a constraint against radical interpretivism. In refuting radical interpretivism, Dworkin makes direct recourse to the Kantian distinction between judgment, which is constrained, and taste, which is not. From there he makes exactly the same move into political interpretivism as Kant, by suggesting that 'judgment' in a community situation necessitates what Dworkin terms an 'overlap' between alternative judgments. The similarity with Rawls's 'overlapping concensus' is clear, although Dworkin will later suggest that his consensus is different in its principled foundations, and thus, of course, more Kantian. In the absence of objective interpretive truth, as a Kantian interpretivist, rather than dissolving into a spiral of external skepticism, Dworkin advocates an internal skepticism which, being wholly internal, approaches an immanent rationality of the text (Dworkin 1985, pp.167-75).

Interpretive constructivism then leads to the redefinition of political liberalism:

> My project does take a certain view of the role of political theory in politics. It supposes that liberalism consists in some constitutive political morality that has remained roughly the same over some time and that continues to be influential in politics. It supposes that distinct liberal settlements are formed when, for one reason or another, those moved by that constitutive morality settle on a particular scheme of derivative positions as appropriate to complete a practical liberal theory... I do not mean that the constitutive morality of liberalism is the only force at work in forming liberal settlements, or even that it is the most powerful, but only that it is sufficiently distinct and influential to give sense to the idea, shared by liberals and their critics, that liberalism exists, and to give sense to the popular practice of arguing about what it is. (Dworkin 1985, p.186)

The core of such a liberalism is equality, and Dworkin distinguishes liberalism from conservatism precisely in its primacy of equality; a principle which he explicitly attributes to Kantian authority. Liberal morality, for Dworkin, is a truly Kantian immanently rational and internally driven morality. Only individual rights can protect against a false ends based equality; although he is equally quick to stress that such rights, rather than encouraging an individual or egoistic ethic, are in fact an expression of 'constitutive morality' (Dworkin 1985, pp.188-204).

Dworkin's Empire

The publication of *Law's Empire* represented Dworkin's 'first full-length feature film' (Hutchinson 1988, p.58). It stands as a testament to Dworkin's open and complete conversion to interpretivism. Criticism came from all sides of the jurisprudential fence. It has been suggested that this interpretivism remained essentially foundational and merely represented a subtle change of tactic (Hutchinson 1988, pp.74-5). There is certainly no denying the foundationalism implicit in what is effectively an hermeneutic theory of interpretivism. This conversion to a fully fledged interpretivism was emphasised in the opening pages of *Law's Empire*. Whereas *Taking Rights Seriously* had attacked the phenomenology of legal positivism in particular, that phenomenology is now replaced by an interpretive method (Dworkin 1986, pp.vii-viii).

The 'adjudicative principle' is replaced by Heideggerian principles of interpretation and of 'fidelity'. The bogey is still the same, the 'plain fact view' of law, but now Dworkin concentrates on the 'argumentative' character of the legal reasoning: 'Legal practice, unlike many other social phenomena, is argumentative. Every actor in the practice understands that what it permits or requires depends on the truth of certain propositions that are given sense only by and within the practice; the practice consists in large part in deploying and arguing about these propositions.' (Dworkin 1986, p.13) The practice is both external and internal. That is historical and social certainly, but also immanently rational. In other words it enjoys an 'internal aspect'; it creates its own rationality. Dworkin maintains his own interpretivist theory within a classically hermeneutic framework; theories 'that ignore the structure of legal argument for supposedly larger questions of history and society are... perverse.' (Dworkin 1986, p.14) Interpretation is a literary enterprise and legal adjudicators must become literary theorists. By reintroducing literary theory into theories of jurisprudence, it is Dworkin's avowed hope that he will also reintroduce philosophy; because the charge of indeterminacy so familiar in theories of interpretation is a philosophical charge.

Dworkin repeatedly aligns himself with a constructivist theory of interpretation, as opposed to a free-standing conversational theory. The key to a constructivist interpretation is a constructivist community; that is a community with an 'interpretive attitude'. There is a 'deep connection between all forms of interpretation', so the constructive form is represented as a directed form of conversational interpretation, but crucially, it is directed from within and not from without. Thus any end is an immanently derived end. Constructive interpretation is the interaction between purpose and object and this, of course, makes it an eminently 'creative' interpretation; precisely what Kant asserted in his critique of teleological judgment. In his advocacy of this constructive approach to interpretation, Dworkin expressly acknowledges the influence of Gadamer, and his assertion that in 'applying' an intention in the interpretation of a text, we are at once creating by the very fact of doing the interpretive exercise. He also expressly approves Gadamer's suggestion that interpretation is always to some extent an historical enterprise, even if the legal hermeneutic is peculiar in its foundational consistency (Dworkin 1986, pp.50-5, 73-5).

Founding the community attitude is, of course, the problem for Dworkin, as it was for Kant, for Radbruch, for Rawls and so on. Dworkin attempts to redress this problem in precisely the same way, by advocating some sort of 'pre-interpretive' stage of 'consensus'. Once this 'consensus' is established, Dworkin then goes on to present a classically Kantian synthetic model of concept and conception, form and substance. Dworkin suggests that his use of concept and conception is different from that familiar to philosophy. It is however, precisely that familiar to Kantian legal philosophy. The concept provides the frame of meaning, and the conception then mediates between the controversies of meaning. Above all, as Dworkin notes, the concept-conception model has proved a 'structure' for meaning, exactly as any other Kantian constructivist theory does (Dworkin 1986, pp.65-6, 70-3). This basic constructivist model of interpretation, therefore, provides the basis for law's 'empire'. Each judge's 'interpretative theories are grounded in his own convictions' about the 'purpose or goal or principle' of their adjudicative role. This necessarily provides for a legal culture of difference and plurality, which necessitates a basic consensus or foundation for any interpretive theory. Here Dworkin employs his concept-conceptions model, so as to present a 'preinterpretive identification of the domain of law', and so that 'legal' rights then complement moral responsibilities. The sense of this being a synthetic modelling enterprise, providing both the abstract and the practical framework, is overwhelming.

This sense is enhanced by Dworkin's clear restatement that this 'model' is designed as a refutation of established jurisprudential theories of natural law or legal positivism, and that the basis of this distinction lies with the idea of principled justice and the morally driven individual. At the very end of his critique of established jurisprudence, Dworkin again asserts the distinction between the conception of grounds of law and particular instances of the force of law. The alternative to pragmatism, he suggests, is a critical 'non-metaphysical' theory of rights, based on the morally driven individual, and a constructive 'two-way stage of reasoning' between this individual and the 'particularly deep personification of the community'. This necessarily leads Dworkin to consider the nature of responsibility, both individual and group. It is this conception, ultimately, which determines the principled from the pragmatic theory of law, because the conception is a moral conception and, as such, is prior to its political counterpart (Dworkin 1986, pp.151-750. Again it is the Kantian model, concept and conception, which Dworkin uses in order to distinguish principle from its skeptical alternatives.

Dworkin presents his own constructive theory of law 'as integrity' as an alternative to the pragmatic and skeptical. He first establishes a specifically community based idea of political integrity. The move is precisely that taken by Kant in his attempt to present a legal theory which could found the plurality of the human situation in a sense of community. There are two essential 'principles' of political integrity; legislative coherence and adjudicative integrity. As he has suggested before, integrity is a matter of principle, and the desire for integrity is an instinctive 'political virtue', and thus a quality which is to be added to the Rawlsian idea of justice as fairness (Dworkin 1986, pp.176-83). The 'deep' sense of community, as a 'moral agent' is pivotal. Such a community, one that accepts integrity, is at once empowered, creative and able to change. The key conception is the 'ideal of self-government'. These qualities Dworkin expressly associates with Kant. Dworkin's description of this ideal is worth quoting at length. It is a classic statement of neo-Kantian political theory:

The ideal of self-government has a special aspect that integrity promotes directly, and noticing this will lead us into our main discussion of legitimacy and political obligation. Integrity expands and deepens the role individual citizens can play in developing the public standards of their community because it requires them to treat relations among themselves as characteristically, not just spasmodically, governed by these standards. If people understood formal legislation as only a matter of negotiated solutions to discrete problems, with no underlying commitment to any more fundamental public conception of justice, they would draw a sharp distinction between two kinds of encounters with fellow citizens: those that fall within and those that fall outside the scope of some past political decision. Integrity, in contrast, insists that each citizen must accept demands on him, and may make demands on others, that share and extend the moral dimension, of any explicit political decisions. Integrity therefore fuses citizens' moral and political lives: it asks the good citizen, deciding how to treat his neighbour when their interests conflict, to interpret the common scheme of justice to which they are both committed just in virtue of citizenship. (Dworkin 1986, pp.189-90)

It is, thus, a community based on integrity rather than upon contract alone; which distinguishes it from a Rawlsian community. However, these principles are based on the same Rawlsian conception of 'equal concern'. Moreover, Dworkin is again using the model of a private contract, which Kant always suggested was purely of metaphorical rather than practical value (Dworkin 1986, pp.200, 206). This then is the nature of the constructed community; one developed from principle rather than simple compromise, and one constructed by an argumentative community, which argues on a foundation proved by the basic political concepts of principle. Despite Dworkin's passing comments on the contract model, the fact that Dworkin is himself presenting a Kantian model of a 'strong' community is undeniable:

It insists that people are members of a genuine political community only when they accept that their fates are linked in the following way: they accept that they are governed by common principles, not just by rules hammered out in political compromise. Politics has a different character for such people. It is a theater of debate about which principles the community should adopt as a system, which view it should take of justice, fairness, and due process, not the different story, appropriate to other models, in which each person tries to plant the flag of his convictions over as large a domain of power or rules as possible. Members of a society of principle accept that their political rights and duties are not exhausted by the particular decisions their political institutions have reached, but depend, more generally, on the scheme of principles those decisions presuppose and endorse... In short, each accepts political integrity as a distinct political ideal and treats the general acceptance of that ideal, even among people who otherwise disagree about political morality, as constitutive of political morality. (Dworkin 1986, p.211)

Political integrity is both an interpretive and an unmistakably Kantian theory of law; judges should adjudicate by seeing law as it is 'created' by the community as a moral agent. Such a process of adjudication is 'relentlessly interpretive'. It recognizes the power of historicity, not history, because historicity encapsulates the creative and empowering nature of the assertive self. Interpretation, being historicist, is thus creative, though also constrained in the same way. It is constrained not just by the past, but also by the 'purpose' of the adjudication. The metaphor Dworkin uses is of the 'chain-novel', where each chapter is written with integrity, and therefore enjoys an immanent rationality, creative, but constrained by the past and the 'purpose' of the future. This is not only what Gadamer suggested as being the nature of the legal hermeneutic, but also precisely what Hannah Arendt suggested was the peculiar fate of the modern and historically interpretive human condition. Interpretive historicity thus consolidates rather than disrupts the immanent rationality of law, and its adjudicative ambition: 'Law as integrity asks judges to assume, so far as is possible, that the law is structured by a coherent set of principles about justice and fairness and procedural due process, and it asks them to enforce these in the fresh cases that come before them, so that each person's situation is fair and just according to the same standards. That style of adjudication respects that ambition integrity assumes, the ambition to be a community of principles.' (Dworkin 1986, p.243)

Judges thus engage in an indisputably 'constructive' process of 'interpretation' which, as an exercise in integrity, attempts to establish the 'best' possible adjudication. To do otherwise, and here Dworkin lifts a phrase directly from Sartre, would be to act in 'bad faith'. In other words, it would be to act irrationally, and against the principle of responsibility. In the hardest of hard cases, the judge will develop political morality, but will do so in a particular 'direction' established by precisely that morality (Dworkin 1986, pp.255, 258). It is a reciprocal process, and thus an immanent one, and it is this immanence which distinguishes it from the raw creativity of skeptical theories of judicial interpretivism. The spirit of skepticism can be retrieved, but only once the false spectre of indeterminacy is laid to rest. Indeterminacy empowers: it does not weaken the principle of law as integrity. Skepticism must be retrieved by internalisation (Dworkin 1986, pp.274-5). Such skepticism is, of course, the spirit of Kantian philosophy.

The interpretation of a text is not simply a matter of understanding history, but rather is the appreciation, and here Dworkin expressly approves Gadamer, of historicity; in other words, the life, not just the history, of the text. Historicism is retrieved precisely so as to consolidate the argument of political morality. This historicism is an internal quality of philosophy, because it understands the creative component of history. Thus an historicist adjudication, based on principles of political morality, is always 'drawn from the most philosophical reaches of political theory' (Dworkin 1986, pp.363-9, 380). The vision of law's 'empire' is Kant's. The starting point is the nature of indeterminacy. Law as integrity fosters substantive indeterminacy: 'Law as integrity therefore not only permits but fosters different forms of substantive conflict or tension within the overall best interpretation of law.' (Dworkin 1986, p.404) What Dworkin now advances, as a further refinement of the principle of integrity, is 'inclusive' and 'pure' or 'abstract' integrity. This is, of course, a classical and necessary piece of Kantian modelling, emphasising as it does the internal nature of reasoning from within established legal principles, as opposed to the more abstract metaphysical approach of pure juridical coherence.

In other words, it invites the distinction between the form and the substance of legal reasoning. It is an exercise in interpretive philosophy, and thus 'Law's Empire' is determined by an 'attitude', an 'interpretive self-reflected attitude'. It is the nature of this attitude which at once empowers the creative moral person, establishes the concept of responsibility and 'constructs' the political community as a moral agent: 'Law's attitude is constructive: it aims, in the interpretive spirit, to lay principle over practice to show the best route to a better future, keeping the right faith with the past. It is, finally, a fraternal attitude, an expression of how we are united in community though divided in project, interest, and conviction. That is, anyway, what law is for us: for the people we want to be and the community we aim to have.' (Dworkin 1986, p.413) It is difficult to imagine a more eloquent appeal for a Kantian conception of law.

As Dworkin's idea of political liberalism has developed since *Law's Empire* it has become ever more overtly Kantian. His *Liberal Community*, as a constitutive community, is classically Kantian in its distinguishing the idea of community from the conception of community: 'The collective acts of a community constitute its communal life. On the metaphysical view of integration, a community is a super-person, and its collective life embodies all the features and dimensions of a human life. But the practice view defines a community's communal life more narrowly: it includes only the acts treated as collective by the practices and attitudes that create the community as a collective agent.' (Dworkin 1989, p.495) The idea of the community as agent is precisely that which provides the foundation in *Law's Empire*. The conception of the 'practice view', moreover, determines the communal agent from the individual, and maintains the integrity of the individual interest. The 'communal life' is thus restricted to 'political issues' and not to moral issues.

The idea that Dworkin advances of this 'integrated citizen' as someone with both an individual and a contributive and constitutive community persona is thoroughly Kantian. The truth of this assertion is born out by the fact that the binding agent in the community is the treating of everyone with 'equal concern', which is exactly what both Kant and Rawls use in their constitutive communities (Dworkin 1989, pp.500-1). In the 1990 Tanner Lectures Dworkin again stressed the development of the community principle around the fulcrum concepts of equality and equal respect; central to his declared aim to try to retrieve Rawls. Pivotal is the increased reliance on the role of a 'reflective equilibrium' as a mechanism for founding a community ethics. Thus Dworkin moves inexorably towards Rawls, and then beyond towards a 'comprehensive' theory. It is this movement which announces Dworkin's inevitable ultimate engagement with ethics. It is the unavoidable result of the increasingly Kantian nature of Dworkin's community (Dworkin 1990, Guest 1992, pp.292-305).

The Dominion of Ethics

This engagement has climaxed in Dworkin's theory of the moral self presented in *Life's Dominion*, a text which represents the most eloquent statement of a Kantian philosophy of ethics in contemporary jurisprudence. It represents the application of Dworkin's evolved theory of political morality to two burning contemporary ethical issues, and employs all the weapons developed over the previous three decades, culminating in the association of the moral person and the constructed interpretive community. The ambition of *Life's Dominion* is to transcend contemporary 'opinions' on ethical issues by means of establishing overriding principles. What Dworkin does not want is a simple compromise. What he does want is a 'principled compromise'. The distinction is, of course, vital, because what it does is demand a comprehensive theory, rather than simply the kind of 'overlapping consensus' presented by Rawls, and which Dworkin has repeatedly suggested must be developed into a consensus founded on principle. With regard to the specific issue of a 'right to life', Dworkin adopts what he terms a 'detached objection', which he suggests means that the right to life is an 'intrinsic' right derived from an absolute value of life. The alternative non-principled compromise is the 'derivative objection', which suggests that the 'right to life' is simply based around the need to 'protect' the fetus, and tends to revolve around 'when' a fetus might become a 'creature' (Dworkin 1993, pp.6-13). It is thus an internally generated 'right'; in Kantian parlance, an immanent ethical right, and thus a rational right. It is, moreover, as Dworkin stresses, the basis of the moderate liberal position on abortion, which is determined by any 'liberal community' (Dworkin 1993, pp.32-4).

The USA is characteristic of such a society; in its pervasive communal pluralism and its essentializing of individual rights. This pluralism, Dworkin hastens to add, does not describe alienated society, but rather a society whose very differentness is held together by principle. The essentializing of the individual right, and its association with an 'intrinsic' value of life, leads Dworkin to accept the clear distinction between the legal and the ethical which is demanded of any Kantian philosophy, and which, of course, was represented in the basic structure of *The Metaphysics of Morals*. Indeed, Dworkin suggests that the imposition of a community position on abortion, generated by some sort of 'social solidarity' and effected by 'the jackboots of the criminal law', is a 'terrible form of tyranny' and nothing less than 'destructive of moral responsibility' (Dworkin 1993, p.15). The association of tyranny with the suppression of moral responsibility is of course wholly Kantian, and most eloquently described by Hannah Arendt.

The starting point for an examination of ethics in the modern state is a discussion of individual right as protected and threatened by the US Constitution. In his analysis of *Roe v Wade*, Dworkin detects two projected arguments which authorised the state to override individual rights; the 'strong' argument and the 'weak'. The 'weak' argument is that represented by the Fourteenth Amendment, which authorises the state to intervene if there is a 'reason' to do so. It is 'weak' because it provides 'weak' protection of individual rights. The 'strong' argument is the necessity of 'compelling' reasons. Much then depends on the origins of this right, because it will determine the strength of its position in the Constitution. Dworkin introduces the nature of the 'sacred', which is realised through a decision-making process which creates an opinion as a 'collective solution to the political controversy. The principles might pre-exist, but the solution does not (Dworkin 1993, pp.71-106). So the question remains of how this 'collective solution' stands in regard of a strong right. The relationship is governed by the precise jurisprudence which Dworkin developed in *Law's Empire*; of interpretation and fit. Thus the interpretation of the Constitution must be tested in two ways; first, by the 'dimension of fit', which determines whether an interpretation is in accordance with legal practice or 'experience', and then second, by the test of 'justice', which demands that the principles of justice must reflect moral rights as reinterpreted by each generation. The exercise, on both counts, is an eminently historical, as well as a principled, one (Dworkin 1993, pp.108-14).

The introduction of interpretation returns Dworkin once again to dismiss the challenge of original intent. The alternative to an original intent conception of interpretation which addresses historical detail, is a form of interpretation which instead concentrates on 'stable principle'. This approach, according to Dworkin, is essential in any democratic state because it maintains the integrity of a legal order against the external skepticism which can be introduced by the acceptance of wholly 'contingent' historical, as opposed to historicist, interpretation. Thus, Dworkin insists that 'judges must justify their decisions through arguments of principle and integrity' (Dworkin 1993, pp.119-24). In his dismissal of original intent theory, Dworkin reveals again his interest in the internal nature of language and its ability to signal meaning over and against original intent. He also repeats the assertion that the creativity demanded by interpretive integrity is in fact a 'responsibility', and a rationally constrained empowerment of the individual (Dworkin 1993, p.145). Life's 'dominion', like law's 'empire', is one governed by argument. This argument on its most important level is one conducted between the judiciary and the community, and founded on moral principle. Moreover, it then empowers the judge to judge, but only with due regard to integrity. Integrity in law has various dimensions. In particular 'it insists that judicial decision be a matter of principle, not compromise or strategy or political accommodation', that it also it 'holds vertically', that is in accordance with established consititutional principles, and also 'horizontally', in that a judge will then accept the constraint of his own creation (Dworkin 1993, p.146).

With his jurisprudential method laid bare, Dworkin addresses the two particular ethical issues of abortion and euthanasia. The solutions that Dworkin presents combine integrity with the 'detached' approach to contemporary ethics. 'Political practice', he suggests, demands the 'detached' support for the argument of 'intrinsic value'. The alternatives are either responsibility or conformity, freedom in the Kantian sense or coercion. The 'detached' argument, as we have already seen, champions responsibility and freedom. Thus, according to Dworkin, the 'detached' argument, in the matter of abortion, favours a 'principle of procreative autonomy'. Accordingly, integrity both demands its recognition in the courts and the recognition of the ultimate principle of Kantian ethics, moral individualism. Moreover, Dworkin adds, this result 'follows from any competent interpretation of the due process clause' of the US Constitution. This right of 'procreative autonomy' is rooted in western political thought, as Dworkin acknowledges, because it is founded by the ideas of moral right and moral responsibility. It is demanded of us because we live in a community of morally driven individuals. Thus *Roe* was rightly decided on 'procreative autonomy' grounds, in accordance with these eminently Kantian fundamental principles of freedom and responsibility (Dworkin 1993, pp.148-51, 158-60, 166-72).

Exactly the same arguments and principles lie at the heart of Dworkin's consideration of the second ethical issue, euthanasia. Again the only principled resolution is one provided by respect for 'autonomy' and 'respect' for the individual's critical faculty. Decisions are reached by such individuals in respect of goodness and morality, as opposed to hedonistic or egoistic motives. Such a process for decision-making in the arena of ethics is then constrained and constructed by principle. It becomes immanent as a 'structure' of 'coherent choice'. Living in accordance with these principles thus becomes a matter of living with integrity to one's own asserted convictions. The justification is, of course, exactly Kant's. Two passages in Dworkin's discussion of euthanasia encapsulate the idea of the Dworkinian moral person, and reveal its philosophical descent. First, with particular regard to indeterminacy and the nature of 'the process of judgment':

The first of these two ideas - that our critical interests are personal - seems to pull us towards the annihilating idea that critical interests are only subjective, only matters of how we feel. The second seems to pull us toward the equally unacceptable idea that everyone's critical interests are the same, over all history, that there is only one truly best way for anyone to live. The remedy is to embrace neither of these extreme positions but instead to remind ourselves of how it feels to believe that a given life is the right one. We feel this not as a discovery of a timeless formula, good for all times and places, but as a direct response to our own specific circumstances of place, culture, and capacity. The response, however, includes conviction: it is important both that we find a life *good* and that we *find* it good. Integrity plays two parts of this story: it is the mark of conviction, of commitment, not just past choice; it also reflects investment, the idea that the value of a life lies in part *in* its integrity, so that its having already been established as one kind of life argues, though of course far from conclusively, that it should go on being that kind of life. (Dworkin 1993, p.206)

Second, concentrating particularly on the notion of individual responsibility and an individual's decision to die: 'So the appeal to the sanctity of life raises here the same crucial political and constitutional issue that it raises about abortion. Once again the critical question is whether a decent society will choose coercion or responsibility, whether it will seek to impose a collective judgment on matters of the most profound spiritual character on everyone, or whether it will allow and ask its citizens to make the most central, personality-defining judgments about their own lives for themselves.' (Dworkin 1993, p.216) The recognition of the principle of 'autonomy' is a recognition of individual creative potential. Ethical issues, like indeed juridical issues, are matters of freedom and responsibility. We have an obligation to 'live up to our freedom' and, thus, 'freedom of conscience presupposes a personal responsibility of reflection, and it loses much of its meaning when that responsibility is ignored.' Certain moments in life, most especially those which demand the individual resolution of ethical issues, above all 'cry out for self-assertion' (Dworkin 1993, pp.224-5, 239-40).

Life's 'dominion' is very much a Kantian dominion. It is the dominion of the moral self, and Dworkin is its champion. Dworkin presents the critical philosophy of ethics which can exist to complement the alternative varieties of critical political philosophy presented in the Heideggerian and relativist strains. Although Dworkin has himself denied that his is a Kantian jurisprudence, there can be no such doubts that it is a Kantian philosophy of ethics (Posner 1979, p.113, Barron 1992a, pp.152-3). Moreover it is a Kantian theory of the moral self, derived from an explicitly Kantian evolution of the relation between the self and law as an idea of practical reason. In this way, Dworkin's ambition is united with that of Cornell and Derrida, as well as Rawls and Unger. This is certainly Rorty's conclusion. Although Rorty dismisses the kind of 'strong' Kantianism which lies behind a comprehensive theory of the moral self, he is right to stress the shared origins of their ambition (Rorty 1991a, pp.198-201). It brings the Kantian critique of politics full circle, whilst in the nature of its own contingency at the same time confirming its enduring validity.

BIBLIOGRAPHY

Altman, A., 1990. *Critical Legal Studies: A Liberal Critique*, Princeton.

Arendt, H., 1951a. *Antisemitism*, New York.

Arendt, H., 1951b. *Imperialism*, New York.

Arendt, H., 1951c. *Totalitarianism*, New York.

Arendt, H., 1954. *Between Past and Future*, London.

Arendt, H., 1958. *The Human Condition*, Chicago.

Arendt, H., 1963. *Eichmann in Jerusalem: A Report on the Banality of Evil*, London.

Arendt, H., 1971. *The Life of the Mind*, New York.

Arendt, H., 1972. *Crises of the Republic*, New York.

Arendt, H., 1982. *Kant's Political Philosophy*, Chicago.

Arendt, H., 1990. *On Revolution*, London.

Arneson, R., 1989. 'Introduction', 99 *Ethics*, p.695.

Ball, M., 1987. 'The City of Unger', 81 *Northwestern Law Review*, p.627.

Barron, A., 1992a. 'Dworkin and the Challenge of Postmodernism', in A.Hunt (ed.), *Reading Dworkin Critically*, Oxford.

Barron, A., 1992b. 'Lyotard and the Problem of Justice', in A.Benjamin (ed.), *Judging Lyotard*, London.

Beardsworth, J., 1996. *Derrida and the Political*. London.

Beiner, R., 1993. 'Kant, the Sublime and Nature', in R.Beiner and R.Booth (eds.), *Kant and Political Philosophy*, Yale.

Beiser, F., 1992. 'Kant's Intellectual Development 1746-1781', in P.Guyer (ed.), *The Cambridge Companion to Kant*, Cambridge.

Bennington, G., 1988. *Lyotard: Writing the Event*, Manchester.

Bennington, G., 1993. *Jacques Derrida*, Chicago.

Bernasconi, R., 1989. 'Seeing Double: Destruktion and Deconstruction', in D.Michelfelder and R.Palmer (eds.), *Dialogue and Deconstruction*, Albany.

Bernstein, R., 1983. *Beyond Objectivism and Relativism*, Oxford.

Bernstein, R., 1987. 'Serious Play: The Ethical-Political Horizon of Jacques Derrida', 1 *Journal of Speculative Philosophy*, p.94.

Bernstein, R., 1991. *The New Constellation*, Cambridge.

Bhasker, R., 1991. *Philosophy and the Idea of Freedom*, Oxford.

Blanchot, M., 1989. 'Thinking the Apocalypse: A Letter from Maurice Blanchot to Elizabeth David', 15 *Critical Inquiry*, p.475.

Boyle, J., 1985. 'Modernist Social Theory: Roberto Unger's *Passion*' 98 *Harvard Law Review* p.1066.

Boyne, R., 1990. *Foucault and Derrida: The Other Side of Reason*, London.

Brencher, G., 1992. 'Formalism, Postivism and Natural Law in Ernest Weinrib's Tort Theory: Will the Real Ernest Weinrib Please Come Forward?', 42 *University of Toronto Law Journal*, p.318.

Brest, P., 1981. 'The Fundamental Rights Controversy', 90 *Yale Law Journal* p.1063.

Burchell, G., 1991. 'Peculiar Interests: Civil Society and Governing the System of Natural Liberty', in G.Burchell, C.Gordon and P.Miller (eds.), *The Foucault Effect: Studies in Governmentality*, Hemel Hempstead.

Burrows, J., 1990. 'Conversational Politics: Rorty's Pragmatist Apology for Liberalism', in A.Malachowski (ed.), *Reading Rorty*, Oxford.

Canovan. M., 1974. *The Political Thought of Hannah Arendt*, London.

Canovan, M., 1994. *Hannah Arendt*, Cambridge.

Carrington, P., 'Of Law and the River', 34 *Journal of Legal Education*, p.222.

Carroll, D., 1984. 'Rephrasing the Political with Kant and Lyotard: From Aesthetic to Political Judgments', 14 *Diacritics*, p.74.

Cassirer, E., 1944. *An Essay on Man*, Yale.

Cassirer, E., 1946a. *Language and Myth*, New York.

Cassirer, E., 1946b. *The Myth of the State*, Yale.

Cassirer, E., 1949. 'Spirit and Life in Contemporary Philosophy', in P.Schlipp (ed.), *The Philosophy of Ernst Cassirer*, Evanston.

Cassirer, E., 1951. *The Philosophy of the Enlightenment*, Princeton.

Cassirer, E., 1967. 'Remarks on Martin Heidegger's Interpretation of Kant', in M.Gram (ed.), *Kant: Disputed Questions*, Chicago.

Cassirer, E., 1981. *Kant's Life and Thought*, Yale.

Caygill, H., 1989. *The Art of Judgement*, Oxford.

Chroust, A., 1944. 'The Philosophy of Law of Gustav Radbruch', 53 *Philosophical Review*, p.23.

Cornell, D., 1985. 'Toward a Modern/Postmodern Reconstruction of Ethics', 133 *University of Pennsylvania Law Review*, p.291.

Cornell, D., 1987. 'Beyond Tragedy and Complexity', 81 *Nothwestern University Law Review*, p.693.

Cornell, D., 1988. 'Institutionalization of Meaning, Recollective Imagination and the Potential for Transformative Legal Interpretation', 136 *University of Pennsylvania Law Review*, p.1135.

Cornell, D., 1991. *Beyond Accommodation*, London.

Cornell, D., 1992a. *The Philosophy of the Limit*, London.

Cornell, D., 1992b. 'The Philosophy of the Limit: Systems Theory and Feminist Legal Reform', in D.Cornell, M.Rosenfeld and D.Carlson (eds.), *Deconstruction and the Possibility of Justice*, London.

Cornell, D., 1995. *The Imaginary Domain*, London.

Crowther, P., 1989. *The Kantian Sublime: From Morality to Art*, Oxford.

Critchley, S., 1993. 'The Question of the Questions: An Ethic-Political Response to a Note in *De l'esprit*', in D.Wood (ed.), *Of Derrida, Heidegger and Spirit*, Chicago.

Crowther, P., 1993. *Critical Aesthetics and Postmodernism*, Oxford.

Cummings, R., 1981. 'The Odd Couple: Heidegger and Derrida', 34 *Review of Metaphysics*, p.487.

Dahlstrom, D., 1991. 'Heidegger's Kantian Turn: Notes to his Commentary on the *Kritik der Reinen Vernunft*', 45 *Review of Metaphysics*, p.329.

Davidson, A., 1986. 'Archaeology of Foucault', in D.Hoy (ed.), *Foucault: A Critical Reader*, London.

Deleuze, G., 1995. *Kant's Critical Philosophy*, London.

D'Entreves, M., 1994. *The Political Philosophy of Hannah Arendt*, London.

Derrida, J., 1978. 'Violence and Metaphysics', in A.Bass (ed.), *Writing and Difference*, Chicago.

Derrida, J., 1983. 'The Principle of Reason: The University in the Eyes of its Pupils', 13 *Diacritics* p.3.

Derrida, J., 1984. 'Of an Apocalyptic Tone Recently Adopted in Philosophy', 6 *Oxford Literary Review*, p.3.

Derrida, J., 1987a. ' Geschlecht II: Heidegger's Hand', in J.Sallis (ed.), *Deconstruction and Philosophy*, Chicago.

Derrida, J., 1987b. 'The Law of Reflection: Nelson Mandela, in Admiration', in J.Derrida and M.Tlili (eds.), *For Nelson Mandela*, New York.

Derrida, J., 1988. 'The Politics of Friendship', 85 *Journal of Philosophy*, p.632.

Derrida, J., 1989. *Of Spirit: Heidegger and the Question*, Chicago.

Derrida, J., 1990. 'The Force of Law: The Mystical Foundation of Authority', 11 *Cardozo Law Review*, p.925.

Derrida, J., 1991. 'Interview', in R.Mortley, *French Philosophers in Conversation*, London.

Derrida, J., 1992a. 'Before the Law', in D.Attridge (ed.), *Acts of Literature*, London.

Derrida, J., 1992b. *The Other Heading: Reflections on Today's Europe*, Bloomington.

Derrida, J., 1992c. 'Onto-Theology of National-Humanism (Prolegomena to a Hypothesis)', 14 *Oxford Literary Review*, p.5.

Diamond, S., 1985. 'Not-So-Critical Legal Studies', 6 *Cardozo Law Review*, p.693.

Donzelot, J., 1991. 'The Mobilization of Society', in G.Burchell, C.Gordon and P.Miller (eds.), *The Foucault Effect: Studies in Governmentality*, Hemel Hempstead.

Doppelt, G., 1988. 'Rawls's Kantian Ideal and the Viability of Modern Liberalism', 31 *Inquiry*, p.413.

Doppelt, G., 1989. 'Is Rawls's Kantian Liberalism Coherent and Defensible?', 99 *Ethics*, p.815.

Douzinas, C. and R.Warrington, 1991. *Postmodern Jurisprudence: The Law of Text in the Texts of Law*, London.
Douzinas, C. and R.Warrington, 1994. *Justice Miscarried: Ethics, Aesthetics and the Law*, Hemel Hempstead.
Douzinas, C., P.Goodrich and Y.Hachamovitch, 1994. *Politics, Modernity and Critical Legal Studies: The Legality of the Contingent*, London.
Dreyfus, H. and P.Rabinow, 1982. *Michel Foucault: Beyond Structuralism and Hermeneutics*, Chicago.
Dworkin, R., 1977. *Taking Rights Seriously*, London.
Dworkin, R., 1985, *A Matter of Principle*, Oxford.
Dworkin, R., 1986. *Law's Empire*, Harvard.
Dworkin, R., 1989. 'Liberal Community', 77 *California Law Review*, p.479.
Dworkin, R., 1993. *Life's Dominion*, London.
Farias, V., 1987. *Heidegger and Nazism*, Philadelphia.
Feinman, J., 1985. 'The Failure of Legal Education and the Promise of Critical Legal Studies', 6 *Cardozo Law Review*, p.739.
Ferry, L. and A.Renaut., 1990. *Heidegger and Modernity*, Chicago.
Finnis, J., 1985. 'On The Critical Legal Studies Movement', 30 *American Journal of Jurisprudence*, p.21.
Fischer, M., 1990. 'Redefining Philosophy as Literature: Richard Rorty's Defence of Literary Culture', in A.Malachowski (ed.), *Reading Rorty*, Oxford.
Foucault, M., 1977. *Discipline and Punish*, London.
Foucault, M., 1980. *Power/Knowledge*, London.
Foucault, M., 1984. 'What is Enlightenment?' in P.Rabinow (ed.), *The Foucault Reader*, London.
Foucault, M., 1988. 'Truth, Power, Self', in L.Martin, H.Gutman and P.Hutton (eds.), *Technologies of the Self*, London.
Foucault, M., 1990. 'The Return of Morality', in L.Kritzman (ed.), *Michel Foucault: Politics, Philosophy, Culture*, London.
Foucault, M., 1991. 'Governmentality', in G.Burchell, C.Gordon and P.Miller (eds.), *The Foucault Effect: Studies in Governmentality*, Hemel Hempstead.
Foucault, M., 1993. 'Kant on Enlightenment and Revolution', in M.Gane and T.Johnson (eds.), *Foucault's New Domains*, London.
Fraser, N., 1981. 'Foucault on Modern Power: Empirical Insights and Normative Confusions', 1 *Praxis International*, p.272.
Fraser, N., 1983. 'Foucault's Body Language: A Post-Humanist Political Language?', 61 *Salmagundi*, p.55.
Fraser, N., 1985. 'Michel Foucault: A Young Conservative?', 96 *Ethics*, p.165.
Frug, G., 1980. 'The City as a Legal Concept', 93 *Harvard Law Review*, p.1057.

Frug, G., 1984. 'The Ideology of Bureaucracy in American Law', 97 *Harvard Law Review* 1984. p.1277.

Frug, G., 1988. 'Argument as Character', 40 *Stanford Law Review*, p.869.

Frug, G., 1990. 'Administrative Democracy', 40 *University of Toronto Law Journal*, p.570.

Frug, M., 1992. *Postmodern Legal Feminism*.

Gabel, P., 1977. 'Intention and Structure in Contractual Conditions', 61 *Minnesota Law Review*, p.628.

Gabel, P., 1980. 'Reification in Legal Reasoning', 3 *Research in Law and Sociology*, p.25.

Gabel, P., 1984. 'The Phenomenology of Rights-Consciousness and the Pact of the Withdrawn Selves', 62 *Texas Law Review*, p.1563.

Gabel P. and D.Kennedy, 1984. 'Roll Over Beethoven', 36 *Stanford Law Review*, p.1.

Gadamer, H., 1975. *Truth and Method*, London.

Gadamer, H., 1989. 'Back from Syracuse?', 15 *Critical Inquiry*, p.428.

Galston, W., 1987. 'False Universality: Infinite Personality and Finite Existence in Unger's *Politics*', 81 *Northwestern University Law Review*, p.751.

Galston, W., 1989. 'Pluralism and Social Unity', 99 *Ethics*, p.711.

Gasche, R., 1986. *The Tain of the Mirror: Derrida and the Philosophy of Reflection*, Harvard.

Gawronsky, P., 1949. 'Cassirer: His Life and Work', in P.Schlipp (ed.), *The Philosophy of Ernst Cassirer*, Evanston.

Goodrich, P., 1991. 'Specula Laws: Image, Aesthetic and Common Law', 2 *Law and Critique*, p.236.

Goodrich, P., 1992. 'Critical Legal Studies in England: Prospective Histories', 12 *Oxford Journal of Legal Studies*, p.195.

Gordon, C., 1991. 'Governmental Rationality', in G.Burchell, C.Gordon and P.Miller (eds.), *The Foucault Effect: Studies in Governmentality*, Hemel Hempstead.

Gordon, R., 1981. 'Historicism in Legal Scholarship', 90 *Yale Law Journal*, p.1017.

Gordon, R., 1982. 'New Developments in Legal Theory', in D.Kairys (ed.), *The Politics of Law*, New York.

Guest, P., 1992. *Ronald Dworkin*, Edinburgh.

Guignon, C. and D.Hiley (eds.). 'Biting the Bullet: Rorty on Private and Public Morality', in A.Malachowski (ed.), *Reading Rorty*, Oxford.

Guyer, P., 1993. *Kant and the Experience of Freedom: Essays on Aesthetics and Morality*, Cambridge.

Haber, F., 1994. *Beyond Postmodern Politics*, London.

Habermas, J., 1986. 'Taking Aim at the Heart of the Present', in D.Hoy (ed.), *Foucault:A Critical Reader*, London.

Habermas, J., 1989. 'Work and *Weltanschauung*: The Heidegger Controversy from a German Perspective', in 15 *Critical Inquiry*, p.443.

Halpin, A., 1994. 'New Rights for Old?', 53 *Cambridge Law Journal*, p.573.
Hamburg, C., 1949. 'Cassirer's Conception of Philosophy', in P.Shlipp (ed.), *The Philosophy of Ernst Cassirer*, Evanston.
Hampton, J., 1989. 'Should Political Philosophy be done without Metaphysics?', 99 *Ethics*, p.791.
Hansen, P., 1993. *Politics, History and Citizenship*, Oxford.
Harries, K., 1975. 'Heidegger as a Political Thinker', 29 *Review of Metaphysics*, p.643.
Hawthorn, G., 1987. 'Practical Reason and Social Democracy: Reflections on Unger's *Passion* and *Politics*', 81 *Northwestern University Law Review* p.766.
Hayman, R., 1986. *Writing Against: A Biography of Sartre*, London.
Heidegger, M., 1962. *Being and Time*, Oxford.
Heidegger, M., 1978. *Basic Writings*, London.
Heidegger, M., 1981. 'Only a God can save us', in T.Sheehan (ed.), *Heidegger: The Man and the Thinker*, Chicago.
Heidegger, M., 1983. 'Facts and Thoughts', 36 *Review of Metaphysics*, p.483.
Heidegger, M., 1985. 'The Self-Assertion of the German University', 38 *Review of Metaphysics*, p.470.
Heidegger, M., 1990. *Kant and the Problem of Metaphysics*, Bloomington.
Heidegger, M., 1992. *Basic Problems of Phenomenology*, Bloomington.
Heller, A. and F.Feher, 1988. *The Postmodern Political Condition*, Oxford.
Heller, T., 1984. 'Structuralism and Critique', 36 *Stanford Law Review*, p.127.
Henrich, D., 1992. *Aesthetic Judgment and the Moral Image of the World*, Stanford.
Hermann, D., 1982. 'Phenomenology, Structuralism, Hermeneutics and Legal Study', 36 *University of Miami Law Review*, p.379.
Hill. T., 1989. 'Kantian Constructivism in Ethics', 99 *Ethics*, p.752.
Hinchman, L. and P.Hinchman, 1984. 'In Heidegger's Shadow: Hannah Arendt's Phenomenological Humanism', 56 *Review of Politics*, p.183.
Hoeffe, O., 1992. 'Even a Nation of Devils Needs the State: the dilemma of natural justice', in H.Williams (ed.), *Essays on Kant's Political Philosophy*, Cardiff.
Hollis, M, 1990. 'The Poetics of Personhood', in A.Malachowski (ed.), *Reading Rorty*, Oxford.
Hoy, D., 1979. 'Forgetting the Text: Derrida's Critique of Heidegger', 8 *Boundary2*, p.223.
Hoy, D., 1985. 'Interpreting the Law: Hermeneutical and Poststructuralist Perspectives', 58 *Southern California Law Review*, p.135.
Hunt, A., 1990. 'The Big Fear: Law Confronts Postmodernism', 35 *McGill Law Journal*, p.508.
Hutchings, K., 1996. *Kant, Critique and Politics*, London.
Hutchinson, A., 1984. 'Of Kings and Dirty Rascals', *Queens Law Journal*, p.273.

Hutchinson, A., 1988. *Dwelling on the Threshold: Critical Essays in Modern Legal Thought*, Toronto.
Hutchinson, A., 1989. 'The Three Rs: Reading/Rorty/Radically', 103 *Harvard Law Review*, p.555.
Hutchinson, A., 1990. 'A Poetic Champion Composes: Unger (Not) on Ecology and Women', 40 *University of Toronto Law Journal*, p.271.
Hutchinson, A., 1995a. 'A Postmodern Hart: Taking Rules Sceptically', 58 *Modern Law Review*, p.789.
Hutchinson, A., 1995b. *Waiting for CORAF*, Toronto.
Hutchinson, A. and P.Monahan, 1984a. 'Law, Politics, and the Critical Legal Scholars: The Unfolding Drama of American Legal Thought', 36 *Stanford Law Review*, p.200.
Hutchinson, A. and P.Monahan, 1984b. 'The Rights Stuff: Roberto Unger and Beyond', 62 *Texas Law Review*, p.1477.
Ingrams, D., 1992. 'The Postmodern Kantianism of Arendt and Lyotard', in A.Benjamin (ed.), *Judging Lyotard*, London.
Jaspers, K., 1962. *Kant*, London.
Kant, I., 1781/1787. *Critique of Pure Reason* (ed. N.Smith), London.
Kant, I., 1785. *Groundwork of the Metaphysics of Morals* (ed. H.Paton), London.
Kant, I., 1788. *Critique of Practical Reason* (ed. L.Beck),. London.
Kant, I., 1790. *The Critique of Judgement* (ed. J.Meredith), Oxford.
Kant, I., 1797. *The Metaphysics of Morals* (ed. M.Gregor), Cambridge.
Kaufman, F. 1949. 'Cassirer, Neo-Kantianism and Phenomenology', in P.Schlipp (ed.), *The Philosophy of Ernst Cassirer*, Evanston.
Kelman, M., 1984. 'Trashing', 36 *Stanford Law Review*, p.321.
Kersting, W., 1992. 'Kant's Concept of State', in H.Williams (ed.), *Essays on Kant's Political Philosophy*, Cardiff.
Klare, K., 1979. 'Law-Making as Praxis', 49 *Telos*, p.123.
Klare, K., 1978. 'Judicial Deradicalization of the Wagner Act and the Origins of Modern Legal Consciousness', 62 *Minnesota Law Review*, p.265.
Klare, K., 1981. 'Labor Law as Ideology: Toward a New Historiography of Collective Bargaining Law', 4 *Industrial Relations Law Journal*, p.479.
Klare, K., 1982. 'The Quest for Industrial Democracy and the Struggle Against Racism: Perspectives from Labor Law and Civil Rights Law', 61 *Oregon Law Review*, p.157.
Knippenberg, J., 1993. 'The Politics of Kant's Philosophy', in R.Beiner and R.Booth (eds.), *Kant and Political Philosophy*, Yale.
Kramer, M., 1991. *Legal Theory, Political Theory and Deconstruction*, Bloomington.
Krell, D., 1993. 'Spiriting Heidegger', in D.Wood (ed.), *Of Derrida, Heidegger and Spirit*, Chicago.

Kress, K., 1989. 'Legal Indeterminacy', 77 *California Law Review*, p.283.
Kritzman, L., 1990. 'Foucault and the Politics of Expeience', in L.Kritzman (ed.), *Politics, Philosophy, Culture*, London.
Kukathas, C., and P.Pettit, 1990. *Rawls: A Theory of Justice and Its Critics*, Cambridge.
Kymlicka, W., 1989. 'Liberal Individualism and Liberal Neutrality', 99 *Ethics*, p.883.
Lacoue-Labarthe, P., 1984. 'Talks', 14 *Diacritics*, p.24.
Lacoue-Labarthe, P., 1990. *Heidegger, Art and Politics*, Oxford.
Langer, S., 1949. 'On Cassirer's Theory of Language and Myth', in P.Schlipp (ed.), *The Philosophy of Ernst Cassirer*, Evanston.
Laursen, J., 1986. 'The Subversive Kant: The Vocabulary of Public and Publicity', 14 *Political Theory* p.593.
Lyotard, J-F., 1984. *The Postmodern Condition: A Report on Knowledge*, Manchester.
Lyotard, J-F., 1988a. *The Differend*, Manchester.
Lyotard, J-F., 1988b. *Peregrinations: Law, Form, Event*, Columbia.
Lyotard, J-F., 1989. 'Judiciousness in Dispute, or Kant after Marx', in A.Benjamin (ed.), *The Lyotard Reader*, London.
Lyotard, J-F., 1990. *Heidegger and the jews*, Minnesota.
Lyotard, J-F., 1991. *Lessons on the Analytic of the Sublime*, Stanford.
Lyotard, J-F., 1992. *'Sensus Communis'*, in A.Benjamin (ed.), *Judging Lyotard*, London.
Lyotard, J-F., 1993. *Political Writings*, London.
MacCarthy, T., 1991. *Ideals and Illusions: Reconstruction and Deconstruction in Contemporary Legal Theory*, Cambridge, Mass.
McBridge, W., 1991. *Sartre's Political Theory*, Bloomington.
Meyerson, D., 1991. 'Fundamental Contradictions in Critical Legal Studies', 11 *Oxford Journal of Legal Studies*, p.444.
Michelfelder, D. and R.Palmer (eds.), *Dialogue and Deconstruction: The Gadamer-Derrida Encounter*, Albany.
Michelman, F., 1981. 'Politics as Medicine: On Misdiagnosing Legal Scholarship', 90 *Yale Law Journal*, p.1224.
Miller, J., 1993. *The Passion of Michel Foucault*, London.
Moore, M., 1989. 'The Interpretive Turn in Modern Theory', 41 *Stanford Law Review* p.871.
Mortley, R., 1991. *French Philosophers in Conversation*, London.
Murdoch, I., 1987. *Sartre: Romantic Rationalist*, London.
Norris, C., 1987. *Derrida*, London.
Norris, C., 1990. *What's Wrong With Postmodernism: Critical Theory and the Ends of Philosophy*, London.
O'Neill, O., 1986. 'The Public Use of Reason', 14 *Political Theory* p.523.

O'Neill, O., 1992. 'Reason and Politics in the Kantian Enterprise', in H.Williams (ed.), *Essays on Kant's Political Philosophy*, Cardiff.

Ott, H., 1994. *Heidegger: A Political Life*, London.

Parsons, C., 1992. 'The Transcendental Aesthetic', in P.Guyer (ed.), *The Cambridge Companion to Kant*, Cambridge.

Peller, G., 1985. 'The Metaphysics of American Law', 73 *California Law Review*, p.1151.

Poeggeler, O., 1978. 'Being as Appropriation', in M.Murray (ed.), *Heidegger and Modern Philosophy*, Yale.

Pos, H., 1949. 'Recollections of Ernst Cassirer', in P.Schlipp (ed.), *The Philosophy of Ernst Cassirer*, Evanston.

Posner, R., 1979. 'Utilitarianism, Economics and Legal Theory', 8 *Journal of Legal Studies*, p.113.

Poster, M., 1986. 'Foucault and the Tyranny of Greece', in D.Hoy (ed.), *Foucault: A Critical Reader*, London.

Price, A., 1989. 'Taking Rights Cynically: A Review of Critical Legal Studies', 48 *Cambridge Law Journal*, p.271.

Putnam, H., 1987. 'Why Relativism Can't Be Naturalized', in K.Baynes (ed.), *After Philosophy: End or Transformation?*, Harvard.

Rabinow, P., 1984. *The Foucault Reader*, London.

Radbruch, G., 1936. 'Anglo-American Jurisprudence through Continental Eyes', *Law Quarterly Review*, p.530.

Radbruch, G., 1950. *Legal Philosophy*, in E.Patterson (ed.), *The Legal Philosophies of Lask, Radbruch and Dabin*, Harvard.

Rappaport, H., 1989. *Heidegger and Derrida: Reflections on Time and Language*, Lincoln.

Rawls, J., 1971. *A Theory of Justice*, Oxford.

Rawls, J., 1975. 'Fairness to Goodness', 84 *Philosophical Review*, p.536.

Rawls, J., 1980. 'Kantian Constructivism in Moral Theory', 77 *Journal of Philosophy* p.515.

Rawls, J., 1985. 'Justice not Fairness: Political not Metaphysical', *Philosophy and Public Affairs*, p.223.

Rawls, J., 1987. 'The Idea of an Overlapping Consensus', 7 *Oxford Journal of Legal Studies*, p.1.

Rawls, J., 1993. *Political Liberalism*, New York.

Readings, W., 1991. *Introducing Lyotard: Art and Politics*, London.

Reiss, H., (ed.), 1991. *Kant: Political Writings*, Cambridge.

Riley, P., 1986. 'The Elements of Kant's Practical Philosophy', 14 *Political Theory* p.555.

Riley, P., 1992. 'Hannah Arendt on Kant, Truth and Politics', in H.Williams (ed.), *Essays on Kant's Political Philosophy*, Cardiff.

Rorty, R., 1980. *Philosophy and the Mirror of Nature*, Princeton.

Rorty, R., 1982. *The Consequences of Pragmatism*, Minneapolis.
Rorty, R., 1986. 'Foucault and Epistemology', in D.Hoy (ed.), *Foucault: A Critical Reader*, Oxford.
Rorty, R., 1989. *Contingency, Irony, and Solidarity*, Cambridge.
Rorty, R., 1991a. *Objectivism, Relativism, and Truth*, Cambridge.
Rorty, R., 1991b. *Essays on Heidegger and Others*, Cambridge.
Rorty, R., 1993. 'Human Rights, Rationality, and Sentimentality', in S.Shute and S.Hurley (eds.), *On Human Rights: The Oxford Amnesty Lectures 1993*, New York.
Rosenfeld, M., 1990. 'Deconstruction and Legal Interpretation: Conflict, Indeterminacy and the Temptations of the New Legal Formalism', 11 *Cardozo Law Review*, p.1211.
Sallis, J., 1987. *Spacings - of Reason and Imagination*, Chicago.
Sartre, J-P., 1962. *Literary and Philosophical Essays*, New York.
Sartre, J-P., 1967. *What is Literature?*, London.
Sartre, J-P., 1989. *Existentialism and Humanism*, London.
Schalow, F., 1992. *The Renewal of the Heidegger-Kant Dialogue*, Albany.
Schneewind, J., 1992. 'Autonomy, obligation and virtue: An overview of Kant's moral philosophy', in P.Guyer (ed.), *The Cambridge Companion to Kant*, Cambridge.
Scott, P., 1990. *The Question of Ethics: Nietzsche, Foucault, Heidegger*, Bloomington.
Sheridan, A., 1980. *Michel Foucault: The Will to Power*, London.
Sherover, C., 1971. *Heidegger, Kant and Time*, Bloomington.
Silverman, H., 1989. 'Derrida, Heidegger and the time of the line', in H.Silverman (ed.), *Derrida and Deconstruction*, London.
Singer, J., 1984. 'The Player and the Cards: Nihilism and Legal Theory', 94 *Yale Law Journal*, p.60.
Smith, B., 1990. 'Judgment after the Fall', 11 *Cardozo Law Review*, p.1291.
Smolin. D., 1986. 'Roberto Unger's Theory of Personality, Law and Society: Critique and Proposal for a Revised Methodology', 55 *Cincinnati Law Review*, p.427.
Sullivan, R., 1989. *Immanuel Kant's Moral Theory*, Cambridge.
Sullivan, R., 1994. *An Introduction to Kant's Ethics*, Cambridge.
Sunstein, C., 1987. 'Routine and Revolution', 81 *Northwestern Law Review*, p.882.
Taylor, C., 1990. 'Rorty in the Epistemological Tradition', in A.Malachowski (ed.), *Reading Rorty*, Oxford.
Tushnet, M., 1981. 'Legal Scholarship: Its Causes and Cure', 90 *Yale Law Journal*, p.1205.
Tushnet, M., 1984. 'An Essay on Rights', 62 *Texas Law Review*, p.1363.
Tushnet, M., 1991. 'Critical Legal Studies: A Political History', 100 *Yale Law Journal*, p.1515.
Unger, R., 1975. *Knowledge and Politics*, New York.
Unger, R., 1976. *Law in Modern Society*, New York.
Unger, R., 1983. *The Critical Legal Studies Movement*, Harvard.

Unger, R., 1984. *Passion: An Essay on Personality*, London.
Unger, R., 1987a. *Social Theory: Its Theory and Its Task*, Cambridge.
Unger, R., 1987b. *False Necessity*, Cambridge.
Unger, R., 1996. 'Legal Analysis as Institutional Imagination', 59 *Modern Law Review*, p.1.
Vekley, R., 1993. 'The Crisis of the End of Reason in Kant's Philosophy and the *Remarks* of 1764-1765', in R.Beiner and R.Booth (eds.), *Kant and Political Philosophy*, Yale.
Ward, K., 1972. *The Development of Kant's View of Ethics*, Oxford.
Watson, D., 1992. *Arendt*, London.
Watson, S., 1990. 'On the Critical Tribunal', 11 *Cardozo Law Review*, p.1471.
Weinrib, E., 1985. 'Enduring Passion', 94 *Yale Law Journal*, p.1825.
Weinrib, E., 1987a. 'Law as a Kantian Idea of Reason', 87 *Columbia Law Review*, p.471.
Weinrib, E., 1987b. 'The Intelligibility of the Rule of Law', in A.Hutchinson and P.Monahan (eds.), *The Rule of Law: Ideal or Ideology?*, Toronto.
Weinrib, E., 1988. 'Legal Formalism: On the Immanent Rationality of Law', 97 *Yale Law Journal*, p.949.
Weinrib, E., 1992. 'Why Legal Formalism?', in R.George (ed.), *Natural Law Theory*, Oxford.
Williams, J., 1987. 'Critical Legal Studies: The Death of Transcendence and the Rise of the New Langdell's', 62 *New York University Law Review*, p.429.
Wolf, E., 1958. 'Revolution or Evolution in Gustav Radbruch's Legal Philosophy', 3 *Natural Law Forum*, p.1
Wolin, S., 1978. 'Stopping to Think', *New York Review of Books* 26/10/78, p.18.
Yack, B., 1993. 'The Problem with Kantian Liberalism', In R.Beiner and R.Booth (eds.), *Kant and Political Philosophy*, Yale.
Yeatman, A., 1994. *Postmodern Revisionings of the Political*, London.
Young-Breuhl, E., 1982. *For Love of the World*, Yale.
Yovel, Y., 1980. *Kant and the Philosophy of History*, Princeton.

INDEX

Altman, A. 113.
American revolution 18, 55.
Arendt, H. 2-3, 5, 12, 18-9, 22, 38-40, 45-56, 58-9, 65, 69, 81-2, 96-7, 99, 101, 106, 112, 114-5, 118-9, 132, 152, 155.
On Revolution 55.
Origins of Totalitarianism 51-2.
The Human Condition 54-5.
The Life of the Mind 46-7, 52.
Truth and Politics 51.
Aristotle 78, 123.
Augustine, St. 48.
Auschwitz 68-9.
Austin, J. 138.

Barron, A. 71.
Barthes, R. 116.
Beiner, R. 17, 50.
Bennington, G. 67, 73, 77.
Bentham, J. 138.
Bernstein, R. 74, 77, 79, 88-9, 97, 118, 127.
Bhaskar, R. 87.
Boyle, J. 111, 116, 119.
Boyne, R. 66.
Brest, P. 114-5.
Burchell, G. 65.
Burrows, J. 88.

Canovan, M. 47, 54.
Carroll, D. 68.
Cassirer, E. 3, 37, 65-6, 79, 85, 133-8.
Essay on Man 136.
Language and Myth 136.
The Myth of the State 137-8.
The Philosophy of the Enlightenment 65, 134, 140-1.
Caygill, H. 17.
Chomsky, N. 62.
Chroust, A. 141.
Cohen, H. 133, 137.
Cornell, D. 2, 112, 126-32, 145, 157.
The Philosophy of the Limit 128.
The Imaginary Domain 132.
Critchley, S. 74.
Critical Legal Studies (CLS) 111, 113-7, 120-2, 130.
Crowther, P. 17.

Dahlstrom, D. 36.
Davidson, A. 66.
Deleuze, G. 13, 17, 61.
D'Entreves, M. 47.
Derrida, J. 1-2, 17-8, 40, 42, 45, 59, 66, 71-8, 80, 83-6, 115-9, 127-32, 145, 157.
Of Grammatology 71, 73.
Of Spirit: Heidegger and the Question 73-4.
The Force of Law 75, 77.
The Other Heading 75-6.
Dewey, J. 78-80, 82-3.
Diamond, S. 115.
Donzelot, J. 65.
Doppelt, G. 98.
Douzinas, C. 118.
Dreyfus case 52.
Dworkin, R. 3, 50-1, 53, 64, 66, 86, 97, 117-8, 124-8, 133, 145-57.
Law's Empire 149-55.
Life's Dominion 154-7.
Taking Rights Seriously 145-9.

Eichmann, A. 51-2.
Enlightenment, the 4-5, 16, 18, 21, 55, 64, 78-9, 82, 85, 97, 118, 134, 136.

Farias, V. 45.

Feher, F. 118.
Feinman, J. 113.
Feldman, S. 116-7.
Ferry, L. 45, 74.
Final Solution 52.
Finnis, J. 110.
Fischer, M. 88.
Foucault, M. 2, 18, 60-7, 76, 78, 80, 82-5, 115-7, 123, 125.
Discipline and Punish 61.
History of Sexuality 61-3.
Madness and Civilization 61.
The Archaeology of Knowledge 61.
Fraser, N. 66, 75.
Freiburg university 40-2.
French revolution 18-9, 25, 55.
Frug, G. 114-6, 125.
Frug, M. 131.

Gabel, P. 2, 114, 116-7, 119-22, 124.
Gadamer, H-G. 13, 15-6, 45, 72-3, 79, 81, 87, 117, 129, 149-50, 152-3.
Galston, W. 97-8, 111.
Gasche, R. 84.
Geertz, C. 85.
Glucksmann, A. 65.
Goodrich, P. 15, 118-9.
Gordon, C. 65-6.
Gordon, R. 115.
Guignon, C. 88.
Guyer, P. 17, 34.

Haber, F. 88.
Habermas, J. 66.
Halpin, A. 111.
Hampton, J. 97.
Hansen, P. 46, 55.
Hart, H.. 145.
Hawthorn, G. 111.
Hegel, G. 127-8.
Heidegger, M. 1-2, 17-8, 36-58, 60-2, 66-7, 69-86, 97, 102, 108, 114, 116-21, 127-33, 136, 138..
Being and Time 36-8, 41, 43, 45, 57, 83.
The End of Philosophy and the Task of Thinking 41, 43-4.
Kant and the Problem of Metaphysics 36, 38-9.
Rektorat 37, 40-6, 73, 76.
Heidelberg university 46.
Heller, A. 118.
Heller, T. 115.
Herder, G. 16-7.
Hiley, D. 88.
Hill, T. 97.
Hitler, A. 44-5, 137.
Hobbes, T. 53.
Hollis, M. 88, 97.
Hoy, D. 117.
Hume, D. 4, 6, 16.
Hunt, A. 117, 119, 121.
Husserl, E. 36.
Hutchings, K. 18, 35.
Hutchinson, A. 2, 111, 122-6.

Jameson, F. 67.
Jaspers, K. 34, 45-6.

Kafka, F. 72, 108
Kant, I. 1-41, 44, 46, 54, 57, 60-1, 63-9, 71-2, 77-88, 90, 93-4, 97-9, 101, 105-6, 109, 114-5, 117, 119,123, 128-9, 131, 133-47, 150-4, 156.
Critique of Judgement 1, 6, 12-23, 26, 34-5, 37-9, 45, 47, 49-51, 67, 69-70, 72, 79, 87, 91, 96, 107, 119, 133-6, 149.
Critique of Practical Reason 6, 10, 12-3, 35, 134-5.
Critique of Pure Reason 5-6, 10, 17, 19, 23, 36-7, 39, 69.

Groundwork of the Metaphysics of Morals 6, 9, 11, 22, 26-7, 35.
Metaphysics of Morals 1, 11-2, 20, 25-35, 44, 49, 61, 69, 99-100, 104, 155.
Kelman, M. 115.
Kennedy, D. 117, 119, 121.
Kierkegaard, S. 42.
Klare, K. 113, 125.
Krell, D. 73.
Kress, K. 115.
Kritzman, L. 66.

Lacoue-Labarthe, P. 42, 45, 69.
Levinas, E. 130.
Locke, J. 105.
Lyotard, J-F. 1-2, 17, 34, 59, 66-72, 74, 84-5, 118-9, 131.
Heidegger and the 'jews' 69.
Lessons in the Analytic of the Sublime 70.
Peregrinations 69-70.
The Differend 67-8, 131.
The Postmodern Condition 67-8.

MacCarthy, T. 79, 87.
Mandela, N. 76.
Marburg university 46, 50, 133.
Marcuse, H. 40.
Marx, K. 46.
Marxism 55, 59, 100, 113, 117, 125.
McBride, W. 58.
Meyerson, D. 110.
Michelman, F. 115.
Monaghan, P. 111.
Moore, M. 116.
Murdoch, I. 57-9.

Nabokov, V. 86.
National Socialism 40-1, 44-5, 51-3, 57, 69, 141.
Nietzsche, F. 41, 45, 48, 73, 81-3.
Norris, C. 72.
Nuremberg laws 52.

O'Neill, O. 6, 13.
Orwell, G. 86-7.

Parekh, B. 47, 51.
Peller, G. 116.
Pietism 4.
Plato 18, 45
Poeggeler, O. 45.
Poster, M. 65.
Proust, M. 82, 108.
Putnam, H. 87.

Radbruch, G. 3, 133, 138-42, 144-6.
Philosophy of Law 138-42.
Rawls, J. 2, 50-1, 53, 66, 71, 78, 81-2, 84-5, 86-98, 100, 111, 118, 128-30, 132, 145-7, 149, 150, 154.
A Theory of Justice 89-93, 145.
Political Liberalism 95-7.
Readings, W. 71.
Renaut, A. 45, 74.
Riley, P. 51.
Rorty, R. 2, 65-6, 78-89, 92, 97-8, 100-2, 110, 115, 123, 126-7, 144, 157.
Contingency, Irony, and Solidarity 81.
Philosophy and the Mirror of Nature 78-9, 81, 87.
Rosenfeld, M. 75.
Rousseau, J-J. 4, 19, 21, 105, 135.

Sartre, J-P. 2, 54, 57-60, 64-5, 80, 85-6, 108, 111, 114, 116, 119-20, 127, 153.
Being and Nothingness 57

Existentialism and Humanism 57-60.
What is Literature? 58-9.
Schalow, F. 36, 38-9.
Schmitt, C. 44.
Scott, C. 66.
Sherover, C. 36, 40.
Singer, J. 116.
Smith, B. 75.
Socrates 5.
Steiner, G. 57.
Sullivan, R. 34.

Taylor, C. 88.
Tushnet, M. 113-5.

Unger, R. 2-3, 34, 66, 78, 81, 84-6, 97-114, 116, 118-20, 123-9, 132, 144-5, 157.
Knowledge and Politics 98-104, 107, 109, 127.
Law in Modern Society 102-4, 107.
Passion 99, 105, 108, 142.
Politics 99, 105.
The Critical Legal Studies Movement 104-5.

Vietnam 60.

Warrington, R. 118.
Watson, D. 46.
Watson, S. 75.
Weinrib, E. 3, 111, 133, 142-6.
White, J. 124.
Williams, J. 116.
Wittgenstein, L. 78-9.
Wolin, S. 46.

Yeatman, A. 118.

Law and Philosophy Library

1. E. Bulygin, J.-L. Gardies and I. Niiniluoto (eds.): *Man, Law and Modern Forms of Life.* With an Introduction by M.D. Bayles. 1985 ISBN 90-277-1869-5
2. W. Sadurski: *Giving Desert Its Due.* Social Justice and Legal Theory. 1985 ISBN 90-277-1941-1
3. N. MacCormick and O. Weinberger: *An Institutional Theory of Law.* New Approaches to Legal Positivism. 1986 ISBN 90-277-2079-7
4. A. Aarnio: *The Rational as Reasonable.* A Treatise on Legal Justification. 1987 ISBN 90-277-2276-5
5. M.D. Bayles: *Principles of Law.* A Normative Analysis. 1987 ISBN 90-277-2412-1; Pb: 90-277-2413-X
6. A. Soeteman: *Logic in Law.* Remarks on Logic and Rationality in Normative Reasoning, Especially in Law. 1989 ISBN 0-7923-0042-4
7. C.T. Sistare: *Responsibility and Criminal Liability.* 1989 ISBN 0-7923-0396-2
8. A. Peczenik: *On Law and Reason.* 1989 ISBN 0-7923-0444-6
9. W. Sadurski: *Moral Pluralism and Legal Neutrality.* 1990 ISBN 0-7923-0565-5
10. M.D. Bayles: *Procedural Justice.* Allocating to Individuals. 1990 ISBN 0-7923-0567-1
11. P. Nerhot (ed.): *Law, Interpretation and Reality.* Essays in Epistemology, Hermeneutics and Jurisprudence. 1990 ISBN 0-7923-0593-0
12. A.W. Norrie: *Law, Ideology and Punishment.* Retrieval and Critique of the Liberal Ideal of Criminal Justice. 1991 ISBN 0-7923-1013-6
13. P. Nerhot (ed.): *Legal Knowledge and Analogy.* Fragments of Legal Epistemology, Hermeneutics and Linguistics. 1991 ISBN 0-7923-1065-9
14. O. Weinberger: *Law, Institution and Legal Politics.* Fundamental Problems of Legal Theory and Social Philosophy. 1991 ISBN 0-7923-1143-4
15. J. Wróblewski: *The Judicial Application of Law.* Edited by Z. Bańkowski and N. MacCormick. 1992 ISBN 0-7923-1569-3
16. T. Wilhelmsson: *Critical Studies in Private Law.* A Treatise on Need-Rational Principles in Modern Law. 1992 ISBN 0-7923-1659-2
17. M.D. Bayles: *Hart's Legal Philosophy.* An Examination. 1992 ISBN 0-7923-1981-8
18. D.W.P. Ruiter: *Institutional Legal Facts.* Legal Powers and their Effects. 1993 ISBN 0-7923-2441-2
19. J. Schonsheck: *On Criminalization.* An Essay in the Philosophy of the Criminal Law. 1994 ISBN 0-7923-2663-6
20. R.P. Malloy and J. Evensky (eds.): *Adam Smith and the Philosophy of Law and Economics.* 1994 ISBN 0-7923-2796-9
21. Z. Bankowski, I. White and U. Hahn (eds.): *Informatics and the Foundations of Legal Reasoning.* 1995 ISBN 0-7923-3455-8
22. E. Lagerspetz: *The Opposite Mirrors.* An Essay on the Conventionalist Theory of Institutions. 1995 ISBN 0-7923-3325-X
23. M. van Hees: *Rights and Decisions.* Formal Models of Law and Liberalism. 1995 ISBN 0-7923-3754-9
24. B. Anderson: *"Discovery" in Legal Decision-Making.* 1996 ISBN 0-7923-3981-9

Law and Philosophy Library

25. S. Urbina: *Reason, Democracy, Society.* A Study on the Basis of Legal Thinking. 1996
ISBN 0-7923-4262-3
26. E. Attwooll: *The Tapestry of the Law.* Scotland, Legal Culture and Legal Theory. 1997
ISBN 0-7923-4310-7
27. J.C. Hage: *Reasoning with Rules.* An Essay on Legal Reasoning and Its Underlying Logic. 1997
ISBN 0-7923-4325-5
28. R.A. Hillman: *The Richness of Contract Law.* An Analysis and Critique of Contemporary Theories of Contract Law. 1997
ISBN 0-7923-4336-0
29. C. Wellman: *An Approach to Rights.* Studies in the Philosophy of Law and Morals. 1997
ISBN 0-7923-4467-7
30. B. van Roermund: *Law, Narrative and Reality.* An Essay in Intercepting Politics. 1997
ISBN 0-7923-4621-1
31. I. Ward: *Kantianism, Postmodernism and Critical Legal Thought.* 1997
ISBN 0-7923-4745-5

KLUWER ACADEMIC PUBLISHERS – DORDRECHT / BOSTON / LONDON